# Democracy Declined

CHICAGO STUDIES IN AMERICAN POLITICS

*A series edited by Susan Herbst, Lawrence R. Jacobs, Adam J. Berinsky, and Frances Lee; Benjamin I. Page, editor emeritus*

*Also in the series:*

*Race to the Bottom: How Racial Appeals Work in American Politics*
*by LaFleur Stephens-Dougan*

*America's Inequality Trap: How Economic Inequality Feeds on Itself and Why It Matters*
*by Nathan J. Kelly*

*Good Enough for Government Work: The Public Reputation Crisis in America (and What We Can Do to Fix It)*
*by Amy E. Lerman*

*Who Wants to Run? How the Devaluing of Political Office Drives Polarization*
*by Andrew B. Hall*

*From Politics to the Pews: How Partisanship and the Political Environment Shape Religious Identity*
*by Michele F. Margolis*

*The Increasingly United States: How and Why American Political Behavior Nationalized*
*by Daniel J. Hopkins*

*Legacies of Losing in American Politics*
*by Jeffrey K. Tulis and Nicole Mellow*

*Legislative Style*
*by William Bernhard and Tracy Sulkin*

*Why Parties Matter: Political Competition and Democracy in the American South*
*by John H. Aldrich and John D. Griffin*

*Neither Liberal nor Conservative: Ideological Innocence in the American Public*
*by Donald R. Kinder and Nathan P. Kalmoe*

*Strategic Party Government: Why Winning Trumps Ideology*
*by Gregory Koger and Matthew J. Lebo*

*Post-Racial or Most-Racial? Race and Politics in the Obama Era*
*by Michael Tesler*

*The Politics of Resentment: Rural Consciousness in Wisconsin and the Rise of Scott Walker*
*by Katherine J. Cramer*

# Democracy Declined
## The Failed Politics of Consumer Financial Protection

Mallory E. SoRelle

The University of Chicago Press :: Chicago and London

The University of Chicago Press, Chicago 60637
The University of Chicago Press, Ltd., London

Published 2020
Printed in the United States of America

29 28 27 26 25 24 23 22 21 20     1 2 3 4 5

ISBN-13: 978-0-226-71165-2 (cloth)
ISBN-13: 978-0-226-71179-9 (paper)
ISBN-13: 978-0-226-71182-9 (e-book)
DOI: https://doi.org/10.7208/chicago/9780226711829.001.0001

Library of Congress Cataloging-in-Publication Data

Names: SoRelle, Mallory E., author.
Title: Democracy declined : the failed politics of consumer financial protection / Mallory E. SoRelle.
Other titles: Chicago studies in American politics.
Description: Chicago ; London ; The University of Chicago Press, 2020. | Series: Chicago studies in American politics | Includes bibliographical references and index.
Identifiers: LCCN 2019054879 | ISBN 9780226711652 (cloth) | ISBN 9780226711799 (paperback) | ISBN 9780226711829 (ebook)
Subjects: LCSH: Consumer credit—United States. | Consumer credit—Political aspects—United States. | Consumer protection—United States.
Classification: LCC HG3756.U54 S673 2020 | DDC 381.3/40973—dc23
LC record available at https://lccn.loc.gov/2019054879

♾ This paper meets the requirements of ANSI/NISO Z39.48-1992 (Permanence of Paper).

*To my parents, Drs. James and Cynthia SoRelle,*
*for teaching me to be intellectually curious,*
*especially about questions with the potential to make a difference*

## Contents

## Abbreviations

| | |
|---|---|
| AFFIL | Americans for Fairness in Lending |
| AFR | Americans for Financial Reform |
| APA | Administrative Procedure Act |
| APR | annual percentage rate |
| BBB | Better Business Bureau |
| CAC | Consumer Advisory Council |
| CARD | Credit Card Accountability Responsibility and Disclosure (Act) |
| CFA | Consumer Federation of America |
| CFPB | Consumer Financial Protection Bureau |
| DOD | Department of Defense |
| ECOA | Equal Credit Opportunity Act |
| EFT | Electronic Funds Transfer |
| FCIC | Financial Crisis Inquiry Commission |
| FCRA | Fair Credit Reporting Act |
| FDA | Food and Drug Administration |
| FDIC | Federal Deposit Insurance Corporation |
| FHA | Federal Housing Administration |
| FTC | Federal Trade Commission |
| HOLC | Home Owners' Loan Corporation |
| MLA | Military Lending Act |
| NCLC | National Consumer Law Center |
| NHA | National Housing Act |
| NWRO | National Welfare Rights Organization |
| PCCI | President's Committee on Consumer Interests |

| | |
|---|---|
| PWA | Public Works Administration |
| SEC | Securities and Exchange Commission |
| TILA | Truth in Lending Act |
| UDAP | Unfair or Deceptive Acts or Practices |

# 1 Democracy Declined: The Failed Politics of Consumer Financial Protection

In the summer of 2007, a few months before the United States economy spiraled into the worst recession since the Great Depression, Elizabeth Warren made a prescient observation. She described a paradox familiar to many Americans in a piece that *Washington Post* columnist Ezra Klein (2010) later called the most important policy article written that decade:

> It is impossible to buy a toaster that has a one-in-five chance of bursting into flames and burning down your house. But it is possible to refinance an existing home with a mortgage that has the same one-in-five chance of putting the family out on the street. . . . Similarly, it's impossible to change the price on a toaster once it has been purchased. But long after the papers have been signed, it is possible to triple the price of the credit used to finance the purchase of that appliance, even if the customer meets all the credit terms, in full and on time. (2007)

Americans today probably take for granted both scenarios Warren describes. For decades, U.S. consumers have been able to shop for a dizzying array of products knowing that their purchases met basic, government-mandated safety standards before appearing on store shelves. Americans also shop with the understanding that once they buy something new, retailers won't call them in a week or a month or a year to demand more money on top of the original purchase price.

Of course, Americans haven't always had the benefit of these guarantees. Consumer protections against unsafe goods and unscrupulous sales practices are a relatively modern invention. They began to proliferate in the early twentieth century when government regulators moved to safeguard the health and general welfare of Americans in response to the increasingly complex marketplace of manufactured goods produced by industrialization. More than a century after U.S. policymakers first enacted consumer protections, however, these government-backed assurances that goods are safe and prices are fixed still don't extend to one of the most important and widely used types of consumer products and services in the United States: consumer financing.[1] The rapidly expanding population of borrowers must shop for their credit cards, loans, bank accounts, and other types of financing without the security of a set of government regulations equivalent to those protecting them from appliance fires, tainted food, and faulty car parts.

The absence of safeguards on consumer bank accounts and loans like those we enjoy on goods from children's pajamas to toaster ovens is particularly dangerous because the consequences of bad financial products extend well beyond harms to individuals; they threaten the stability of entire economies. After all, an exploding toaster has never sparked a global economic collapse. But with the storm clouds of impending financial crisis gathering ominously on the horizon as Warren penned her 2007 article—aptly titled "Unsafe at any Rate"—it appeared that the explosion of risky credit products and lending practices in the United States would do just that. Under these circumstances, it made sense for Warren to ask, echoing the same question that had been posed by a chorus of consumer advocates for decades, "Why are consumers safe when they purchase tangible consumer products with cash, but when they sign up for routine financial products like mortgages and credit cards they are left at the mercy of their creditors?"

An array of risky, potentially predatory,[2] credit products and practices like the subprime loans and interest rate hikes mentioned by Warren proliferated in the years leading up to the 2008 financial crisis. For example, on the eve of the crisis in 2007, four of every ten nonmortgage loans originated in the United States were subprime[3] (Zibel and Andriotis 2015). One-third of all credit card users were subject to interest rates exceeding 20 percent. That translates to a vast amount paid in interest when considering that about 44 percent of card users carried a balance from month to month and 20 percent fell behind on their payments (Board of Governors 2017a). Financial products like fee-harvester credit cards, tax refund anticipation loans, and overdraft programs, each possessing the ability to draw consumers into a cycle of debt from which they might have trouble extricating themselves, also multiplied.[4] And all of this took place as Americans' increased reliance on borrowing fueled such a dramatic rise in overall indebtedness that, by 2007, total outstanding household debt had considerably outpaced annual household disposable income in the United States (Dynan and Kohn 2007).

Despite these conditions, federal policymakers—both in Congress and in regulatory agencies—did little to staunch the growth of risky lending; in many cases, they enacted policies that did just the opposite. While U.S. lawmakers have adopted a network of consumer protections combining information disclosure with more stringent safety and inspection protocols for a variety of durable and comestible consumer goods dating as far back as the 1906 Pure Food and Drug Act, they have taken a distinctly different approach to consumer financing. Beginning with passage of the first national consumer credit regulation in 1968—the Truth in Lending Act—federal policymakers have opted to pursue a strategy of consumer financial protection predicated almost exclusively on information disclosure. They have enacted few substantive safety measures that would, for example, prohibit certain lending practices or place limits on excessive fees and interest rates, eventually going so far as to circumvent state consumer protection laws that did adopt such provisions. Federal policymakers adhered closely to this information-based model even as consumer loan terms became increasingly costly, disclosures became increasingly ineffective, and a growing percentage of the population became increasingly reliant on consumer credit to finance their daily lives.

Consumer advocates like Warren recognized the looming potential for economic catastrophe generated by growing American indebtedness under progressively riskier lending terms long before the "Great Recession" began in earnest in December 2007.[5] Alarmed by these trends, which advocates attributed in large part to inadequate government regulation of the consumer finance industry (a view ultimately shared by the federal Financial Crisis Inquiry Commission [FCIC]), a group of public interest organizations set out to mobilize the expanding ranks of affected borrowers toward political action. Advocates hoped that putting grassroots political pressure on policymakers would help secure lasting reform to strengthen consumer financial protections. And mass consumer political mobilization was deemed necessary because, up to that point, Americans had largely restricted their attempts to solve problems with banking and credit to the marketplace, for example, by complaining to a credit card company or searching for a new lender. Disgruntled borrowers had not, for the most part, taken political action in any substantial or sustained way to express their growing displeasure with consumer financial protection in the United States.

A number of consumer, civil rights, labor, and religious groups coalesced in the years immediately preceding the 2008 financial crisis with the goal of engaging ordinary Americans in collective political action to demand lending reform. They established new organizations like Americans for Fairness in Lending (AFFIL) and Americans for Financial Reform (AFR) with the express purpose of mobilizing grassroots political support to combat predatory lending.[6] Bolstered by media coverage and the growing prominence of Warren's advocacy, AFFIL and AFR actively encouraged consumers to engage with their elected officials and federal regulators to support new financial reform being considered in the wake of the 2008 crisis. Despite the power of mobilization to generate political engagement (see Rosenstone and Hansen 1993), however, these new groups failed to "fully mobilize and channel the public rage" toward grassroots political participation in support of financial reform (Kirsch and Mayer 2013: 152). The limited success public interest groups did enjoy came from mobilizing consumers toward targets within the market itself, for example, protests of banks and trade associations.

While consumer groups struggled to get the public to demand political solutions for predatory lending, advocates continued their own lobbying efforts within Congress and during the rulemaking process. Public interest organizations were able to achieve one of their desired legislative reforms in the aftermath of the financial crisis: the creation of the Consumer Financial Protection Bureau (CFPB) in 2010. Indeed, the formation of a new government agency tasked specifically with protecting American borrowers had been the centerpiece of Warren's 2007 article. While the CFPB represented a major change in *who* would be regulating consumer finance, public interest groups were largely stymied in their attempts to secure substantive changes in *how* consumer finance would be regulated, even as policymakers acknowledged the inadequacy of existing protections and the role that risky lending practices played in sparking the financial meltdown (FCIC 2011).[7]

When President Obama signed the Dodd-Frank Wall Street Reform and Consumer Protection Act into law on July 21, 2010, he emphasized the relationship between predatory lending and the economic crisis, saying, "Over the past two years, we have faced the worst recession since the Great Depression. . . . The primary cause was a breakdown in our financial system. . . . Unscrupulous lenders locked consumers into complex loans with hidden costs." But President Obama's remarks unintentionally underscored the new law's lack of substantive policy change, at least with respect to consumer financial protection:

> Now, for all those Americans who are wondering what Wall Street reform means for you, here's what you can expect. If you've ever applied for a credit card, a student loan, or a mortgage, you know the feeling of signing your name to pages of barely understandable fine print. What often happens as a result is that many Americans are caught by hidden fees and penalties, or saddled with loans they can't afford. With this law . . . we'll make sure that contracts are simpler—putting an end to many hidden penalties and fees . . . so folks know what they're signing. . . . So, all told, these reforms represent the strongest consumer financial protections in history. (Obama 2010)

The problem with the President's explanation is that "what you could expect" sounded a lot like what Americans already had. According to the new law, as Obama's signing statement describes it, the existence of high fees and risky lending terms wasn't the main issue; the problem was that those fees and terms were too complex for the average borrower to identify or understand. The solution? Better information disclosure. By taking this approach, federal policymakers continued down the same—arguably ineffective—path embraced by their predecessors half a century before. As one consumer advocate resignedly acknowledged in a speech commemorating the five-year anniversary of the bill signing, "[We] knew even during its passage that the Dodd-Frank bill aimed to preserve the financial system, rather than restructuring it fundamentally to make it serve the real economy" (McGhee 2015).

Adopting a new approach to consumer financial protection would have been a logical response to the economic damages wrought by decades of consistent lending deregulation and the destruction of the financial security of millions of Americans. But instead of reshaping policies to mirror the combination of restrictive remedies and information disclosures applied to other arenas of protective regulation, legislators adopted "reforms" that doubled down on existing information disclosure requirements. The stubborn adherence to preexisting policy remedies is especially perplexing because it stands in stark contrast to federal responses during prior, comparable economic recessions in the United States. For example, crises like the Panic of 1907, the Great Depression, and the recession following the oil shocks of the 1970s all resulted in substantive economic and regulatory policy changes.

Equally perplexing in the aftermath of the crisis, consumer advocates struggled to persuade borrowers who suffered the effects of predatory lending to demand policy change. Public interest groups have historically been successful spark plugs for collective citizen engagement on behalf of other crucial economic policy issues from social security to tax reform (e.g., Campbell 2002). Moreover, the lack of political action doesn't indicate either borrower approval of or apathy toward the financial industry. In fact, borrowers evinced their willingness to engage in individual, and occasionally collective, action to voice opposition to banking and lending practices, but only when the target of that action was a financial institution or trade group. This suggests that borrowers were neither without grievances, nor averse to acting on them; they simply weren't inclined to turn to policymakers for help.

Each of these puzzles—the failure of federal policymakers to change their approach to curb risky lending practices, the (largely ineffective) decision by angry borrowers to focus their energy and action on banks and lenders instead of lawmakers, and the inability of consumer groups to change either of those patterns through mobilization and lobbying—is of significant consequence for American political economy, yet scholars have largely ignored them. What explains these failures in the  politics of consumer financial regulation? What do these trends mean for future policymaking efforts to improve consumer financial protection? What are the consequences for the financial security of ordinary Americans and the nation's economy?

Over the last two decades, scholars have paid increasing attention to the cultural and economic trends associated with growing consumer credit usage in the United States. They have traced the evolution of American attitudes toward borrowing from treating consumer debt as an unpardonable sin to embracing it as an indispensable feature of what Lizabeth Cohen (2003) calls a "Consumers' Republic" (Calder 1999; Hyman 2011). Scholars have also shown that credit is an essential component of the modern U.S. economy, both as a driver of consumption and, more recently, as an enormously profitable industry unto itself (Manning 2000; Krippner 2005, 2011). And in the absence of a more generous "traditional" welfare state, access to consumer credit serves as an essential form of financial support for many Americans (Prasad 2012; Schelkle 2012; Logemann 2012).

Beyond the established cultural and economic implications of consumer credit, however, this book is motivated by an underlying contention that the expansion—both in access and economic significance—of consumer financing in the United States is fundamentally a political issue as well. And while some of the political *causes* of growing consumer credit markets in the United States have been explored by scholars (e.g., Cohen 2003; Hyman 2011; Prasad 2012; Trumbull 2014; Quinn 2019), very little research attends to the explicitly political *consequences* created by an economy built on a foundation of consumer credit.

In this book, I propose a policy-centered explanation for the failed politics of consumer financial protection in the United States. I argue that the politics of U.S. consumer financial protection, from bureaucratic decision making to mass political behavior, are shaped by the historical development of consumer lending policies and the political reverberations, or feedback effects, those policies produced. Expanding on the pathbreaking work of scholars who describe the centrality of consumer finance to the modern U.S. economy (e.g., Hyman 2011; Krippner 2011; Prasad 2012; Quinn 2019), I explore how New Deal policymakers responded to the political and economic constraints of the Great Depression by laying the groundwork for a consumption-driven economy fueled largely by consumer credit. I argue that, in doing so, they unleashed a path-dependent process that would dramatically limit the political incentives for protecting consumers' finances in the future.

Under this system, lawmakers are motivated to maintain wide access to credit in order to support the stability and growth of the U.S. economy, even if it means adopting weak consumer protections that put the financial well-being of individuals at risk. I argue that, constrained by a scheme of their predecessors' invention, policymakers since the New Deal have adopted information disclosure as the primary form of consumer financial protection because they believe it is the only method that encourages a modicum of consumer confidence in borrowing without restricting the overall supply of consumer financing—the supply necessary to sustain a credit-fueled economic system. By the time President Obama confronted the 2008 recession, the transformation to a credit-based economy was largely complete. As the President was forced to acknowledge when signing into law the relatively limited regulatory changes after the crisis, "The fact is, the financial industry is central to our nation's ability to grow, to prosper, to compete and to innovate" (Obama 2010).

Relying on information disclosures has political consequences. The design, implementation, and administration of these disclosure laws produce what I call *regulatory feedback effects* that shape the behaviors of bureaucrats, consumer advocates, and ordinary Americans. First, disclosure requirements are revealed to borrowers in the course of ordinary financial transactions, giving no indication that policymakers play a crucial role in their creation and enforcement; only banks and lenders are visible as the information's source. Second, by suggesting that information can prevent problems with banking and credit, disclosures shift the burden of financial protection to borrowers. Together, I argue that these elements of policy design teach people that banks, lenders, and borrowers themselves are primarily responsible for preventing or managing problems with consumer financing. I contend that this depoliticizes consumer financial protection, encouraging borrowers to engage with market rather than government actors when they encounter problems with credit. The incentives for borrowers to overlook government's culpability for weak financial protection also complicate public interest groups' efforts to spur mass political mobilization. Finally, I propose that these outcomes are exacerbated by Congress' decision to divide the authority to implement federal consumer financial protections across multiple regulatory agencies, most of which are designed to promote the financial security of banks and not individuals. The resulting arrangement puts deregulatory pressure on bureaucrats, limits the influence of public interest lobbying, complicates citizen complaint making, and ultimately weakens borrower protections.

This process of policy development and resulting feedback creates what I call a *political economy of credit* in the United States. The political economy of credit is a self-reinforcing cycle that begins when policymakers embrace broad access to consumer credit to sustain the national economy, thus limiting their motivation to adopt financial protections that might threaten that supply. The cycle is reinforced when policymakers subsequently design and administer weak disclosure-based protections that encourage borrowers to blame themselves and their banks for financial problems, rather than government policymakers, thus minimizing borrowers' incentives to demand reform from elected representatives and federal regulators. Compelled by the need to preserve credit access and without the countervailing force of voter mobilization, policymakers have few reasons to change their approach to consumer financial protection.

In *Democracy Declined* I draw on multiple sources of data—from historical records to survey experiments—to demonstrate the development and ongoing dynamics of the U.S. political economy of credit. I look to the past and the present to explain how this cycle shapes the politics of consumer financial protection. Ultimately, I conclude that the policies promoting and regulating consumer borrowing in the United States create a feedback loop that contributes to lawmakers' ongoing failure to enact more meaningful financial protections and threatens the economic security of individual borrowers and the United States as a whole.

I do, however, identify two potential pathways to mitigate these potentially disastrous consequences. First, I consider several alternative approaches advocacy groups might use to overcome borrowers' unwillingness to turn their energy toward political mobilization. I find that talking about credit as an issue of economic security rather than consumer protection or regulation encourages borrowers to take political action. Second, I argue that the creation of the Consumer Financial Protection Bureau (CFPB) has the potential to restructure the regulatory arena to promote borrower interests and boost government's public profile when it comes to financial protection—if the agency can survive external political attacks and the pendulum swing of leadership changes. This could increase both the success of public interest lobbying and rates of borrower engagement. While neither of these approaches is foolproof, they each offer political pathways to strengthen consumer financial protection. The remainder of this chapter more fully advances the argument of the book and previews how that argument unfolds in the remaining chapters.

: : :

## *The Borrower's Paradox*

Consumer credit[8] refers to loans issued to individual, non-commercial borrowers to help finance the purchase of commodities and services or to refinance existing debt. It can be issued in two primary forms: installment (closed-end) or revolving (open-end) credit. Installment credit includes any loan issued for a set amount that is repaid over a specified time period with scheduled payments of both principal and interest (e.g., a car loan). Revolving credit, by contrast, refers to a loan with a predetermined borrowing limit where the loan is automatically renewed each time the debt balance is paid off (e.g., a credit card). Consumer credit costs money to use. Borrowers pay interest and often finance charges—for example, overdraft fees on checking accounts or late payment fees on credit cards—in order to borrow money or use financial services like banking.[9]

While consumer credit is a fundamental piece of the American economy today, the forms it most commonly takes are a relatively modern invention. As industrialization transformed the United States from an economy based on agrarian production to one supported by manufacturing, the ability of consumers to purchase the dazzling array of new manufactured goods was paramount. Marriner Eccles, chairman of the Federal Reserve under President Franklin Roosevelt, explained succinctly in his memoir (Eccles and Hyman 1951), "mass production has to be accompanied by mass consumption." And, as retailers in the 1920s quickly discovered, mass consumption—particularly for more expensive goods like large appliances and automobiles—required credit. Installment loans grew when retailers observed that they could make greater profits by extending credit to consumers to purchase their products (Olney 1991), a practice that became even more profitable once installment debt became resellable (Hyman 2011).

The 1920s witnessed the proliferation of installment loans provided primarily by retail outlets for the purchase of specific manufactured goods, but legal options for small personal loans to help cover general expenses were scarce. The lack of available small loans was of particular concern for the new and growing class of urban workers who were without a source of financing to weather unexpected costs. Having left behind familial support in their rural hometowns, and with virtually no form of government assistance or welfare available to them, workers turned to loan sharks when facing a financial emergency (Calder 1999; Hyman 2011). The combination of state usury laws, which limited the interest that lenders could collect on a loan, and the relatively high costs of administering even small-dollar loans, made extending consumer credit an unprofitable business for reputable financers (Hyman 2011; Trumbull 2014). That would change, however, during the New Deal.

While explanations for the origin of the Great Depression are plentiful, many reformers active at the time pointed to underconsumption and a lack of liquidity in the market as the roots of the crash (Eccles and Hyman 1951; Jacobs 2011; Prasad 2012). New Deal policymakers, therefore, sought ways to stimulate cash flows and increase consumption to jumpstart the beleaguered economy. Enhancing the purchasing power of consumers became a central focus of New Deal policies (Jacobs 2005, 2011; Cohen 2003). The Roosevelt administration believed that a boost to the construction industry, in particular, would have a significant positive impact on both the producers of raw materials and the labor market. They wanted to encourage the building of new homes and the renovation of old homes, but homeowners lacked sufficient resources to finance this construction boom and financial institutions did not offer credit products for such a purpose. With the passage of Title I of the National Housing Act of 1934 (P.L. 73–479), a home modernization loan program, government stepped in to insure banks that were willing to make small loans for home renovation to protect them against potential default. Interest rates on the small-dollar loans were low, but with the backing of government insurance, bank profits were virtually guaranteed.

Banks' positive experiences with the modernization program showed exactly how profitable small consumer loans could be, and by the end of the 1930s, they were a standard service provided by commercial banks (Hyman 2011). During the Second World War, creative banking strategies to circumvent government limits on installment credit—enacted to restrain consumption in the wartime economy—led to revolving credit. This new form, when combined with improved technology, launched the credit card. In the years that followed, bankers and policymakers alike embraced credit as a major source of fuel for the consumer economy. By 1972, the Congressionally constituted National Commission on Consumer Finance was lauding the "magnitude and the importance of the consumer credit industry, both as a lubricant which oils the wheels of our great industrial machine and as the vehicle largely responsible for creating and maintaining in this country the highest standard of living in the world" (1). The significance of consumer financing to the U.S. economy has only grown since then.

In the last fifty years, consumer financing and its associated debt have become the "lifeblood" of the U.S. economy (Manning 2000: 6; Williams 2004). The so-called FIRE sector (finance, insurance, and real estate), which is funded in large part on the back of consumer credit, comprised almost a quarter of the national GDP in 2000 (Krippner 2005). This outcome would not be possible without a tremendous amount of consumer borrowing. To what extent does the average U.S. household contribute to the borrowing boom? Why do American families borrow, and what economic consequences do they face as a result?

The Survey of Consumer Finances, a cross-sectional study of U.S. household finances conducted every three years by the Federal Reserve, found that more than three in four Americans (77 percent) had some type of outstanding debt on the eve of the 2008 financial crisis. Credit cards comprised the most common form of non-mortgage consumer financing, with 73 percent of American households using them in 2007

(Board of Governors 2017a). According to the U.S. Census Bureau, there were nearly 1.5 billion cards in circulation, held by 176 million cardholders at the onset of the crisis. The average cardholder had at least four separate cards. With such high rates of credit usage, it is clear that borrowing is commonplace among Americans, but do all households use credit at similar rates and for similar purposes?

It turns out that borrowers can be found across the socioeconomic spectrum; however, the likelihood of borrowing increases with income. In 2007, for example, 38 percent of American households in the bottom income quintile had at least one credit card—a significant portion, but the lowest for any income group. A majority of Americans in every other income quintile used at least one card, with 75 percent of middle-income and 94 percent of the most affluent Americans using credit cards (Durkin et al. 2014). And while just over half of all borrowers (56 percent) report that they use credit cards primarily for convenience (Board of Governors 2017a), a substantial number of households rely on their credit cards to ensure their family's security and well-being. About 40 percent of Americans report regularly using credit cards to cover basic expenses from groceries to housing payments to medical care (Traub and Ruetschlin 2012), and 45 percent say that they are most likely to rely on credit cards when they experience a shortfall in income (Board of Governors 2017b). These statistics demonstrate how integral consumer financing has become to support consumer spending across the income spectrum, and they confirm that nearly half of all American families depend on credit both to secure daily necessities and to navigate financial emergencies.

The costs and consequences of borrowing are not evenly distributed across American households. Borrowers from different socioeconomic backgrounds face disparate financing terms and fees. For example, a 2012 study of Federal Reserve data on credit card interest rates found that low-income borrowers, people of color, and single women are most liable to encounter high finance charges (Traub and Ruetschlin 2012). Borrowers in the bottom two income quintiles are twice as liable to have cards with annual percentage rates exceeding 20 percent compared with middle-income borrowers and about four times more likely than the wealthiest borrowers. Black and Latinx borrowers are twice as liable as white borrowers to have interest rates above 20 percent, and single women are similarly twice as liable to see those high rates compared to single men.

The combination of expansive borrowing with expensive finance charges generates a vast amount of consumer debt in the United States.

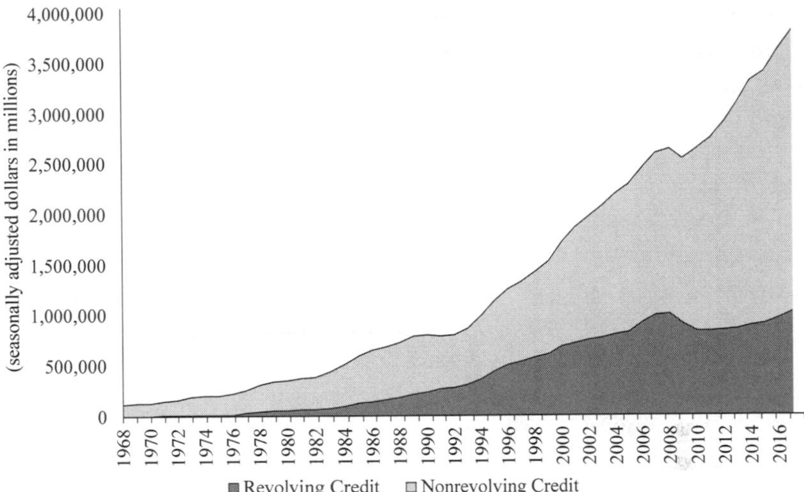


**FIGURE 1.1** Total Outstanding U.S. Consumer Debt (non-mortgage), 1968–2017
Source: Board of Governors of the Federal Reserve System, Consumer Credit-G.19, 2018

As figure 1.1 depicts, the total outstanding debt from both revolving and non-revolving forms of consumer credit has risen dramatically over the last four decades. Non-mortgage consumer debt exceeded 3.8 trillion dollars in 2017, up from two and a half trillion dollars at the onset of the 2008 financial crisis. In fact, by 2016, credit cards surpassed mortgages to become the most widely held type of consumer debt (Board of Governors 2017a).

In the year before the financial crisis, about two-thirds of credit card users carried a balance—meaning that almost half (46 percent) of American households failed to pay off their credit card balance each month (Durkin et al. 2014). The average balance carried by credit card holders who revolved their debt from one month to the next was more than seven thousand dollars—a 30 percent increase from 2004 (Board of Governors 2017a). That generates a tremendous amount of additional interest families must pay to cover their daily expenses, magnifying the impact of unfavorable financing terms for the average American.

Perhaps unsurprisingly, the number of borrowers who carry a balance and the size of that balance vary across socioeconomic groups. For example, in 2007, a majority of households in every income quintile except the most affluent (47 percent) carried a credit card balance from month to month, with middle income households revolving their balance in the highest proportion (65 percent). This demonstrates, once again, the degree to which American families from across the income spectrum rely on credit for financial support. The amount of debt each group carries from one month to the next increases considerably as income rises. In 2007, for example, the mean credit card balance ranged from 4,050 dollars for households in the lowest income quintile to 11,303 dollars in the highest (Durkin et al. 2014). Patterns of debt also vary by race. More black (48 percent) and Latinx (50 percent) households report credit card debt than do white borrowers (42 percent) (Dettling et al. 2017), but they carry a lower average balance—5,784 dollars and 6,066 dollars for black and Latinx card users compared with 7,315 dollars for white borrowers (Traub and Ruetschlin 2012).

These patterns of borrowing and debt accumulation combine to take a significant toll on the financial well-being of American families. The average U.S. household had deleveraged by 2002, meaning their debt surpassed their annual income. On the eve of the financial crisis in 2007, total outstanding debt represented 115 percent of the average household's annual income (Board of Governors 2017a). On a monthly basis, debt payments amounted to about 19 percent of the average debtor's income, and one in ten households devoted more than 40 percent of their monthly paycheck to debt. Perhaps unsurprisingly, one of every five households (21 percent) had fallen behind on their credit card payments, meaning they accrued sizeable late fees on top of their interest charges.

Borrowing clearly shapes the financial fortunes of Americans from across the socioeconomic spectrum, albeit with different consequences for different groups. While affluent families may be better able to pay off their full balance each month, a full 47 percent are revolving huge sums and paying the resulting finance charges. Middle- and working-class families, people of color, and single women are carrying lower balances but are less likely to pay them off each month, and when they revolve credit they are hit with especially costly interest and fees. In fact, the higher finance charges that low-income borrowers, people of color, and single women encounter means they often pay more interest in the long run than more affluent, white, male borrowers who revolve higher balances (Traub and Ruetschlin 2012). Altogether, these patterns suggest that borrowing presents a paradox for American families: credit has become a fundamental financial support and a first line of defense against financial emergencies, but relying on credit with increasingly costly finance charges and weak consumer protections generates mounting debt burdens for American borrowers. The result, as Greta Krippner describes, is that "the citizen-debtor" has supplanted "the citizen-worker" as the iconic figure of late twentieth-century capitalism (2017: 3).

### *Understanding the Politics of Consumer Financial Protection*

Given the importance of consumer financing to the economic well-being of individuals and the national economy, it makes sense that scholars have devoted increased attention to the issue. Early work focused primarily on the cultural changes that made lending palatable (Calder 1999; Mann 2002; Cohen 2003) and the technological advances that made it possible (Jappelli and Pagano 1993, 2002; McCorkell 2002). More recently, however, scholars have turned their focus toward two frequently interwoven political arguments to explain how, in the absence of a naturally occurring consumer credit market, expanded consumer financing came to thrive in the United States: activists agitated for access to credit and policymakers created institutions that facilitated consumer lending.

Collective movements by agrarian populists (Sanders 1999; Prasad 2012), progressive reformers (Calder 1999), and organized labor (Trumbull 2014) were critical to the growth of consumer lending at the turn of the twentieth century. In the absence of more expansive public welfare, these groups lobbied for credit—first to help support small farmers who needed credit to bolster their productive capacity and later to aid the growing ranks of industrial workers who often lacked access to emergency financial support. In the 1960s and '70s, women's, civil rights, and welfare rights groups engaged in renewed mobilization to expand credit access to their constituents, who had historically been excluded from many types of consumer financing (Prasad 2012; Trumbull 2014; Krippner 2017; Thurston 2018). In each instance, political mobilization focused on demanding access to credit for groups who lacked it, rather than improving financial protections for existing borrowers.

A second line of research focuses on the specific government interventions that made lending possible by making it profitable. In a 2011 review of the historiography of the politics of consumption, Meg Jacobs cautioned scholars to move beyond explanations for evolving consumer markets that focus solely on the struggle among interest groups. Echoing a call from Lawrence Glickman (2012) to explore how policy regimes shape consumption, Jacobs suggested, "We need to ask careful questions about how and in what ways the state has influenced consumer markets" (2011: 567). Indeed, from Tocqueville ([1835] 2004) to Polanyi ([1944] 2001), political economists have long acknowledged that governments foster free markets and mass consumption through intentional policymaking. With respect to consumer credit, Louis Hyman, Monica Prasad, and Sarah Quinn exemplify the charge to examine the effect of government intervention on the growth of consumer financing.

Hyman (2011) musters compelling historical evidence to demonstrate how policy innovations establishing and eventually regulating new credit markets led to the growth and proliferation of credit and debt in the twentieth century. Prasad (2012) proposes an astute and encompassing demand-side theory of political economy that ties the American credit boom to policymakers' adoption of credit to promote consumption. Central to Prasad's theory is the choice by policymakers to adopt measures that expanded mortgage credit to support economic growth, an approach she dubs "mortgage Keynesianism." Quinn (2019) places similar emphasis on credit expansion as a policymaking tool for managing the U.S. economy. Focusing primarily on housing finance, she demonstrates how federal policymakers have historically used credit as an indirect tool to manage the federal budget and financial markets broadly.

Each of these accounts explores different political motivations for a common outcome: the choice by U.S. policymakers to use consumer financing as a primary tool to build the American economic system. But what are the consequences of such a system? Far fewer studies grapple with this question, but to the extent that they have, analyses are generally limited to observing how a credit-driven economy either spurred the growth of the financial sector or helped create a "credit-welfare" state. With respect to the first, scholars trace how the U.S. economy has become increasingly dependent on the profits generated from financial products and services (Manning 2000; Williams 2004; Krippner 2005, 2011). One political outcome of this so-called financialization (see Arrighi 1994) is an increase in the political power of financial institutions in the United States (Hacker and Pierson 2010; Krippner 2011; McCarty et al. 2013).

Second, in an innovative addition to the welfare state literature, scholars contend that the financialization of the American economy limits the prospects for a robust public welfare system. They argue that policymakers in the early (Prasad 2012; Trumbull 2014; Quinn 2019) and late (Krippner 2011; Streeck 2011) twentieth century embraced access to credit as a politically viable way to promote consumption while circumventing the complicated politics of welfare expansion. This decision ultimately undermined support for more traditional welfare programs, facilitating welfare retrenchment and neoliberal policy approaches. Both the financialization of the U.S. economy and the formation of a U.S. credit-welfare state have been shown to contribute to increasing income inequality (Phillips 2002; Hacker and Pierson 2010; Prasad 2012).

While these analyses provide invaluable insight into how credit has been leveraged as a "tool of statecraft" (Krippner 2017: 6) in the U.S. context, they raise key policy and political questions that need answering. One of the most notable absences from the existing discourse is an account of how this approach to state building affects the subsequent politics of consumer financial protection, particularly as it relates to the political behavior of ordinary citizens, public interest groups, and the resulting prospects for policy reform.

How have policymakers approached the need to protect individual consumers' finances? This is an especially salient question because, as Prasad (2012) theorizes, macroeconomic systems that rely on credit to support consumer demand require keen regulatory oversight, without which the entire framework is prone to instability. Perhaps even more importantly, how do American borrowers wield political power to ensure that their interests are represented once they attain access to this crucial source of financial support? Scholars have a wealth of data to explain how and why people engage politically around questions of redistribution, yet we have shockingly little evidence to address the same questions for consumer financing, despite its role as welfare surrogate and its outsized influence on the financial security of ordinary Americans.

I suggest that the answers to these questions can be found in tracing the development and subsequent consequences of federal policymakers' decisions to build and maintain an economy fueled by credit in lieu of other forms of consumer purchasing power. While both the support of societal coalitions motivated by the welfare of their members and policymakers' need to circumvent the tricky politics of expanding public assistance may have smoothed the way for the initial creation and later expansion of consumer credit markets in the United States, I argue that the individual welfare of American borrowers has never been the primary consideration in policymakers' efforts to expand and regulate credit. Instead, establishing a viable market for consumer credit was and continues to be driven by the need to promote purchasing power to ensure economic growth and stability.

Does it really matter why policymakers turned to credit? Should we care whether policymakers were motivated primarily by the welfare of ordinary Americans versus the welfare of the national economy if the outcome—expanding access to credit—was the same? This distinction is worth making, I argue, because it led federal lawmakers to prioritize financial protections that look very different from the types of remedies they might have employed if motivated primarily by borrower welfare. By concerning themselves with consumer financing as a way to bolster the national economy, not only have lawmakers locked themselves into a path-dependent set of policy alternatives to maintain that system, but also the resulting decisions they have made with respect to policy design, implementation, and administration have significantly influenced the preferences and behaviors of citizens and constrained the ability of advocacy groups to successfully lobby for reforms to consumer financial protection.

## *A Theory of Regulatory Feedback*

Once enacted, public policies, particularly those that become durable features of the political landscape, have the capacity to shape future politics in many ways (Lowi 1972; Skocpol 1992; Pierson 1993; Mettler and Soss 2004; Mettler and SoRelle 2017). As Suzanne Mettler (1998: 4) explains in her study of the gendered dimensions of New Deal social programs, policies "may legitimate the formation of certain social identities, determine the civic status attached to particular social roles, and produce particular organizational arrangements in society." A growing body of scholarship explores how a policy's design can influence people's conceptions of their own citizenship, including their relationships with the state and with one another (Schneider and Ingram 1993; Mettler and Soss 2004). Furthermore, studies show how policy implementation has the capacity to highlight or obscure government's role in service provision, ultimately shaping people's assumptions about the appropriateness and efficacy of government intervention in certain areas (Mettler 2011). Finally, a number of scholars have detailed how government policies affect the emergence and capacity of interest groups (Walker 1983; Skocpol 1992).

The existing corpus of policy feedback scholarship—a term used to describe work that examines how policy shapes politics—focuses primarily on effects generated from what Theodore Lowi (1972) classified as redistributive policies, particularly social welfare programs (e.g., Soss 1999; Campbell 2002; Mettler 2005a; Michener 2018). These policies, which involve the transfer, or redistribution, of resources, make it relatively easy to establish a direct link between the policy and the beneficiary. Redistributive policies typically benefit (or burden) a specific and easily identifiable group, for example, senior citizens or low-income mothers. They also allow for the direct interaction of beneficiaries with some form of distributive mechanism, like a trip to the unemployment office or a check from the Social Security Administration. There is no reason to assume that these feedback mechanisms only manifest for redistributive policies, but the existing policy feedback literature may not map onto other laws quite so clearly.

Despite any welfare functions consumer credit may fulfill, financial protections fall squarely into the category of protective regulations: policies "designed to protect the public by setting the conditions under which various private activities can be undertaken" (Ripley and Franklin 1987: 24). Protective regulatory policies differ fundamentally from redistributive (and distributive) polices in their design and implementation in two primary ways, each with implications for existing conceptions of policy feedback. First, while many redistributive policies provide benefits directly to recipients, protective regulatory policies promulgate rules that initially affect businesses. The ultimate beneficiary is still the citizen, but she only experiences policy remedies once they have been filtered through private transactions.

Second, while redistributive policies usually target a distinct group (e.g., Medicare recipients), protective regulatory polices typically affect anyone who interacts with the regulated industry, meaning that beneficiaries are diffuse (Lowi 1972) and frequently defined by their transactions rather than their group traits. In the case of consumer financial regulation, for example, the breadth of policy beneficiaries will generally be defined by the use of the regulated financial product or service. So, a credit card regulation may well affect nearly two hundred million Americans. These beneficiaries are unlikely to enjoy the common characteristics that targets of a redistributive policy share.

Beyond these two distinctive features of policy design and implementation, protective regulations have another key political feature that is underdeveloped in existing feedback scholarship: federal bureaucratic agencies play a particularly important role in the development and enforcement of regulations. This means that the bureaucracy is an essential site for political contestation, so the administrative arrangement for a specific regulatory scheme bears significant weight on the ability of individuals and groups to influence policymaking. To date, policy feedback scholarship has overlooked the potential for a given policy's administrative arrangement to produce feedback effects that influence the politics of bureaucrats, interest groups, and citizens during

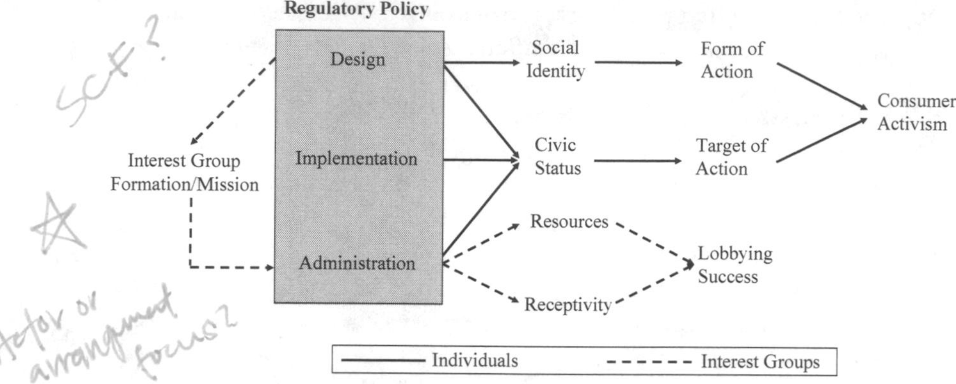


FIGURE 1.2 Regulatory Feedback Effects for Individuals and Interest Groups

the rulemaking process. Would an interest group's lobbying strategy differ, for example, if the power to regulate credit cards was handed to the Treasury Department versus the Consumer Financial Protection Bureau? What if they both have to agree on any new regulation, but a third agency—like the Federal Trade Commission—has to enforce it?

The following section develops an explicit theory of regulatory feedback effects, applying it to consumer financial protections. I adapt insights from the policy feedback literature to the distinctive design, implementation, and administrative features of protective regulations. Figure 1.2 charts the pathways along which regulatory feedback effects influence individuals (solid line) and interest groups (dotted line).

### Social Identity

As figure 1.2 depicts, government policies can shape people's conceptions of their own identity as it relates to that of others, promoting or depressing specific characteristics (Mettler and Soss 2004). Steve Engel (2016) describes the feedback effect of policy on identity formation as "a lens through which the regulatory authorities of the state see and define the individual." The particular language and remedies inherent in a regulatory policy's design can, therefore, teach beneficiaries lessons about their identity as both consumers and citizens. This is achieved primarily through the construction of target groups to whom policies apply and the associated norms and benefits ascribed to those groups (Schneider and Ingram 1993). Typically, policymakers begin crafting policy by specifying a particular group to whom their policy applies—often based on some subset of shared characteristics. The policy spells out who is a member of the identified group and who is not (Schneider and Ingram 1993; Mettler and Soss 2004). Often, members of the group form identities, or constituencies, surrounding their beneficiary status and will coalesce to preserve and expand their benefits (Pierson 1993; Campbell 2002).

This process is fairly straightforward for consumer financial regulations that provide protections to a specific subset of the population. For example, the 2006 Military Lending Act (P.L. 109–364) imposed a usury cap of 36 percent on certain types of loans extended to service members and their families. The military families who benefit from these protections may come to understand that government recognizes them as a specific population—easily identifiable on the basis of the shared characteristic of military service—that is deserving of protection. This identity would be relatively easy for its members to mobilize around to protect or expand their policy benefits.

Most consumer financial protections, however, apply to such a large and diverse segment of the population—for example, basic information disclosure requirements for debit cards—that no such collective constituency is activated. Instead of providing benefits to a group with shared characteristics, regulations like this provide benefits on the basis of a set of transactions. As a result, people affected by these policies may come to understand their identity as a function of the transaction rather than as a function of group characteristics. For example, two borrowers who are both subject to disclosure requirements on their debit cards are hardly likely to feel an affinity with one another because they both use ATMs to get cash. "ATM user" is not a particularly salient identity group for people. So, consumer financial protections that provide benefits in a transactional manner may well personalize the procurement and usage of credit while suppressing any sense of collective group identity. By contrast, more traditionally targeted regulations might activate collective consumer identities—an important prerequisite for creating an engaged constituency.

### Civic Status

Beyond their effects on identity formation, figure 1.2 shows how regulatory policy designs also transmit norms about the relationship between citizens and the state for a particular set of issues, suggesting to beneficiaries the degree to which their citizenship is valued (Mettler and Soss 2004). For example, exposure to consumer financial safeguards that encourage "voluntary" regulation suggest that government is not invested in mandating that consumers be protected from harmful financial products. Similarly, if regulations primarily focus on providing remedies that maintain fair market competition—rather than intervening in the function of supply and demand by outlawing the sale of certain credit products or the use of specific finance charges—people may learn that, as long as transactions are "fair," borrowers are accountable for their own financial fortunes as responsible players in an increasingly complex market of financial products.

But norms generated by policy design are not the only feedback mechanism through which regulatory policies can affect individuals' attitudes about government intervention. People's direct experiences with policy disbursement agencies have also been shown to influence their attitudes about government efficacy and further their resulting political engagement (Soss 1999; Campbell 2002; Mettler 2005a, 2011; Weaver and Lerman 2010). Of particular relevance are findings that a lack of obvious interaction with government during the implementation of a policy can encourage citizens to underestimate the role government plays in that policy area, thus disincentivizing direct political action for that issue (Mettler 2011). If a policy intentionally obscures government's role in supplying a certain type of benefit, the policy generates different norms from one that provides clear evidence of government activity in the provision of benefits.

This is especially important for understanding the feedback effects of regulatory policies because the direct recipients of government regulations are not consumers themselves. Businesses are the actual target of government regulation, so ordinary Americans are not responsible for knowing or complying with most regulatory policy mandates. The result is that consumers, despite being the intended beneficiary of protective regulations, only indirectly experience them once they have been mediated through a private company. When the policy does not highlight government's regulatory power, for example, through a label or notice of inspection by a government agency, people may not be aware that government played a role in regulating the transaction at all.

The administrative arrangement for a regulatory policy may further illuminate or obfuscate government's authority for a given issue. If a single administrative agency is granted oversight for a policy area, people may come to associate that agency with its respective policy jurisdiction. For example, most Americans, as I demonstrate later in the book, know that the Food and Drug Administration is responsible for overseeing new prescription medications before they make their way onto pharmacy shelves. Thus, it is relatively easy for individuals to identify the appropriate government actor to communicate with if they experience problems with medication. By contrast, when the regulatory authority for a policy area is dispersed across multiple agencies, it may

be far more complicated for citizens to identify the appropriate government body responsible for addressing a particular concern. The degree to which agencies engage actively in citizen outreach, for example, through well-publicized field hearings or even social media use, may also serve to boost recognition of government intervention for a regulatory issue.

Douglas Arnold (1990) argues that the electorate must be able to link policymaking to a specific political actor in order to engage politically on that issue. His assessment is consistent with attribution theory: the idea that people develop beliefs about cause and effect relationships (Heider 1958) and that those beliefs ultimately have the potential to shape their preferences across a range of issues (Weiner 2006) including many political contexts. A similar argument might be made for borrower responses to financial regulations. The combined effects of policy design, implementation, and administration on borrower perceptions of government's appropriate role in the protection of consumer finances can ultimately shape ideas about what grievances and goals should be pursued through political versus market means. So, when a regulatory policy obscures the role of government in consumer financial protection, leaving only the work of the market visible, it will teach people to attribute blame to market actors and subsequently to target those actors with their complaints. By contrast, consumer financial regulations that highlight the role of government in consumer banking and lending, or emphasize government protection of citizens, will encourage people to target political actors when expressing their grievances.

### Organizational Capacity

Beyond the ability of regulatory policies to affect individual beneficiaries, they also have the capacity to shape the emergence, activities, and efficacy of interest groups. As Paul Pierson explains in one of the first articulations of policy feedback's specific mechanisms, "The activity of interest groups often seems to follow rather than precede the adoption of public policies" (1993: 598). Indeed, Jack Walker, the noted scholar of interest group politics, argued that many interest groups emerge after the enactment of new polices because they can benefit from some form of patronage produced by the policy. Andrea Campbell's work on Social Security (2002) provides another explanation for the ability of a policy to spark the formation of new interest groups, arguing that new benefits produce new constituency groups with incentives to lobby on behalf of those benefits. As figure 1.2 suggests, the emergence of new sites of regulation may induce a similar process for groups concerned with the regulated industry. It is also possible that the absence of government policymaking for a particular issue may incentivize existing agencies to restrict their activities to non-political realms.

Beyond this, however, I argue that the specific administrative arrangement for a regulatory policy has the capacity to shape the landscape of contestation on which public interest groups engage. Theda Skocpol (1992: 47) notes that "patterns of bureaucratic development influence the orientations of educated middle-class groups as well as the possibilities for all social groups to 'do things' through public authority." The arrangement of bureaucratic authority for a given issue, therefore, has the ability to ease or complicate participation in the ongoing rulemaking process that determines the contours of most forms of protective regulation. Figure 1.2 demonstrates the two mechanisms by which I argue this occurs.

First, the degree to which oversight and enforcement authority are concentrated in a single agency may shape the application of interest group resources, with fragmented authority making it more costly and more difficult for advocates to develop and maintain relationships with regulators. Furthermore, the mission of administrative agencies tasked with overseeing a policy may shape how receptive regulators are to interest group lobbying. When an agency is designed primarily to engage in protective regulation, those enacted for consumers' benefits, bureaucrats will be more attuned to claims made on behalf of consumers. When an agency is designed primarily with a competitive regulatory mission—a mission focused on maintaining industry competition and stability—regulators may not be predisposed to consider consumer-based concerns to the same degree. These two features can combine to lead to regulatory arbitrage, or the race to the bottom that occurs when multiple regulators, often lacking a legally compelled interest in consumer protection, must agree to the appropriate form of protective regulation on an issue. I contend that regulatory arbitrage may further diminish the success of interest group lobbying.

In sum, I argue that a regulatory policy's ability to shape the social identities and civic status of individuals and the organizational capacity of groups can explain much about the current state of consumer financial protection politics.

*Creating and Sustaining the U.S. Political Economy of Credit*

This book argues that the failed politics of consumer financial protection in the United States are the result of a political economy of credit:

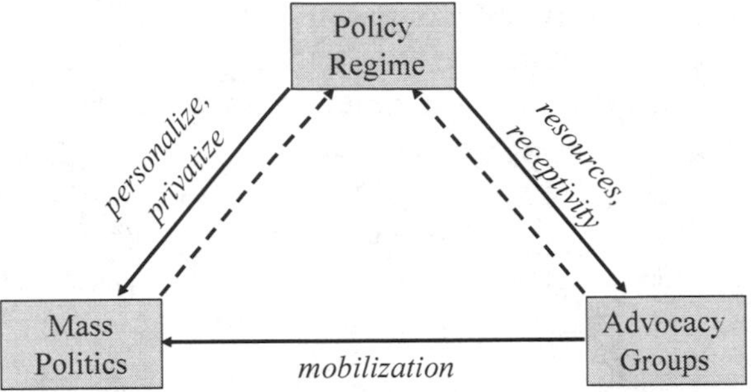


**FIGURE 1.3** The Political Economy of Credit

an ongoing cycle of policy development and regulatory feedback effects that ultimately limit the incentives and abilities of policymakers, public interest groups, and borrowers to fight for stronger consumer financial protections. Figure 1.3 illustrates this model of the U.S. political economy of credit, and the following pages explain how that cycle is unpacked in the remaining chapters.

Chapter 2 investigates the development of the U.S. consumer financial protection regime. It demonstrates how the evolution of a political economy of credit encourages federal policymakers to embrace disclosure requirements as the primary way to protect borrowers. The chapter traces how New Deal policymakers built a government-backed infrastructure to jumpstart consumer credit to boost the construction industry and drive economic revitalization in the wake of the Great Depression. I argue that, in so doing, policymakers began a path-dependent process whereby consumer financial protections were and continue to be designed to promote broad purchasing power in support of the national economy rather than adopting individual consumer protections that might restrict the supply of credit. Drawing on archival records from the Franklin Delano Roosevelt and Lyndon Baines Johnson Presidential Archives and comprehensive legislative analyses of all major consumer credit policies enacted from 1934 to 2010, I explore how the mission to promote broad-based purchasing power translated to federal lawmakers' adoption of specific policy design features.

Two critical tradeoffs were consistently made with respect to the design and implementation of U.S. consumer credit policies and financial protections. First, in the absence of a naturally occurring market for legal small loan lending, New Deal policymakers chose to provide financial institutions with sufficient government support to establish a private marketplace for consumer lending rather than to issue direct government loans. Second, in an effort to broadly expand access to credit to boost the purchasing power of consumers, policymakers needed to ensure that consumers felt sufficiently confident in their abilities to acquire and use credit without constraining its overall supply. They accomplished these two goals by requiring that companies provide borrowers with information about financial products and services in order to minimize adverse selection, rather than by employing any sort of restriction on lending terms that might limit credit access. I argue that, having arrived at this equilibrium solution, policymakers today embrace a limited range of regulatory strategies because of the process set in motion by their New Deal colleagues, helping to explain their failure to take stronger action against risky lending practices.

I argue in chapter 3 that these aspects of policy design, which I explore in more detail, produce regulatory feedback effects that diminish the political engagement of borrowers by privatizing and personalizing the issue of consumer financial protection. It is privatized in part because government-backed market institutions, rather than government agencies themselves, lend to borrowers. This obscures government's key role in creating and regulating modern consumer credit. That role is further hidden by the implementation of financial protection regulations through regular market transactions such that consumers have no indication of government's oversight or regulatory function. Regulations of the consumer lending industry personalize consumer financial protection because they largely assume a model of the consumer as an atomistic, rational market actor, treating the procurement and usage of financing as a personal decision in which the onus is placed on the consumer to make appropriately informed decisions. I hypothesize that, in combination, these feedback effects promote individual market action while discouraging citizens from engaging in both individual and collective politics to address problems with consumer finance. Figure 1.4 illustrates how these preferences combine to shape borrower action around financial protection.

When regulations provide language and remedies that make borrowers think of themselves as individual, responsible consumers, while obscuring the role of government, borrower preferences will align with transactional methods of pursuing grievances. Transactional responses to grievances all take the form of normal market dealings like complaining directly to lenders or trade associations or moving business to another company. When policies rely on market remedies but provide them to, or deny them from, an identifiable target population, consumerism is more likely to occur. This form of action includes taking part in boycotts and buycotts, or other mass responses directed at market actors.

| Type of Action | | Target of Action: Market | Target of Action: Government |
|---|---|---|---|
| | Individual | *Transactional*<br>• borrowing & service decision<br>• complain to lenders<br>• complain to trade association<br>• change lender<br>• file lawsuit | *Political*<br>• contact public official<br>• vote<br>• complain to federal agency<br>• submit rulemaking comment<br>• file lawsuit |
| | Collective | *Consumerism*<br>• join boycott<br>• join buycott<br>• join class action lawsuit | *Civic*<br>• participate in protest<br>• participate in lobbying day<br>• join class action lawsuit |

**FIGURE 1.4** Regulatory Feedback and Consumer Mobilization Strategies

Note: This typology is adapted from Maney and Bykerk 1994. Lawsuits can be considered either market or political action since they work through political institutions but use contract law central to functioning markets.

Conversely, when policies provide sufficient evidence of government intervention, borrowers might be more likely to turn to public officials. When these policies provide transactional benefits, borrowers will be most likely to engage in individualized political action. By contrast, when these policies provide remedies to a target population, collective political action, or civic behavior, may ensue. Borrowers are, of course, exposed to multiple policies at a time, so the resulting lessons may be derived from the cumulative exposure to policies governing consumer financial protection rather than from each individual policy. I leverage original and existing public opinion data on consumer credit and regulation to explore the substance and effect of policy-generated attitudes about who bears responsibility for problems with financing on people's willingness to engage in different types of action to support financial protection.

In chapter 4, I explore how these regulatory feedback effects on individuals have inhibited advocacy groups' attempts to mobilize borrowers toward political participation. Public interest groups need to utilize collective action frames that are salient to and resonate with the beliefs of potential participants to effectively mobilize consumers (Klandermans 1997; Benford and Snow 2000). That means a collective action frame defining borrowers as victims of corporate abuse and encouraging them to seek redress from government will work only if those themes either resonate with people's experiences or reshape them. I argue that this is particularly challenging because borrowers' experiences with financing both personalize and privatize its use.

To explore whether public interest groups' attempts to mobilize borrowers politically are stymied by a mismatch between consumer beliefs and advocacy appeals, I explore the cases of Americans for Fairness in Lending (AFFIL) and Americans for Financial Reform (AFR), two prominent campaigns against predatory lending launched in the lead-up to and aftermath of the 2008 financial crisis. I draw on interviews with consumer advocates and archival material from the Consumer Movements Archives to identify the mobilization strategies these groups employed. I then use original survey and experimental data to examine the effect of a typical appeal on an individual's willingness to take political action to support a proposal for stronger consumer financial protection. Finally, additional experiments explore whether alternative messaging strategies can, at least temporarily, increase people's willingness to take political action to combat predatory lending.

In chapter 5, the book considers the dynamics of policy development, feedback, and mobilization specifically for marginalized borrowers. I explore policymakers' efforts to "democratize" credit for women, communities of color, and lower-income borrowers beginning in the 1970s. I argue that the process of expanding access to marginalized borrowers was a natural consequence of the creation of a political economy of credit. But loosening credit regulations to facilitate democratization created a bifurcated lending system wherein privileged borrowers benefit from more favorable terms, while marginalized borrowers are subject to costlier and riskier credit products. I return to the survey and experimental data from the previous chapters to demonstrate that, beyond the considerable economic implications of this unequal arrangement, marginalized borrowers also experience demobilizing feedback effects from their encounters with financial regulation—effects that might be even more consequential for groups who are especially vulnerable to predatory lending. I find that, unlike their more privileged peers, however, marginalized borrowers are more responsive to appeals that encourage them to consider government an appropriate target of action, indicating their potential for increased political mobilization.

Chapter 6 considers how all of these dynamics coalesce within one of the most important sites of policymaking: regulatory agencies. Again, making use of archival material and legislative histories, I describe how policymakers chose to administer consumer financial protections through a fragmented regulatory arrangement that privileges the profit and stability of financial institutions over the protection of borrowers. As credit products proliferated, legislators delegated the primary rulemaking and enforcement authority for financial protection to executive agencies. Instead of concentrating authority within a single agency, however, Congress distributed that authority across seven preexisting agencies on the basis of the type of financial institution that administered a particular product. Most of these agencies were tasked with prudential, or competitive, regulation and not with protecting consumers (Levitin 2013; Carpenter 2014).

I argue that this fragmentation of regulatory authority for consumer financial protection across multiple agencies, all tasked with guarding industry interests, produced three significant regulatory feedback effects that diminished prospects for stronger consumer protection rulemaking: First, it led to regulatory arbitrage, whereby financial institutions were often able to play different agencies against one another to secure the least burdensome regulation (see Carpenter 2014). Second, it constrained the ability of consumer advocacy organizations to successfully lobby for more stringent consumer financial protections by raising the costs of and diminishing lawmaker receptivity to public interest lobbying. Third, this arrangement depressed citizen engagement in the regulatory process by making it especially complicated for borrowers to identify the appropriate political target for their participation. I explore these dynamics through interviews with consumer advocates and analysis of consumer complaint data.

The book concludes with a discussion of the CFPB's potential to create a critical juncture, reshaping the future politics of consumer credit. While substantive changes to the design of regulatory policies enacted by Congress largely failed, the emergence of the CFPB alters the administrative environment in meaningful ways. The CFPB centralizes rulemaking and enforcement authority for most consumer financial protections in an agency with a primary mission of promoting consumer interests, potentially raising the public profile of government in these financial transactions and reversing the political obstacles to public interest lobbying and participation. I also weigh the substantial obstacles to this result, most notably introduced by Republicans' ongoing attempts to subvert the CFPB's undertakings.

## *Expanding What We Know about Financial Regulation*

The financial precarity of American families has come into sharper scholarly focus over the last two decades. One of the more pressing

tasks for political scientists has been illuminating patterns of policy-making and political engagement with respect to these issues. Relatively absent from that narrative, however, has been consideration of the politics of consumer financial protection. *Democracy Declined* addresses the political dynamics of this crucial, though severely understudied, aspect of U.S. political economy. In so doing, it advances two distinct bodies of scholarship—studies of policy feedback and of consumer finance more specifically—and offers insights for policy practitioners.

With respect to the former, the theory articulated in this book expands the current, and rapidly growing, discourse on policy feedback effects in three important ways. First, it contributes to our understanding of how policies shape politics for a fundamental, though previously unexplored, piece of the U.S. political economy: consumer financial protection. Second, the book moves beyond the existing scholarly focus on policy feedback effects for redistributive policies (see Mettler and SoRelle 2017) to consider the unique dynamics of regulatory policy. The theory of regulatory feedback effects articulated here can help us understand how the design and implementation of regulatory policies more broadly shape politics for issues that touch virtually every aspect of our daily lives—from the food we eat to the air we breathe. Finally, this book introduces an important innovation that is largely absent from the existing policy feedback literature: I show that regulatory policies can influence politics through the administrative arrangements they adopt. Expanding our understanding of policy feedback effects to encompass this venue is essential because the rulemaking process accounts for as much as 90 percent of all federal policies enacted each year, yet it is too often overlooked by both scholars and citizens.

The book also contributes to the vital multidisciplinary work on consumer credit, debt, and the politics of consumption. The concept of the political economy of credit I explore in the following chapters extends current scholarship by providing the first major analysis of the political consequences of credit policy for public interest groups and borrowers. It also centers a different set of questions about the elements of financial regulation we should be attentive to. For example, most work on U.S. consumer financial regulation charts the changing volume and orientation of financial regulation over time (e.g., Vogel 2003; Prasad 2012), paying less attention to the specifics of those policies. Relatedly, much of the existing social science research on U.S. credit policy treats the expansion of mortgage and non-mortgage programs that emerged in the New Deal as two outcomes of a single broad, underlying phenomenon. This approach overlooks the fact that mortgage and non-mortgage policies are designed in fundamentally different ways—and they accomplish distinct political goals with distinct political consequences.

Generalizing about the details of consumer financial regulations in each of these ways, while important for exploring broad patterns of political development, limits our ability to understand the politics that are likely to emerge from discrete policy arrangements in a given historical moment. For example, federal home loan programs historically do not hide government's role in providing or regulating benefits to the same degree that consumer credit policies do. As a result, the theory of regulatory feedback I advance in this book would predict a greater degree of political engagement around mortgage finance and foreclosure defense than consumer credit and financial protection. By focusing on the details, rather than the broad strokes of policy design, the potential emerges for distinctive political futures to unfold from types of regulation that scholars frequently evaluate together.

## *Why the Politics of Consumer Financial Protection Matters*

The United States is a nation that runs on consumer finance. American consumers rely on an ever-evolving array of banking and credit products to pay for their food, clothing, shelter, transportation, and other daily necessities. Furthermore, the development of a profitable lending industry has itself become a key contributor to the growing American economy. Despite its political and economic significance, however, policymakers have largely failed to protect consumer financial interests, and borrowers have largely ignored the political arena as a viable forum for pursuing grievances with increasingly risky forms of lending. Not even calls from advocacy groups have been successful in turning borrowers toward sustained political action.

Consumers have accumulated some victories in recent years pursuing market mobilization on behalf of comestible and durable goods—particularly when that mobilization is targeted toward a single producer and there are sufficient alternatives within the market. By selectively boycotting or buycotting, consumers of products like fast food or shoes may be able to get individual producers to offer redress or change their way of doing business. But the ability of market mobilization to achieve success seems to rely on two factors: the choice and availability of other products in the market for consumption and the ability of consumers to get by without the product in question. For example, if a critical mass of consumers boycotts a fast food chain because it uses trans fats, they may have success in changing the company's policy because 1) consumers have plenty of alternative venues from which to satisfy their fried food cravings and 2) even without those alternatives, consumers would be able to meet their daily needs without the fast food products. The presence of these two criteria allows consumers to take meaningful market action.

These two conditions are unlikely to be met so easily for consumer financing. First, there are relatively few meaningful choices when it comes to financial products and services—particularly for middle- and low-income Americans. While information disclosures are intended to help borrowers "shop around" for the best credit deals, the federal preemption of stricter state consumer protections that began in the 1980s, coupled with the fact that most banks are now headquartered in states with minimal restrictions for those few statutes that have not been preempted, means that, while interest rates and overdraft fees may vary slightly by lender, the general trend is an industry-wide aversion to consumer-friendly terms and practices. This does not allow consumers to forego products from one financial institution in favor of better terms from another lender because the terms are comparable.

And, unlike with fast food, access to consumer finance is a virtual necessity for many Americans. The U.S. economy is predicated on providing citizens with bountiful access to credit in lieu of a strong social welfare system or guaranteed wage increases. Because consumers need credit to cover their day-to-day expenses—especially lower- and middle-income borrowers who may not have sufficient savings on hand to deal with emergencies—people cannot simply boycott their credit cards or refuse to pay off their student loans to protest excessive fees without risking both current and future financial insecurity. The necessity of consumer financing, coupled with the lack of meaningful choice, render market mobilization relatively toothless as a means to combat weak consumer financial protection.

Political mobilization, and its accompanying electoral accountability mechanism, may well be a more effective manner of successfully pursuing consumer financial reform. Thus, the fact that borrowers largely ignore this alternative has significant implications for the ability of both borrowers and consumer advocates to secure any significant change to lending practices. Despite the existence of political opportunities and organizations with the resources and expertise to generate borrower political action, the inability of advocates to construct collective action frames encouraging political mobilization that will resonate with today's borrowers, combined with a fragmented regulatory structure that is largely apathetic to the concerns of consumer protection, seriously hamper the implementation of meaningful reform.

The consequences of failing to enact better protections for consumers are severe. As events of the 2008 financial crisis ably demonstrated, growing debt borrowed under increasingly risky lending terms threatens not only the financial security of individuals but also that of the nation as a whole. Beyond these catastrophic events, the current system of consumer financial regulation also has the potential to consistently exacerbate the already staggering socioeconomic inequality in the United States in multiple ways.

The current lending system contributes to the ever-widening gap between the bottom 80 percent of Americans and the top 20 percent of wealthier citizens. While disclosure requirements provide insufficient protection regardless of income, banks and lenders can privilege wealthy borrowers by offering lower interest rates, grace periods, and many other services that less affluent borrowers are not privy to. By contrast, middle- and low-income borrowers are subject to more costly credit, a plethora of high fees for minor mistakes, and an effective zero-tolerance policy before fees kick in. The result is that wealthier borrowers are more insulated from the lack of stronger protective policy than are their less affluent peers.

No amount of government-mandated fine print can make the terms of these loans more affordable or equitable. As Elizabeth Warren (2007) observes, "If toasters are dangerous, they may burn down the homes of rich people or poor people, college graduates or high-school dropouts. But credit products are not nearly so egalitarian." Ultimately, the lack of stronger consumer financial protections—and the failure of Americans to demand such reforms—has the potential to disproportionately affect the economic fortunes of Americans who fall outside of the upper echelons of the socioeconomic elite, thus continually widening the gap between the haves and have nots in American society.

# 2 Full Disclosure: Building the U.S. Political Economy of Credit

After nearly a decade of failed attempts, on May 22, 1968, Congress finally enacted the Consumer Credit Protection Act (P.L. 90–321). President Lyndon Johnson signed it into law one week later. More commonly referred to by the name of its first provision, the Truth in Lending Act (TILA), this law marked the first major federal regulation of the growing consumer credit industry in the United States. Its passage was a watershed moment for consumer activists, and it is the law under which almost all subsequent financial protections for consumer credit are incorporated. The law attempts, as its opening declaration clearly states, "to assure a meaningful disclosure of credit terms so that the consumer will be able to compare more readily the various credit terms available to him and avoid the uninformed use of credit" (§102). Perhaps the most significant piece of information the new law required lenders to disclose was an annual percentage rate, or APR, to convey the cost of borrowing to consumers.

One decade after TILA's implementation, the Federal Reserve Board commissioned a study to see how well the law's disclosure provisions were working. As part of the 1977 Survey of Consumer Finances, borrowers were asked questions to gauge both their awareness of the use of APRs in credit contracts and their ability to meaningfully use that information to shop for the best credit deals. The study found that 70 percent of card users had heard of the term APR (Board of Governors 1977). Unfortunately for policymakers, knowing that APRs existed did not translate to knowing how to use them. A summary of the 1977 results worries:

> The only troublesome finding among these favorable, although possibly slow, trends [in APR awareness] is the discovery that the ability to use percentage rates to calculate dollar finance charges remains relatively uncommon. . . . Heightened consumer awareness has not been accompanied by an increase in credit shopping. (7)

In short, the new disclosures didn't make ordinary Americans better credit shoppers. The authors of the report concluded that revisions to the landmark law's regimen of disclosures might be necessary to more adequately protect Americans' finances. Instead, the exact opposite occurred in the decades that followed. Unwilling to throw out the proverbial baby with the bathwater, federal policymakers continued to rely almost exclusively on disclosure requirements to protect consumer financial transactions. They did so despite mounting evidence that disclosures were unsuited to the task. As Elizabeth Warren explained in a plea for a new approach to regulation:

> Financial products have become more dangerous in part because disclosure has become a way to obfuscate rather than to inform. . . . In the early 1980s, the typical credit card contract was a page long; by the early 2000s, that contract had grown to more than thirty pages of incomprehensible text. (2007)

Even as policymakers wrestled to rescue the financial industry in 2008, whose collapse stemmed in part from unsustainable debt generated by risky consumer lending practices that disclosures hadn't prevented, the major financial reform measures lawmakers adopted failed to depart from a model of consumer protection via information. Why, despite increasing evidence that disclosures are an insufficient form of consumer protection, have federal policymakers continued to rely on them as the primary—and in many cases the only—remedy designed to aid borrowers? This pattern of political decision making is especially mysterious considering how significant consumer credit has become as a source of financial support for the average American family and for the national economy. It is equally perplexing because it is unusual:

most other consumer goods and services are regulated by a combination of federally mandated information disclosures *and* robust safety restrictions and inspection standards that outlaw harmful products. The second prong of that approach is glaringly absent from the realm of consumer financial protection.

A common explanation for policymakers' reliance on information disclosures is the broad acceptance in policymaking communities of a behavioral economic approach to regulation, one that prioritizes disclosure above all else (Beales et al. 1981; Hadfield et al. 1998). Others might argue that this perplexing regulatory response is the result of Wall Street's dominant influence over policymakers (Hacker and Pierson 2010; Johnson and Kwak 2010). While those factors undoubtedly play a role in maintaining the status quo, I argue that the continued adoption of a failed policy, and indeed the unique reliance on disclosure to the exclusion of other protections, cannot be justified purely as a rational economic choice nor a result of interest group influence.

Instead, policymakers' continued dependence on information disclosures to protect the interests of borrowers is grounded in the political development of the American economy. This chapter explores the evolution over the course of the twentieth century of what I argue are the origins of a political economy of credit in the United States. Federal policymakers deliberately embraced an economic arrangement whereby governing institutions established and continue to support a consumption-based economy fueled in large part by Americans' access to consumer credit. In so doing, policymakers focused their attention on preserving national economic stability rather than protecting individual consumer welfare. It is the required maintenance of this arrangement, one predicated on wide access to consumer financing, often in lieu of other forms of purchasing power like higher wages or more generous welfare support, that I argue has set into motion the distinctive, path-dependent imperative for information disclosure as the major regulatory approach to consumer financial protection.

The chapter begins by reviewing evidence that information disclosures have failed to adequately protect borrowers. Turning to my proposed theory, the chapter next traces the evolution of the consumer financial protection policy regime in the United States.[1] I explore archival records from the Franklin Delano Roosevelt and Lyndon Baines Johnson Presidential Archives and the Consumer Movement Archives, congressional materials, invaluable historical and sociological scholarship on consumer credit, and a comprehensive analysis of federal consumer credit policies to explore why and how New Deal policymakers chose to establish a government-backed infrastructure to jumpstart consumer credit in order to drive economic revitalization. Having addressed the foundation of a political economy of credit, I then trace how subsequent attempts to enact borrower protections were constrained by the perceived need to preserve and expand consumer purchasing power to support the national economy. Finally, the chapter considers the far-reaching consequences of this policy legacy not only for federal policymakers, but also for the political behavior of borrowers, consumer advocacy organizations, and bureaucrats as well.

### *The Trouble with Truth in Lending*

The traditional explanation for adopting disclosure requirements in market transactions is largely rooted in principles of behavioral economics. According to this theory, information disclosure is the most efficient and least onerous method of combating adverse selection—when sellers have more information about products than buyers—and leveling the playing field between consumers and businesses (see Hadfield et al. 1998). So long as the consumer has access to sufficient information, the argument goes, the burden is on them to make smart decisions. The economic rationale for creating a fair market is no doubt part of the reason that lawmakers embrace information as a policy remedy to combat risky lending practices. Indeed, federal policymakers adopted labeling and disclosure requirements for food, drugs, and other consumer products over the course of the twentieth century for similar reasons.

The key difference, however, is that food, drugs, and most other consumer goods also became subject to increasing inspection and safety protocols, which prevent potentially harmful products from ever reaching the shelf. These types of safety standards remain largely absent from consumer credit. As Elizabeth Warren (2008) articulated, "Missing from the financial products market . . . are basic safety regulations that protect consumers in other markets from exploding toasters, collapsing car seats, and tainted meat" (453). And, as this chapter will demonstrate, even when a small contingent of federal policymakers have attempted to enact more restrictive credit protections over the years, they have rarely been successful. Of course, if information disclosures alone were an effective means of protecting borrowers from unscrupulous lending practices, then the absence of safety regulations would be understandable. But evidence suggests they are not.

As early as 1977, policymakers had reason to doubt people's ability to use the information mandated by TILA to protect their own financial

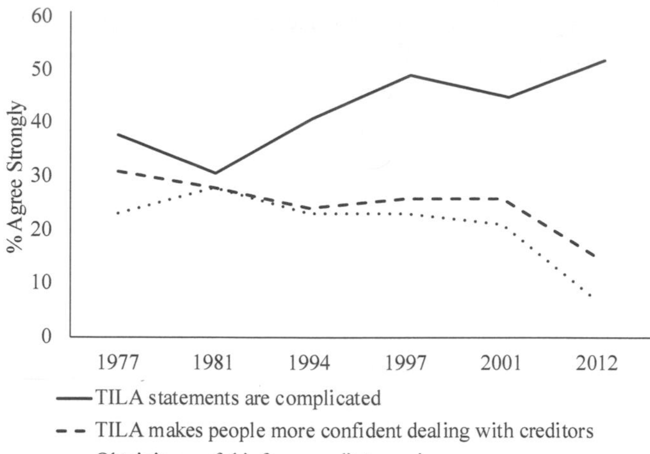


**FIGURE 2.1** Evaluations of Truth in Lending Disclosures, 1977–2012
Source: Board of Governors of the Federal Reserve System, Survey of Consumer Finances, 1970–2016

interest when shopping for credit. The Survey of Consumer Finances has continued to ask respondents to assess the efficacy of TILA's growing disclosure requirements over time. Figure 2.1 presents responses to three statements about credit disclosure requirements from 1977 to 2012: 1) TILA statements are too complicated, 2) TILA makes people more confident when dealing with creditors, and 3) obtaining useful information on credit terms is easy. People's answers suggest that shortcomings with disclosure-driven consumer protections have not abated over time. In fact, they appear to have gotten worse.

The number of respondents reporting that they "strongly agree" that TILA statements are complicated rose by about 20 percentage points from a low of 31 percent in 1981 to a majority (51 percent) by 2012. And these increasingly complicated disclosures don't appear to be making borrowers more confident in their credit decisions. To the contrary, the number of respondents who strongly agreed that TILA made them more confident in their interactions with creditors halved between 1977 and 2012, from 31 percent to 15 percent. Relatedly, a shrinking group of respondents thought that disclosures made it easy for consumers to find useful information on credit terms. While borrowers have always felt disadvantaged finding helpful information on credit terms—only a quarter (23 percent) strongly agreed that they could do so in 1977—that number declined to under 10 percent by 2012 despite the growth of required information disclosure. The conclusion seems clear: information disclosures are not an adequate or effective form of protecting borrowers in their credit dealings.

So why have they remained the primary remedy for federal policymakers? The reliance on information is especially puzzling because policymakers have expanded their protective efforts to safety and inspection protocols for other types of consumer goods and services. If neither the logic of behavioral economics nor the efficacy of the policy can explain the distinctive governmental reliance on information disclosure for consumer credit regulation, perhaps the failure to introduce more restrictive protections stems from the lobbying power of the financial industry.[2] Scholars have demonstrated that the financial industry can influence policymaking across a variety of domains including regulation (e.g., Hacker and Pierson 2010; Johnson and Kwak 2010). Upon closer inspection, however, this explanation also falls short.

This alternative assumes first that policymakers always consider multiple regulatory strategies and second that the financial industry is more permissive of disclosure requirements than of other alternatives. However, in many cases, as the legislative record discussed in the following pages demonstrates, policymakers preemptively narrow the alternatives under consideration to include only varying degrees of information disclosure, suggesting a form of policy learning at play. For example, during debate over TILA, described in greater detail in subsequent sections, Congressional leaders were clear from the start that the bill was restricted to considering disclosure. The debate that followed was fought specifically over how much, how little, and what type of information should be required and for what types of credit. Furthermore, there is little evidence to indicate that, even if policymakers do consider alternate approaches, lenders readily acquiesce to new disclosure requirements as some form of compromise. To the contrary, the financial industry has consistently fought to minimize disclosures and the regulatory burdens they impose.

Attributing the continual adoption of disclosure requirements to the power of industry lobbying also presupposes that banks and lenders hold a steady position of privilege relative to consumer groups across time. This, however, seems historically inaccurate. While consumer creditors today are powerful and well organized, they have not always enjoyed such advantages. Prior to the 1970s, when early federal consumer financial protections were being drafted and enacted, and when the financialization of the American economy was in its fledgling stages, lending interests—and the business lobby more broadly—were relatively disorganized compared to consumer coalitions (Pertschuk 1982). Even today, when the financial industry has gained considerable political power (Hacker and Pierson 2010), conditions of crisis can temporarily weaken that power to open up opportunities for reform (see Kingdon 1984; Baumgartner and Jones 1993). In response to a financial crisis, for example, we should not expect the financial industry to wield the same capacity to dictate policy terms that they otherwise might. Yet, through all of these periods, policymakers have been relatively single minded in their choice of information disclosures.

Two comparisons provide additional evidence that something beyond the power of the financial industry is at play in securing this pattern of policymaking. If policymakers' continued adoption of information disclosure to the exclusion of more restrictive protections were the sole result of Wall Street's lobbying power, we might see similar patterns of regulation for other consumer products backed by formidable industry. But, for example, the expansive power and resources of the pharmaceutical industry[3] haven't prevented lawmakers from imposing restrictions on drug manufacturers—including safety and inspection protocols—in addition to the labeling requirements that medications are subject to. Even within regulation of the financial sector more broadly we see varied strategies of consumer protection. For example, the 2010 Dodd-Frank Act introduced new restrictions for both mortgage and securities markets. It was, in fact, only for non-mortgage consumer credit—the type that I will argue has become a fundamental fuel for the consumption economy—that disclosure remained the go-to remedy.

For a final indication that the wishes of the financial industry are not driving this peculiar pattern of federal credit regulation we can look to the states. If powerful interest groups were solely responsible for the adoption of a specific approach to regulating consumer credit, we might expect those forces to influence state policymakers as well. After all, national and state-chartered banks and lenders all have a vested interest in the state rules restricting their lending practices. That means states should also be likely to rely on information disclosures to protect their residents' finances. In fact, given the competition among states to lure major financial corporations to make a home within their borders, states might be even more susceptible to the whims of the banking lobby, suggesting they would be especially likely to enact weak, disclosure-based consumer protections. But the reality of state policymaking looks quite different.

States have a long history of adopting and enforcing stringent consumer credit regulations, often enacting policies that place limits on the type of loans available and the cost of borrowing money. For example, one of the most common types of protective restrictions is a usury cap—a limit on the amount of interest a lender can charge. Usury laws, unlike information disclosure requirements, do not place the burden of shopping for a good deal on borrowers alone. Instead, these laws prohibit loans that the state deems too costly, risky, or unfair for borrowers. State usury laws date back to colonial times, and they vary widely today. In Pennsylvania, for example, the legal limit on consumer interest is 6 percent (PA Tit. 41 §§201, 202); in Arkansas, the limit is 17 percent (Arkansas State Constitution Article 19 Section 13).[4] The presence of usury laws like these, however much they may vary from state to state, demonstrates that neither pressure from the financial lobby, nor, for that matter, the appeal of behavioral economics, explains state lawmaker decision making.

Taken together, these details offer compelling evidence that, while the power of Wall Street undoubtedly influences the regulation of consumer finance, it cannot be responsible for such a distinctive pattern of federal policymaking on consumer financial protection. As Nolan McCarty and his coauthors similarly contend in their account of the post-2008 federal response to failures in the mortgage and securities markets, explanations that reduce financial regulation to suggesting that "Wall Street has captured Washington and always gets what it wants and gets it right away . . . [are] far too simple. Politicians and policymakers do often behave in ways that are not reducible to carrying water for Wall Street" (2013: 6). If federal policymakers' reliance on information disclosures to the exclusion of other, potentially better, remedies cannot solely be attributed to economic arguments or powerful financial interests, then what explains it? I argue that the answer lies in the path-dependent effects of adopting a specific approach to building and sustaining the national economy.

### *Policy Consequences in a Political Economy of Credit*

By concerning themselves primarily with consumer credit as a way to bolster an economic system reliant on mass consumption, I argue that policymakers have had to make specific decisions with respect to the design and implementation of consumer financial protections. In particular, as I identified in the previous chapter, policymakers faced a series of tradeoffs in their treatment of consumer credit, and at each point they prioritized measures that would privilege access over consumer protection and the financial security of institutions over that of individuals.

| ECONOMIC SYSTEM | PURCHASING POWER | SOURCE OF SUPPORT | FORM OF REGULATION |
|---|---|---|---|
| Production vs. **Consumption** → | Redistribution/Wages vs. **Financing** → | Public vs. **Private** → | Safety vs. **Information** |

**FIGURE 2.2** Policy Tradeoffs in the U.S. Political Economy of Credit

These decisions have had major consequences for both policy and politics.

Figure 2.2 summarizes the policy tradeoffs that will be discussed in greater detail in this chapter. First, New Deal policymakers embraced mass consumption to revive a staggering economy, thus reorienting policymakers' focus from promoting a production-based to a consumption-based economy. Doing so required sufficient purchasing power to jumpstart industries that literally had been put out of business by the Depression. Policymakers could have introduced new forms of government social welfare, higher wages, or other schemes of redistribution to provide citizens with sufficient capacity to purchase goods. While some new policies did just that, members of Congress and the Roosevelt administration eventually opted to pursue consumer financing as a major means of generating new purchasing power—an approach that has been embraced more fully in subsequent decades, while policies to improve wages or expand welfare have simultaneously experienced stagnation and retrenchment.

Policymakers next were faced with decisions about how to provide credit in the absence of a naturally occurring national market for legal, small loan lending. Rather than creating a new government agency to directly lend to consumers, an approach with waning political support after the creation of so many New Deal programs in that mold, Congress opted instead to introduce a system of government insurance to incentivize private companies to lend to borrowers. As Marriner Eccles justified to Congress during hearings for the implementation of the National Housing Act (NHA), "There is no lack of money. It seems to me, however, that it lacks velocity" (U.S. House 1934: 7). With the passage of Title I of the NHA, federal policymakers attempted to give "velocity" to the money sitting in banks. They created a system of home modernization loans designed to stimulate the construction industry, whereby the government would insure private lenders willing to participate in the program in lieu of providing the funds themselves.[5] It worked like a charm.

As banks discovered that consumer lending could be exceedingly profitable, the next two decades witnessed the evolution of several novel forms of consumer financing, most notably the credit card. With the growing use of these new forms of consumer credit came growing opportunities for abuse by lenders. Congress, having firmly embraced credit as a way to support an economy of mass consumption (and increasingly to circumvent some of the sticky political questions associated with welfare provision), needed to find a way to inspire consumer confidence in credit products, much as they had done decades before with manufactured goods. But having tied the country's fortunes to credit-fueled consumption, policymakers had to tread carefully. They needed to find an approach to regulation that would not restrict access to consumer credit—the all-important economic fuel. In the absence of such an imperative, policymakers might have adopted restrictions on financing terms, like a national usury cap, to ensure that Americans could borrow with confidence. Regulations that prohibited the issuance of certain types of credit, however, could limit the credit supply—particularly for middle- and low-income borrowers, so Congress turned instead to information disclosures as the primary remedy to promote consumer confidence, thereby maintaining widespread credit access.

The process of development that unfolds is, I argue, one of positive path dependence. That is to say, policymakers beginning in the New Deal instigated an "irreversible branching process"[6] whereby the decision to adopt credit to fuel a consumption economy, and the financial and technological developments that followed as a direct result, introduced both economic and political costs that would constrain the regulatory alternatives available to future policymakers. Significant economic costs emerged in two potential forms. First, any alternative that reduced access to credit had the potential to create a corresponding drop in consumption that might lead to macroeconomic instability or stagnation. Second, providing alternative modes of purchasing power to replace a political economy of credit, for example, by expanding public assistance, would require significant government investment. The political costs were equally high. Restricting credit would force policymakers to confront the far more politically dangerous issue of traditional welfare provision or mandatory wage increases necessary to support those who might lose access to credit should more restrictive financial protections be introduced.

The following pages describe in greater detail the political battles that led to these policy tradeoffs, focusing on policies enacted between 1934 and 2010. In order to systematically assess the presence of the distinctive policy features that I argue resulted from the creation of a political economy of credit, I also explore an original dataset of all significant consumer financial protections passed during this period.

### *Consumer Borrowing in Agrarian America*

The practice of consumer lending and a government's eventual decision to regulate it may well be as old as any policy legacy in recorded history. Provisions against usury were codified in the Code of Hammurabi around 1750 B.C.E. By the time the United States declared its independence from England in 1776, most states had usury provisions that capped interest rates on loans at around 6 percent (Ackerman 1981). But the types of consumer loans made in the fledgling nation bear little resemblance to modern forms of consumer credit.

From the colonial period through the late nineteenth century, "open book" credit was the primary vehicle for lending (Calder 1999; Gelpi and Julien-Labruyère 2000). Conducted without legal contracts, wholesalers would extend loans, typically for comestible goods, to those customers who relied chiefly on seasonal income. This form of consumer lending happened primarily within the realm of retail transactions. The provision of open book credit was essential to support an agrarian economy and, later, to facilitate westward expansion. Farmers required tools and seeds to cultivate their land, and they relied on credit to purchase those supplies from local merchants (Quinn 2019). Many such credit transactions, however, were predicated on the goodwill of shop owners and the trustworthy reputation of individuals within the community.

Even in the nineteenth century, the United States largely lacked both a unified national economy and a centralized state with the capacity to regulate either commercial or consumer financial affairs. After gaining independence, the United States existed for more than a century with the bulk of governance occurring in a piecemeal fashion at the state level in the so-called "state of courts and parties" (Skowronek 1982). Commercial financial disputes were typically managed within the court system (Glaeser and Shleifer 2001), and despite the presence of state usury laws, consumer financial affairs were dealt with almost exclusively between citizens and individual lenders.

Mobilization of agrarian interests in the latter decades of the nineteenth century marked the first significant attempt to engage the federal government in the regulation of credit (Sanders 1999; Prasad 2012; Quinn 2019). But this mobilization was designed to secure credit primarily to facilitate production. Of course, consumption and production are not mutually exclusive activities. For example, smallholder farmers serve a productive function, but to the extent that they purchase supplies or transportation for their crops, they are also consumers. Nonetheless, the distinction is still an important one to make because at this point in time it was the economic and political interests of producers that were of primary import to government policymakers. It wasn't until the 1930s that they became meaningfully concerned with consumer interests (Creighton 1976; Cohen 2003).[7]

### *Financing Industrialization*

The late nineteenth and early twentieth centuries witnessed a significant shift in the predominant form of production in the United States, and that change necessitated two new types of consumer credit. The industrialization of the U.S. economy led to the rapid manufacture of myriad new consumer goods, but in order to be economically successful, manufacturers needed ordinary Americans to buy those goods. Extending credit to consumers for the purchase of specific manufactured products became a profitable solution, particularly for businesses selling large-scale durable commodities like furniture, appliances, and especially automobiles (Olney 1991; Calder 1999). Originating in the United Kingdom in the form of "hire purchase"—a practice that resembles today's rent-to-buy schemes—American retailers began to issue installment loans (Olney 1991; Calder 1999; Hyman 2011). Interestingly, installment credit wasn't subject to usury laws because neither the state nor the courts viewed it as a traditional loan (Carruthers and Ariovich 2010; Hyman 2011). The result was that installment loans could be issued with fees exceeding what state usury laws permitted.

But the interest of retailers in financing the mass consumption of manufactured goods wasn't the only way that industrialization compelled new forms of consumer lending. The influx of workers to urban manufacturing centers disrupted many of the existing networks of personal financial support that existed within agrarian communities (Calder 1999). This new class of urban labor, primarily white males, no longer had access to familial sources of financial support to cover emergency expenses or brief periods of unemployment (Hyman 2011; Trumbull 2014). Nor did the burgeoning American welfare system offer benefits to this particular cohort to cover occasional financial shortfalls (Skocpol 1992). What these workers needed was a way to borrow small sums for unrestricted purposes that could be repaid once the borrower had overcome his temporary economic shock.

Unfortunately for workers, usury caps made the legal provision of such a loan unprofitable. At the turn of the twentieth century, the administrative cost to issue a small personal loan was roughly the same as that of a much larger loan. With state usury caps in place, the potential profit generated from interest on a small loan was, therefore, insufficient to overcome their burdensome administration fee, so reputable lenders simply didn't extend small loans (Hyman 2011; Trumbull 2014). Instead, a more nefarious entrepreneur entered the market to fulfill the demand. Loan sharks provided credit to urban workers secured by their future earnings and incurring exorbitant, and illegal, interest rates (Calder 1999). Between 1880 and 1920, loan sharks became an incredibly lucrative element of U.S. organized crime (Gelpi and Julien-Labruyère 2000).

Change was ultimately sparked by the idea that affordable consumer credit could serve as an ersatz form of welfare support for urban labor and an alternative to the "loan shark evil" (see Fleming 2012) and the associated doubling of outstanding debt that occurred between 1900 and 1920 (Williams 2004). Progressive reformers and organized labor coalesced to pursue change first through market incentives and later through state-level legislation that allowed for new forms of legal small loan lending (Fleming 2012). Progressives embraced this battle as part of a larger campaign to improve the conditions of the urban environment. Unions mobilized because they believed the availability of small loans not only would allow workers to combat occasional economic shocks but also would facilitate organized workers' ability to strike (Trumbull 2014).

These groups initially turned to charitable foundations to help provide alternative, less predatory small loans (Hyman 2011; Trumbull 2014), an understandable decision given the total absence of federal policymakers from the regulation of consumer credit. In early twentieth-century New York City, for example, "as much as 10 percent of all relief dispensed by the New York Charity Organization Society was provided in the form of credit" (Fleming 2012: 1078). Reformers hoped that charitable loans might stimulate market competition among financial institutions, but that hope wasn't borne out. The question of profitability still remained, so reformers set out to find a way to make legal small loans lucrative for private financial enterprises.

The vehicle to do just that emerged from the Russell Sage Foundation in 1916 (Hyman 2011; Fleming 2012; Trumbull 2014). The brainchild of Arthur Ham, the Uniform Small Loan Law was proposed as a way to counteract state usury prohibitions while maintaining reasonable limits to interest charged on small loans. The model law suggested allowing lenders to charge a monthly interest rate of three and a half percent—a ceiling of forty-two percent annually—for loans under $300 (Gelpi and Julien-Labruyère 2000; Hyman 2011). State legislatures were targeted because, in a period of dual federalism, the primary authority for day-to-day governance still rested with the state (Grodzins 1966).

With the backing of Progressives, unions, and a number of lenders themselves (Trumbull 2014), four states had adopted a version of the small loan law within a year. By 1928, twenty-five states had a small loan law on the books (Hyman 2011). Interestingly, while a few commercial banks began making small loans after the passage of these laws (Trumbull 2014), the bulk of the loans were issued by a new class of financial institutions, which called themselves a number of things including industrial banks, personal finance companies, or licensed lenders (Hyman 2011). By the 1930s, small loan lending had become both a profitable and a respectable business, with lenders numbering in the thousands. But the infrastructure for consumer lending was still relatively small in scope, restricted to the activities of retailers and their installment loans and these new small dollar lenders. With the enactment of a seemingly minor provision of a single law, however, Congress and President Roosevelt would take the first steps toward plunging the federal government in 1934 into the expansion and regulation of consumer credit, forever changing the consumer loan market in the United States.

## *"Modernizing" Consumer Credit*

The bank failures, massive unemployment, and widespread economic collapse that accompanied the Great Depression were too large for individual states to combat alone. As a result, a greater degree of policy-making authority than ever before was ceded to the federal government (Higgs 1987). President Roosevelt's new administration was tasked with creating programs that would help the country climb out of the economic crisis and subsequent recession. While the New Deal policies promulgated by the Roosevelt administration incorporated an array of intellectual approaches (Moley 1966), Roosevelt's famed brain trust was particularly convinced that underconsumption was a major contributor to the economic collapse (Cohen 2003).

Central figures in the administration quickly embraced the belief that consumers and mass consumption were of fundamental importance to the American political economy. Roosevelt himself, in an address at Oglethorpe University in May 1932, professed, "In the future we are going to think less about the producer and more about the consumer." Secretary of Labor Frances Perkins regularly referred to a "consumption economy." This type of thinking marked a shift from considering the economy in terms of production to that of consumption. And by this logic, if policymakers were to jumpstart the ravaged economy, they needed to ignite consumption (Cohen 2003; Hyman 2011).

Winfield Riefler proposed the method to carry out such a task. An eleven-year veteran economic advisor for the Federal Reserve, Riefler argued that restarting the stalled construction industry was the key to turning around the economy (U.S. Senate 1934). As Harry Hopkins, the Federal Emergency Relief Administrator, explained during congressional hearings for the NHA, "The building trades in America represent by all odds the largest single unit of our employment. . . . More than one-third of all of the 4,000,000 families on the relief rolls are identified with building trades" (U.S. House 1934: 1). By focusing on putting the construction industry back to work, therefore, New Deal policymakers were convinced that the recession could be reversed. Rather than subsidizing the construction industry directly—a production-oriented policy approach—they began to explore potential programs to stimulate construction by incentivizing the repair of the nation's housing stock, which had become increasingly dilapidated as homeowners squirreled away their meager savings during the Depression.

Of course, members of the Roosevelt administration were not the only ones to recognize the potential for a home modernization campaign to reignite the building trades. Companies like Hines and Johns-Manville launched advertising campaigns and promotions to encourage consumers to modernize (Harris 2012). But these businesses ran into the same problem that dealers of pricey durable goods had encountered years before, one that was compounded by the economic havoc wrought by the Depression: their customers lacked the cash for repairs, but an appropriate form of credit to cover the purchases didn't exist. Once again, it was left to the government to step in. This time, however, it was the federal rather than state governments that would intervene to provide an appropriate form of consumer credit to purchase these products and services.

The Home Owner's Loan Corporation (HOLC), established by the Roosevelt administration in 1933 to rescue mortgages in default, also, incidentally, provided limited funds directly to homeowners for the completion of necessary repairs (Harris 2012). The demand for these funds was substantial, and the experience shaped proposals for part of a new bill being developed to improve the nation's housing with an eye toward reinvigorating construction. The resulting National Housing Act of 1934 (P.L. 73–479) is perhaps best known for creating the Federal Housing Administration (FHA) and transforming mortgage lending in the United States, but it was the law's lesser-known Title I Home Modernization Loan Program that helped to revolutionize American consumer lending.

The goal of Title I was to encourage financial institutions to make loans to consumers for the specific purpose of home repair and renovation. Rather than issuing the funds directly to homeowners through a government agency as HOLC had done, however, Title I provided government insurance to private lenders for up to 20 percent of the total value of loans made by a participating lender. Individual loans for modernization were not to exceed $2,000. While policymakers recognized the potential benefit of the policy for homeowners, it was at best a secondary goal.

The acknowledged mission of the policy was to boost consumption of the products and services provided by the construction industry. In a message to Congress on May 14, 1934, President Roosevelt urged passage of the Act, stating, "The purpose of this program is twofold: First, to return many of the unemployed to useful and gainful occupation; second, to produce tangible, useful wealth in a form for which there is great social and economic need." Similarly, witness after witness during congressional hearings for the bill echoed Hopkins' statement that "a fundamental purpose of this bill is an effort to get these people back to work . . . an effort to move the heavy industries" (U.S. House 1934: 2). Even news coverage of the Act made the goal of boosting consumption to put people back to work explicit to readers:

> A government which has struck the fetters from millions of dollars in frozen credit today is begging its citizenry to modernize. It is calling on its citizens, as patriots, to take loans and buy new roofs for their homes, new heating plants, new wall coverings, new baths, to refurbish and build extensions and convert waste space into usable space. It is trying, in a nutshell, to end the depression by putting millions of men to work. (FHA 1934b)

The home modernization program was a clear attempt by federal policymakers to use credit to drive consumption in order to support the national economy. But why, if the appropriate credit market did not occur naturally, did policymakers turn to private entities to provide the loans necessary to support the desired consumption? Why not, instead, provide this "patriotic" credit directly through a government agency? The answer is twofold: policymakers believed that government-backed private loans were both more efficient and more politically feasible.

Roosevelt and his advisors learned important lessons from early New Deal attempts to replace functions of the market with direct government intervention. For example, both the Public Works Administration (PWA) and HOLC relied upon direct government involvement in the creation and preservation of housing. Championed by Secretary of the Interior and head of the PWA Harold Ickes, government intercession in the traditional role of private industry was adopted because, as Ickes argued, "We have left it so far to private enterprise, and the conditions we have are the result" (*New York Times* 1933). But early federal housing programs proved only a limited ability to achieve their goals, and private actors were not pleased with the government's entrance into what they perceived to be the domain of business (Hyman 2011). As a result of these dynamics, the NHA adopted a different approach. Hopkins explained to members of the House Committee on Banking and Currency, "We believe it is essential that we unloose private credit rather than public funds in the repairing of those houses and the building of new houses" (U.S. House 1934: 2).

The reasoning was framed primarily in practical terms. Eccles, then the Assistant to the Secretary of the Treasury, reported to Congress that financial institutions already had the capital to lend; it was simply a matter of encouraging them to do so—particularly for commercial banks that had largely avoided extending personal consumer loans to date:

> There is hardly a section of this country but what there are excess funds not working—not working, first, because the banks won't take the risks involved and, secondly, because there is no adequate form of credit available on a sufficiently attractive basis over a period of time to induce borrowers to use that credit. (U.S. House 1934: 7)

All government needed to do, therefore, was to provide an attractive loan vehicle and assuage banks' concerns about the riskiness of issuing the new product. Furthermore, according to Eccles, insuring bank loans was much more cost-effective than providing the money directly to consumers:

> The cost to the Federal Government is limited to $200,000,000 if a total of a billion dollars is loaned on these modernization

> and repair receivables, assuming that 20 percent of all the loans which are made are lost—which is almost inconceivable. . . . If a billion dollars is put out in this manner, it would have the same effect by the Government putting out a hundred million as it would if the Government directly put out, through its relief agency or other agencies, a billion dollars. . . . So if 200 million can act as a cushion to create the effect of a billion, it seems to me it is good business and good economy for the Government to provide that necessary cushion, rather than be forced, due to pressure of unemployment, to provide it all. (U.S. House 1934: 8)

In short, the government could spend much less to insure private lenders—even if they had to pay out the maximum amount of insurance—than it would to make the loans themselves. This message resonated with members of Congress, but practicality was not the only reason for routing the loans through private banks. Policymakers were concerned with the political viability of the program as well. Witnesses did not shy away from drawing distinctions between the proposed legislation and previous, and increasingly untenable, federal programs designed to intervene directly in housing and other forms of economic support. In response to a question from Representative T. Alan Goldsborough (D-MD) about the economic soundness of subsidizing loans, John Fahey, chairman of the Federal Home Loan Bank Board, responded:

> In my judgment, it is a far better policy to risk the comparatively small sum of money involved here to induce employment and stimulate and encourage really constructive work, as against facing the possibility of appropriating another $500,000,000 or $900,000,000 or $1,000,000,000 to maintain people in comparative idleness through the P.W.A. (U.S. House 1934: 26)

The modernization loan scheme provided by the NHA also had the support of business interests, who immediately saw the opportunity for profit with very limited risk. As Louis Hyman explains, "By working through private channels, the FHA did not seem like another one of Roosevelt's unnecessary, possibly socialist, or fascist, boondoggles, but a valid capitalist enterprise" (2011: 59). And to make the program even more attractive to private interests, Roosevelt tapped James Moffett, the former director of Standard Oil in New Jersey, to head the new FHA and the Title I program. Moffett subsequently staffed the agency with businessmen from a variety of industries (Hyman 2011).[8] While some members of Congress were concerned with the possibility that consumers would use this new type of credit as a way to "keep up with the Joneses" (U.S. House 1934: 32), the Act passed both chambers with bipartisan support on a vote of 176–19 in the House and 71–12 in the Senate (Congressional Record 1934a, 1934b).

The result was the creation of a government-backed private loan program designed to stimulate consumption within the construction industry in order to bolster the national economy. The program would be implemented through existing financial institutions, with the new FHA overseeing the process. The significance of this policy to the Roosevelt administration's effort to restart the economy through credit-backed consumption is evident in plans for its roll out. Both Eccles and Walker referred to a "campaign" to implement the program during congressional hearings (U.S. House 1934). Each walked back their statements to assure reluctant members of Congress that they did not mean for the government to engage in high-pressure loan sales.

But that is exactly what the FHA tried to do. The agency hired Ward Canaday, a businessman with experience working in auto finance companies, to run their public affairs program. It was, in essence, a government advertising campaign to encourage Americans to take out private loans. Canaday helped to design a Better Housing Campaign to encourage businesses and consumers alike to make use of the new modernization loans. In a letter to Press Secretary Early sent on August 23, 1934, Canaday passed along a selection of newspapers with sample "Better Housing" sections, noting that he encouraged these papers to combine their real estate and housing sections "into regular Better Housing sections" to "build up the nucleus of a program of advertising." An additional 45,000 radio broadcasts were run in the first six months of the program to publicize the loans (Harris 2012). The FHA also produced sample Better Housing brochures that communities could adopt to encourage their residents to make use of the modernization loans:

> For several years past, homes all over America have been steadily going down hill. Many property owners have been unable to pay for normal upkeep and repairs. . . . Now is the time to make those improvements. The National Housing Act was designed to help you improve your property and increase its value and usefulness. Through one of the simplest and most reasonable systems of financing ever devised, the Act makes it possible for

> you to make delayed repairs and provide better surroundings for your family. (FHA 1934a: 4)

While the program didn't single-handedly revive the economy, it was very successful. By October 1934, a mere four months after the Act was signed into law, news outlets around the country were touting the program's achievement. For example, an excerpt from a *New York Times* article published on October 17, 1934, proclaimed:

> A total of $1,001,091 has been lent to date by the National City Bank for home modernization purposes under provisions of the National Housing Act. . . . [The bank] added that property owners whose first monthly deposits had become due had shown the "best payment record in the history of the bank's personal loan department." (*New York Times* 1934)

Indeed, banks were incredibly pleased by the profits generated from the program. By 1935, about 254,000,000 dollars in modernization loans had been issued, comprising almost half of the total volume of funds generated by FHA programs, including the better-known mortgage financing (FHA 1935). Whereas only a few banks had personal lending departments in 1920, by 1940 at least 5,000 banks were registered as making Title I modernization and, importantly, a variety of other personal loans (Trumbull 2014). With this policy, the federal government clearly embraced a consumption-driven economy fueled by consumer credit. They also ignited a new phase of consumer lending in the United States that could be marshaled to support ordinary Americans' purchasing power. Having adopted these policies, the federal government laid the foundation for an economic system that, in order to maintain, would restrict subsequent policymaking efforts to implement financial protections.

### *Credit, Consumption, and the Wartime Economy*

Between the growing use of installment credit and the personal loan boom that followed from the Title I program, consumer credit continued to fuel mass consumption throughout the thirties (Hyman 2011). As the country rerouted its productive capacity toward war making with the outbreak of World War II in 1939, the federal government had to reckon with this new economic approach. This time, however,

President Roosevelt sought to restrict the supply of credit in order to drive down demand for consumer goods so that industry could focus on the production of war materiel (Trumbull 2014). Roosevelt enacted Executive Order 8843 on August 9, 1941. Claiming authority based on an extremely expansive reading of the Trading with the Enemy Act, the order directed the Federal Reserve to enact regulations to restrict installment credit (CQ Almanac 1947).

The resulting policy took form in Regulation W. It required consumers to make down payments of at least one-third of the total purchase price for a number of consumer goods as a condition for taking out an installment loan. The total period of the loan was restricted to between twelve and fifteen months (CQ Almanac 1947). Regulation W was designed primarily by Rolf Nugent and Leon Henderson, who had worked together in the Remedial Loan Department of the Russell Sage Foundation before taking jobs in the Roosevelt Administration (Hyman 2011). As Moffett had done, they were careful to cultivate the opinions of prominent retailers so as not to alienate businesses that had come to rely heavily on credit. The result was a relatively weak law with lackluster enforcement. The Federal Reserve Board lifted most of the credit restrictions on December 1, 1946, and President Truman advised Eccles, who was by then chairman of the Board of Governors for the Federal Reserve, to lift the remaining controls in the spring of 1947 (CQ Almanac 1947).

The enactment of Regulation W is relevant to our story for two reasons. First, while it briefly departed from the trend in federal policies toward expanding consumer credit, the creation of Regulation W is further evidence that policymakers realized how fundamental consumer lending had become as a driver of the American economy. Its regulation was, therefore, seen as key to the successful rationing of consumption. It is additionally important for the unintended consequences Regulation W wrought on the landscape of consumer financing in the United States. Regulation W focused on installment loans because its goal was to reduce credit specifically for the purchase of manufactured goods, whose raw materials were necessary for the war effort. While retailers were relatively complicit in the regulation's construction, their acquiescence did not preempt attempts to work around the new rules. If the policy put limits on closed-end accounts, the obvious answer was to devise an open-ended credit plan to circumvent restrictions. That is exactly what retailers did. They began utilizing new Charga-Plate technology to issue revolving credit to their customers, paving the way for the introduction and rapid proliferation of credit cards (Hyman 2011).

Credit usage, including the new credit cards, would skyrocket in the consumption boom of the postwar economy.

### *Regulating Credit to Promote Economic Stability*

By the early 1960s, the foundation for a political economy of credit was laid. About half of all U.S. households used some form of revolving credit in addition to existing closed-end consumer loans (Durkin and Staten 2002). As consumer financing continued to grow in the postwar era, so too did the potential for abusive lending practices, particularly because revolving credit was often exempt from state usury laws. In a special message to Congress on March 15, 1962, President John Kennedy acknowledged, "Consumer debt outstanding, including mortgage credit, has almost tripled in the last decade and now totals well over $200 billion . . . in many instances, serious abuses have occurred." But President Kennedy's sole concern was not how lending abuses affected consumers themselves. Instead, he explained, "Excessive and untimely use of credit arising out of ignorance of its true cost is harmful both to the stability of the economy and to the welfare of the public." Once again, the importance of consumer credit to the national economy received top billing.

In response to a perceived need for a voice for consumers within government, President Kennedy established a Consumer Advisory Council (CAC) under the purview of the Council of Economic Advisors (Creighton 1976). Helen G. Canoyer, dean of the New York State College of Home Economics at Cornell University, was appointed to lead the eleven-member council. The CAC was divided into multiple subcommittees, one of which was dedicated to consumer credit. There are several indications that the committee also recognized the relationship between consumer financing and economic stability. One of their core assignments was to "study the effect of consumer credit on the national economy" (CAC 1963). Meeting minutes from CAC member Caroline Ware, a long-time consumer advocate, note, "I think it is appropriate that we should give particular attention to consumer spending or the meeting of consumer needs and wants, as a generator of economic growth" (Ware 1962).[9]

While the advocacy community initially greeted the CAC with excitement, it ultimately had little real effect. A 1963 *New York Times* piece articulated the CAC's shortcomings, describing it as "an advisory group to an advisory group" and noting that "the Administration does not quite know what to do with the Consumer Council and is trying to limit its activity as much as possible" (Loftus 1963). On January 3, 1964, President Lyndon Johnson made a fresh attempt to establish an executive body tasked with consumer protection. He created the President's Committee on Consumer Interests (PCCI) and appointed Assistant Secretary of Labor Esther Peterson to oversee the group as the Assistant for Consumer Affairs (Johnson 1964). But in a message to Congress on February 5, 1964, introducing the PCCI, President Johnson's remarks once again implied that the reason to protect consumers was primarily to protect the economy. He opened his speech saying, "America's economy centers on the consumer" and went on to argue, "the consumer credit system has helped the American economy to grow and prosper." He voiced support for legislative proposals to regulate credit to protect the confidence of borrowers in order to maintain that economic prosperity.

### *The Birth of Truth in Lending*

The Truth in Lending Act (TILA) was the primary legislative vehicle to accomplish the President's stated goals. It was designed to deal with mounting concerns about consumer lending abuse and an associated diminution of consumer confidence. Initially proposed by Senator Paul Douglas (D-IL) in 1959, TILA required the disclosure of a "simple annual rate" of interest calculated on the basis of all charges levied to borrowers (S. 2755). Only four states—Massachusetts, Washington, Connecticut, and Maine—had comparable legislation at the time. Proponents of TILA believed it could alleviate growing concerns about the deceptive pricing of loans. Opponents of the legislation, primarily retail businesses and banks, argued that revealing an annual rate rather than the traditional monthly rate might confuse consumers and lead them to forego using credit (CQ Almanac 1967).

Several iterations of the Douglas bill remained mired in the Senate Banking and Currency Committee for nearly a decade. The bill's failure was, in part, the result of staunch opposition to the measure from committee chairman Senator A. Willis Robertson (D-VA) (CQ Almanac 1967). The Eisenhower administration had also opposed the bill when it was first unveiled. TILA finally began to gather steam when Presidents Kennedy and Johnson, and their respective consumer committees, voiced support for the legislation. Indeed, TILA was one of the four major proposals backed in the first (and only) CAC report issued in 1963. In the summary prepared by the Consumer Credit committee, the need for disclosure was supported with the following justification: "There is reason to believe that consumers who are informed about credit will use it with greater confidence, and thereby exercise a greater stabilizing force on the economy than will uninformed consumers" (CAC 1963: 6). Like its predecessor, the PCCI also recommended passage of TILA, with members presenting key testimony during congressional hearings on the bill.

Ultimately, however, TILA's passage was enabled by the 1966 electoral defeats of both Senators Douglas and Robertson, whose longstanding feud over the legislation had poisoned its prospects (CQ Almanac 1967). Senator William Proxmire (D-WI) took up TILA's mantle. During seven days of hearings on the bill (S. 5) held before the Senate Banking and Currency Committee in April and May of 1967, supporters were quick to note that the legislation was not intended to restrict or limit the terms creditors could offer, rather to provide information to enable consumers to shop in a fair marketplace. Proxmire opened the proceedings with the following statement:

> We are considering a full-disclosure bill and nothing more. The bill does not regulate credit. The bill does not tell lenders how much they can charge. The bill contains no assumptions that credit is bad. . . . Instead, the bill aims at providing consumers with the facts they need to make intelligent decisions on the use of credit. (U.S. Senate 1967: 1)

Similar to testimony presented during hearings on the National Housing Act more than thirty years before, TILA's supporters emphasized the limited nature of the proposed intervention. They highlighted how information disclosure was a minor correction to the free market, rather than a more onerous government restriction of free enterprise. Even Senator Douglas, the first witness during the Senate hearings, echoed this line of reasoning in his testimony:

> The basic philosophy behind truth in lending is a belief in free enterprise and in the price system. But if markets are to function properly, there must be a free flow of information. . . . By increasing the amount of information on consumer credit, we will remove a major imperfection in the marketplace. The alternative to regulation by the market is regulation by the government. This tends to be less efficient and leads to an increase in governmental power which conservatives deplore. (U.S. Senate 1967: 50–51)

The hearings also make explicit that TILA's ability to undergird economic stability and maintain access to credit was foremost in policymakers' minds. The following exchange between Senator Proxmire and James Robertson, vice chair of the Federal Reserve, exemplifies this:

> PROXMIRE: Do you think this bill would have adverse impact on the banking industry?
>
> ROBERTSON: My own view is that it ought to help. . . .
>
> PROXMIRE: How about the effect on the economy? After all, consumer credit has become a tremendously important aspect of our economy. It has been a force that has helped grow, develop, and expand our sales. Do you see this slowing down?
>
> ROBERTSON: I certainly do not. . . . This isn't going to curtail consumer credit overall. And as a matter of fact, I think it may very well help. (U.S. Senate 1967: 669–670)

The Senate eventually passed the bill by a vote of 92–0 on July 11, 1967 (Congressional Record 1967), but the compromise crafted by the Banking Committee excluded revolving credit accounts from the new annual rate reporting requirements in order to avoid the most contentious issue in the hearings. It also carved out loans with finance charges lower than ten dollars. Under the leadership of Representative Wright Patman (D-TX), a self-styled populist known for his adversarial relationship with banks (Young 2000), the House Banking and Currency Committee was not so willing to exempt revolving credit. The House version (H.R. 11601) extended the annual rate reporting requirements to revolving credit accounts and eliminated the carve-out for loans with small finance charges. Perhaps unsurprisingly, witnesses from the Administration supported these provisions. Interestingly, however, many business owners became unexpected proponents of the more stringent House bill, expressing the opinion that if a bill was to be passed at all it ought not to discriminate between open- and closed-end credit. Representative Leonor Sullivan (D-MO) described the position of these lenders to a conference of consumer advocates in 1967:

> Believe it or not, our greatest hope right now in getting through a strong bill which would treat all forms of consumer credit alike seems to rest in the efforts being put forward by a group which would really prefer no legislation at all—the small town and big city furniture dealers, who sell on the installment basis, and who

> have warned their Congressmen that they may be put out of business if they have to tell their customers they are charging at the rate of 18 percent a year, say, for credit arrangements similar or identical to those which the department stores, or Sears or the others on revolving credit, can offer at the expressed rate of 1-1/2 percent a month. (Sullivan 1967)

The House eventually passed the bill by a vote of 383–4 (Congressional Record 1968). Eventually, after a months-long stalemate over the revolving credit provisions (CQ Almanac 1968a), a bill was agreed to by the conference committee that required both open- and closed-end credit accounts to report a monthly and an annual rate of interest (U.S. House 1968). It was approved by Congress and signed into law on May 29, 1968. TILA's primary remedy, information disclosure, was to be administered entirely through existing market transactions with no obvious allusion to government's role in the regulation.

Given its reputation as a landmark consumer protection policy, anyone reading the opening rationale for the law might be justifiably confused to discover that the term "consumer protection" does not appear at all. In fact, individual borrowers are not even mentioned until the end of the "Findings and Declaration of Purpose," which reads as follows:

> The Congress finds that economic stabilization would be enhanced and the competition among the various financial institutions and other firms engaged in the extension of consumer credit would be strengthened by the informed use of credit. The informed use of credit results from an awareness of the cost thereof by consumers. (§102)

On the surface it seems strange that the declaration of purpose for the Consumer Credit Protection Act makes no explicit mention of protecting consumers. However, it makes a great deal of sense in the context of the political economy of credit. The law's opening is consistent with the idea that Congress was concerned primarily with protecting the national economy and its constituent financial institutions rather than the welfare of individual borrowers. Even consumer czar Ester Peterson's remarks to a national gathering of consumer advocates, made during the fight to pass TILA, reflect the understanding that informing consumers was ultimately designed not primarily for their own safety but to promote the stability of the national economy:

> In too many cases, the supposedly sovereign consumer is not given all the information necessary to allow him to be master of his kingdom. . . . If our free economy is to work properly, the consumer must have enough information to make rational decisions. . . . An informed buying public is no less essential to a free market system than an informed citizenry is to a free political system. (Peterson 1967)

With a firm foundation for a political economy of credit laid decades earlier, policymakers in 1968 faced a conundrum. They were constrained by the need to assure that sufficient access to credit existed to retain the viability of the system, but they also needed to make sure that consumers would take advantage of that access. Earlier experiences with the tension between state usury caps and the availability of credit led policymakers to believe that restricting the terms and types of credit that were legally permissible would cause banks to limit the supply of credit, particularly for the increasing proportion of middle-income borrowers. By contrast, policymakers believed that requiring lenders to disclose the terms of credit to consumers could inspire the necessary confidence to keep people taking out loans without preemptively limiting the amount and form of credit that banks would extend. In so doing, policymakers also shifted the burden of financial protection largely to borrowers themselves, fully embracing the doctrine of caveat emptor. By mandating the provision of information, it was now in the hands of borrowers to make smart decisions.

In short, because policymakers had adopted an economic system that promoted access over consumer protection, there really was no practicable policy alternative to information disclosure. This phenomenon was born out in congressional debates over the bill. For example, Representative Sullivan, a proponent of more stringent lending restrictions, initially suggested incorporating a provision in TILA that would require a national interest rate cap of 18 percent, but the amendment was quickly dropped after strong opposition from other members of Congress (CQ Almanac 1968a).

### *We Can All Agree on One Thing*

As federal policymakers worked to expand access to consumer financing to maintain the political economy that was set in motion in 1934, lenders found themselves extending an increasing volume of credit to borrowers they deemed risky. A variety of what consumer advocates term "exotic" loan products began to proliferate to serve that expanding population of borrowers. These new loan vehicles often included high and variable rates of interest, substantial fees, and other terms that made borrowing particularly costly for those who were most dependent on credit and least able to afford it. Yet public policy continued largely as it had before. As the following section demonstrates, 18 significant non-mortgage consumer lending regulations were passed between 1968 and the 2008 financial crisis, almost all of which adopted information disclosure as the sole or primary form of "protection."

I analyzed each of the significant non-mortgage consumer financial protection policies passed by the federal government from 1934 (when the National Housing Act was enacted) to 2010 to more systematically explore subsequent congressional efforts to protect borrowers. Significant policies were identified in three steps. First, I compiled the list of policies for which each relevant federal financial regulator has jurisdiction. I then supplemented this list with any additional policies identified in the prominent historical literature on the evolution of consumer credit in the United States (see Calder 1999; Hyman 2011; Prasad 2012; Trumbull 2014). Finally, I searched both the Congressional Record and the Congressional Quarterly Almanac for the relevant time period to identify any other major policy reforms. I have excluded from the dataset policies that provide technical corrections or updates without making substantive policy changes. The result is a dataset consisting of 22 consumer financial protections enacted by Congress between 1934 and 2010.

The following section explores the major remedies introduced by protections enacted prior to the 2008 financial crisis. I created two dummy variables to capture the remedy prescribed by a particular policy. Specifically, each policy remedy is coded using dummy variables to capture whether the policy establishes new information disclosures and whether a policy provides any restrictive remedy, for example, by outlawing certain types of practices or placing limits on the amount of interest charged for a transaction. These two types of remedies are included as separate dummy variables because policies may contain multiple remedies. As table 2.1 reports, 83 percent of the regulations employ information disclosures. In fact, every single consumer financial protection enacted since 1974 includes at least one significant disclosure requirement.

Many of these laws reflect disclosure requirements for new technologies in the consumer lending market. For example, as the use of credit reports increased, Congress enacted a series of laws, beginning

**Table 2.1 Consumer Financial Protection Policy Attributes, 1968–2010**

| Year | Policy | Policy Remedy | |
|---|---|---|---|
| | | *Disclosure* | *Restriction* |
| 1968 | Consumer Credit Protection Act | | x |
| 1968 | Truth in Lending Act | x | |
| 1970 | Fair Credit Reporting Act | x | x |
| 1970 | Provisions Relating to Credit Cards (Title V) | | x |
| 1974 | Equal Credit Opportunity Act | | |
| 1974 | Fair Credit Billing Act | x | x |
| 1976 | Truth in Leasing Act | x | |
| 1977 | Fair Debt Collection Practices Act | x | x |
| 1978 | Electronic Funds Transfers Act | x | x |
| 1980 | Truth in Lending Simplification and Reform Act | x | |
| 1988 | Fair Credit and Charge Cards Disclosure Act | x | |
| 1988 | Home Equity Loan Consumer Protection Act | x | |
| 1991 | Truth in Savings Act | x | |
| 1996 | Omnibus Consolidated Appropriations Act | x | |
| 1996 | Consumer Credit Reporting Reform Act | x | x |
| 1996 | Credit Repair Organizations Act | x | x |
| 2003 | Fair and Accurate Credit Transactions Act | x | x |
| 2006 | Military Lending Act | x | x |
| | Total | 83% | 56% |

with the Fair Credit Reporting Act of 1970 (FCRA), that mandate the disclosure of credit reporting information to consumers. The most recent, and perhaps most widely known, update was the 2003 Fair and Accurate Credit Transactions Act, which allows consumers to request a free credit report once every twelve months. As with TILA, Congress justifies these additional disclosure laws in terms of protecting the stability of the financial system rather than individual borrowers. As the declaration of purpose for the FCRA explains:

> The banking system is dependent upon fair and accurate credit reporting. Inaccurate credit reports directly impair the efficiency of the banking system, and unfair credit reporting methods

> undermine the public confidence which is essential for the continued functioning of the banking system. (§602)

Another major addition to the growing slate of consumer credit disclosure requirements was enacted in the Fair Credit and Charge Card Disclosure Act of 1988. The "Schumer Box," named for the bill's sponsor then-Representative Charles Schumer (D-NY), requires a credit card issuer to provide specific information about the card's APR, annual fee, and other interest charges in a standard format in any promotional material.

Most of the credit laws enacted after 1968 fall in a similar vein, designed to increase regulation through additional disclosure requirements. But three laws passed during the deregulatory turn that accompanied the election of President Ronald Reagan were actually designed to roll back some of the existing requirements (P.L. 96–221; P.L. 104–208). While many scholarly narratives focus on the deregulation of consumer finance that began in the 1980s,[10] it is interesting to note that even these attempts primarily revolved around disclosure requirements. Both the Truth in Lending Simplification and Reform Act of 1980 and the credit provisions of the Omnibus Consolidated Appropriations Act of 1996 attempted to deregulate through the reduction of disclosure requirements.

While the overwhelming majority of these policies embrace information disclosure as the primary form of consumer protection, just over half (56 percent) include some form of restrictive measure. That may seem like a significant number of non-disclosure remedies, but unlike the case of disclosure requirements codified in these policies, many of the restrictions are relatively minor aspects of each law. For example, the main restrictive remedy created by the 1968 Consumer Credit Protection Act includes a prohibition on wage garnishment to pay off creditors. This title was a relative afterthought in the bill compared to the disclosure requirements central to the same law, not least of which was the creation and required reporting of the APR. The wage garnishment prohibition also had little ability to affect the supply of credit as it was a direct ban not on a lending product, but on a method of debt collection. Even this provision, however, was justified in terms of the national economy, noting that garnishment might "hinder the production and flow of goods in interstate commerce" (§302).

Several other restrictive remedies follow this mold. The FCRA limits what can be included on a credit report (§605), but that provision is directly related to the larger disclosure elements of the act. The Fair Credit Billing Act of 1974 is predominantly a law to mandate that consumers are furnished with certain information on their monthly statements, but it also includes a provision that allows consumers to dispute any billing errors (§302)—another remedy directly tied to information disclosure. The Electronic Funds Transfer Act of 1978 is once again focused on disclosure requirements for EFTs, but it also includes a short provision stating that an EFT cannot be made compulsory for a borrower or account holder (§905). More than half of all the restrictive measures accounted for in this data are ancillary to the primary focus on disclosure requirements in the law.

There are, however, three notable exceptions that provide significant, and central, restrictive remedies. First, Title V of the FCRA, "Provisions Relating to Credit Cards," prohibits the issuance of unsolicited credit cards and sets the maximum liability for unauthorized use of such a card at 50 dollars. This act was passed in response to the growing practice among credit card companies of sending people active credit cards in the mail with no prior application on the part of the recipient. Not only did this custom influence people's credit scores, but it also led to significant credit card fraud as cards were stolen out of mailboxes or after being discarded. Outlawing this practice did not so much reduce the availability of credit as it reduced its fraudulent—and costly—use.

The Fair Debt Collection Practices Act of 1977 is the second law that introduced a major protective remedy. In this case, the law implements a number of rules that debt collectors are obliged to adhere to when trying to collect a debt. For example, they cannot call outside the hours of 8 AM and 9 PM local time, nor can they communicate with a borrower at work upon the borrower's request (§805–808). Once again, the restriction predictably has little effect on the overall supply of credit since it regulates activities that take place after the point of sale for a new loan or credit product. Instead, it enacts necessary measures to prevent the harassment of borrowers after they have already accumulated debt.

But perhaps the most significant piece of legislation to rely primarily on a restrictive remedy was the Military Lending Act (MLA). Part of the larger defense appropriations for 2007, the MLA placed a 36 percent interest rate cap on a variety of consumer loans made to active duty military and their family members (§605). While this law also included information disclosure provisions, in a rare turnabout these were secondary to the interest rate cap. This act represents the most significant divergence from the tendency to eschew restrictive policy remedies in favor of information disclosure for consumer financial protection. It is also hard to dispute that the MLA's rate cap might limit the supply of available credit, at least for military borrowers.

So why was this provision enacted despite being at odds with the goals of the political economy of credit? In this particular case, another mandate prevailed: national security. Military commanders and the Department of Defense were concerned that the dramatic increase in service member indebtedness posed a real threat to military preparedness. In an August 2006 report issued by the DOD, the department estimated that nearly one of every five military personnel used payday loans. In a particularly damning assessment of the power of information to protect borrowers, the report notes how the DOD and commanders employed several methods to provide information and education to service members about the potential dangers of predatory loans, but that didn't curb the problem. Instead, the DOD endorsed a 36 percent rate cap, concluding that "predatory lending undermines military readiness, harms the morale of troops and their families, and adds to the cost of fielding an all volunteer fighting force" (DOD 2006: 9). At the end of the day, the need for military readiness superseded that of widespread credit access—a logic similar to the grounds given for Regulation W. In this case, however, the tradeoff between credit access and national security was of a much narrower scope—affecting only military borrowers.

The general trend, as the evidence clearly suggests, is that the political economy of credit has produced an imperative for policymakers to ensure that any consumer lending remedy they enact doesn't interfere with the need to promote widespread credit access. The result has been the consistent reliance on information disclosure as the primary policy remedy for consumer financial protection. Interestingly, this mission has largely spanned partisan differences. I recorded the voting records by party for each policy for both the House and Senate. The degree of bipartisan support for many of these policies resulted in voice votes being taken on final passage of the legislation. Even though party polarization has increased dramatically since 1970 (McCarty et al. 2008)—the same period during which these laws were enacted—very few disclosure requirements have been subject to dramatic partisan divides.

As table 2.2 illustrates, only two pieces of legislation, the Fair Debt Collection Practices Act of 1977 and the 1996 omnibus appropriations bill (which included three separate credit acts), secured the support of fewer than half of each party's members in Congress. In the case of the latter, it is hard to know whether the credit acts or other provisions of the appropriations bill were responsible for the partisan gap in support. These trends suggest that the adoption of information disclosures in consumer finance, in addition to being a path-dependent outcome of previous policymaking decisions, also reflects bipartisan consensus.

**Table 2.2 Partisan Support for Consumer Financial Protections, 1968–2008**

| | | House | | | | Senate | | | |
|---|---|---|---|---|---|---|---|---|---|
| | | *Yes* | | *No* | | *Yes* | | *No* | |
| Year | Policy | %R | %D | %R | %D | %R | %D | %R | %D |
| 1968 | Consumer Credit Protection Act | 88 | 89 | .05 | 1 | 100 | 88 | 0 | 12 |
| 1968 | Truth in Lending Act | 88 | 89 | .05 | 1 | 100 | 88 | 0 | 12 |
| 1970 | Fair Credit Reporting Act | 76 | 66 | 0 | 0 | . . . | . . . | . . . | . . . |
| 1970 | Provisions Relating to Credit Cards (Title V) | 76 | 66 | 0 | 0 | . . . | . . . | . . . | . . . |
| 1974 | Equal Credit Opportunity Act | 51 | 78 | 34 | 13 | 90 | 86 | 0 | 0 |
| 1974 | Fair Credit Billing Act | 51 | 78 | 34 | 13 | 90 | 86 | 0 | 0 |
| 1976 | Truth in Leasing Act | 68 | 84 | 17 | 6 | . . . | . . . | . . . | . . . |
| 1977 | Fair Debt Collection Practices Act | 29 | 57 | 67 | 38 | . . . | . . . | . . . | . . . |
| 1978 | Electronic Funds Transfers Act | 75 | 81 | 11 | 6 | . . . | . . . | . . . | . . . |
| 1980 | Truth in Lending Simplification and Reform Act | 80 | 87 | 11 | 8 | 73 | 78 | 10 | 9 |
| 1988 | Fair Credit and Charge Cards Disclosure Act | 78 | 76 | 0 | 2 | . . . | . . . | . . . | . . . |
| 1988 | Home Equity Loan Consumer Protection Act | . . . | . . . | . . . | . . . | . . . | . . . | . . . | . . . |
| 1991 | Truth in Savings Act | . . . | . . . | . . . | . . . | 74 | 63 | 5 | 23 |
| 1996 | Omnibus Consolidated Appropriations Act | 81 | 44 | 14 | 46 | 94 | 47 | 6 | 51 |
| 1996 | Consumer Credit Reporting Reform Act | 81 | 44 | 14 | 46 | 94 | 47 | 6 | 51 |
| 1996 | Credit Repair Organizations Act | 81 | 44 | 14 | 46 | 94 | 47 | 6 | 51 |
| 2003 | Fair and Accurate Credit Transactions Act | 98 | 76 | 1 | 22 | . . . | . . . | . . . | . . . |
| 2006 | Military Lending Act | 97 | 86 | 1 | 11 | . . . | . . . | . . . | . . . |

Note: Empty cells reflect either voice votes or unanimous consent.

## *Preempting State Protections*

Beyond their own legislative activities, federal policymakers confronted another challenge to the maintenance of a political economy of credit. In a federal system of government, where states have tremendous power to set policy within their own borders, the absence of more stringent federal consumer credit protections might be mitigated if states adopt a different approach to lending regulation. Thus, it's no surprise that since the late 1970s, federal policymakers have also proactively sought to weaken the hold of state credit protections, which have historically included a broad range of restrictive measures including caps on interest rates, fees, and other finance charges.[11]

In 1978, the Supreme Court ruled in *Marquette National Bank v. First of Omaha Service Corporation* that nationally chartered banks were subject only to the regulations on credit card interest rates for the state in which they were headquartered, not, as had been practice, the state in which a borrower lived.[12] This allowed nationally chartered banks to relocate their headquarters to states with virtually no consumer financial protections and "export" higher interest rates and fees across the nation. By headquartering in a state with limited consumer credit regulation, nationally chartered banks could charge whatever fees and rates they wished even to borrowers who lived in states with more stringent protections. States like South Dakota and Delaware capitalized on the ruling, promoting their lack of regulation to entice national banks to move to the great benefit of their state economies. South Dakota's tax revenue from commercial banks grew from about three million dollars in 1980 to more than 27 million dollars in 1987, while Delaware's commercial bank tax revenue grew an even more astounding amount, from about two million dollars to 40 million dollars (Staten and Johnson 1995: 22).

With this precedent set, Congress acted quickly to dramatically expand preemption of state consumer financial protections.[13] With §521 of the Depository Institutions Deregulation and Monetary Control Act of 1980 (P.L. 96–221), Congress extended the ability to export interest rates and fees for consumer credit to state-chartered banks that make interstate loans. The effective preemption of state protections became complete with passage of the Riegle-Neal Interstate Banking and Branching Efficiency Act of 1994 (P.L. 103–328) and §731 of the Gramm-Leach-Bliley Financial Modernization Act of 1999 (P.L. 106–102), both of which expanded the population of banks that could export most-favorable national rates for credit contracts. With this series of actions, federal policymakers once again demonstrated their commitment to enabling wider access to credit in lieu of greater borrower

protection, this time by effectively wiping out safeguards adopted at the state level.

### *Consumer Financial Protection after the Crash*

Between 1968, when the first federal consumer credit protection was enacted, and 2006, when the last major credit regulation prior to the financial crisis became law, the trend was clear. Federal policymakers from both parties looked overwhelmingly to information disclosures to balance the mandate for broad credit access produced by the political-economic arrangement with the need for some form of consumer financial protection. They even sought to eliminate policies at the state level that deviated from this approach. But information disclosures did not curb the spread of risky lending practices or the associated growth in consumer debt described in the previous chapter. Nor, it turned out, were these disclosures sufficient to maintain national economic stability.

By 2008, Congress was confronted with the need to restore the stability of the financial system. They also had the opportunity to provide a greater degree of protection for borrowers. While much of the media, and indeed legislative, focus was directed toward resolving problems with subprime mortgage lending and the securities and derivatives markets, two major laws were enacted that dealt specifically with consumer credit. The Credit Card Accountability Responsibility and Disclosure (CARD) Act was adopted in 2009, shepherded through Congress by Representative Carolyn Maloney (D-NY). Dubbed "low-hanging" fruit in one prominent analysis of the policy response to the crisis (McCarty et al. 2013: 207), the CARD Act codified a number of regulations that the Fed was already in the process of implementing (Kirsch and Mayer 2013). Despite the economic situation, the CARD Act did not stray too far from the existing approach to consumer financial protection. It introduced a number of new information disclosure requirements, perhaps most notably a requirement that credit card statements show borrowers how long it will take them to pay off their balance at the current interest rate (Title II). The law did, however, enact some protective restrictions. The Act placed a cap on the fees that companies could levy for late payments (Title I), but it also allowed fees to keep pace with inflation, meaning that caps have risen each year since enactment. Title I also restricted the practice of double-cycle billing.[14] The provision that most clearly violated the tendency toward extending credit access was contained in Title III, which introduced restrictions designed to make it harder for young borrowers to get more credit than they were capable of paying off.

Interestingly, legislative support for the CARD Act more closely mirrored the bipartisan approval secured by previous disclosure laws than it reflected the bitter partisan divides that emerged for a number of other policy issues addressed during President Obama's administration. In the Senate, 88 percent of Republicans and 93 percent of Democrats voted in favor of the bill. In the House, 98 percent of Republicans voted to pass the CARD Act, while only 41 percent of Democrats did so. The curiously low support among House Democrats was likely in response to an amendment added by Senate Republicans—led by Senator Tom Coburn (R-OK)—that allowed people to carry firearms in national parks (§512).

The second major policy enacted in response to the financial crisis was the creation of the new Consumer Financial Protection Bureau (CFPB), which was established by Title X of the Wall Street Reform and Consumer Protection Act (Dodd-Frank). The formation of a federal regulatory agency designed specifically to protect consumer financial transactions was a revelation for its reshaping of the administrative environment, which will be explored in greater detail in chapter 6. In other ways, however, the CFPB preserved the status quo of consumer financial protection via disclosure.

Nine separate congressional hearings were held to debate the controversial proposal between June 24 and September 30, 2009. One of the primary questions for policymakers was whether the CFPB would be empowered to enact new types of protective regulations, or if it would simply enforce and extend the existing infrastructure of information disclosure–based policies. This debate spoke directly to the tradeoff between protecting borrowers and ensuring broad access to credit. Consumer advocates, championed by Elizabeth Warren, proposed an innovative approach to credit regulation as part of Dodd-Frank. They suggested that the CFPB could design a series of "vanilla" loan products as default credit vehicles for lenders to offer (Kirsch and Mayer 2013). These default products would be marketed as standard loans, and any alterations to them would be clearly identified for consumers. The idea was that each potential borrower would be provided with several "safe" loan products with federally preapproved terms and would have to actively select credit that came with alternative, and potentially riskier, terms. Such a provision would have been a significant departure from the existing approach to lending.

Perhaps unsurprisingly, it failed to gain Congressional support. Echoing earlier debates over TILA, even the proposed agency's champions acknowledged that the new bureau would have to be mindful not to institute new protections that would restrict access to financing and thus hinder the credit-fueled economy. Treasury Department official Michael Barr, who played a prominent role in drafting the Obama administration's proposal for the new consumer watchdog, explained that language was included in the bill to require the new agency "not just to look at questions of consumer protection but also questions of access" in its rulemaking (U.S. Senate 2009: 9). The result was the creation of a consumer watchdog tasked primarily with upholding the existing disclosure-based policy regime. As Ellen Seidman, a veteran of several government financial regulatory agencies, lamented about the eventual compromise, "We have to stop relying on consumer disclosure as the primary method of protecting consumers" (Kirsch and Mayer 2013: 16).

### *The Political Consequences of Consumer Financial Protection*

It's hard to believe that even a major financial crisis, perpetuated at least in part by the consequences of high-risk lending and inadequate regulation (FCIC 2011), wasn't enough of an incentive for policymakers to pursue a new consumer financial protection strategy. Instead, policymakers embraced procedural changes to the administration of these policies while holding fast to the disclosure-based approach. I argue that much of the failure to innovate in the realm of consumer credit regulation is tied to the political economy of credit and the New Deal policymakers who set it in motion.

While policies designed to provide access to consumer financing may have had secondary benefits at various points in time, for example, facilitating home modernization or providing a form of politically feasible welfare, the main goal of establishing a viable market for consumer credit was and continues to be promoting purchasing power to drive the growth and preserve the stability of the national economy. By creating a specific set of institutional constraints, most notably a reliance on expansive access to credit to support a consumption economy, federal policymakers felt their hands were bound when it came to protecting borrowers. The result, as I have demonstrated, is that policymakers relied on information disclosure, vesting individual borrowers with the primary responsibility for protecting themselves by making smart decisions with respect to credit use.[15] These dynamics form the backbone of the U.S. political economy of credit.

If the financial crisis did not lead to a significant reevaluation of the political economy of credit and its attendant policy regime, what would? The obvious answer is that voters could mobilize to demand reform. But the foundation of a political economy of credit, it turns out, doesn't only influence the choices of federal policymakers, it also inhibits borrower political activism. The consumer financial protections described in this chapter are the first piece in a larger cycle that perpetuates weak financial protections. The remaining chapters explore how these policies, through their design, implementation, and administration, have subsequently changed the game of consumer financial protection for borrowers, advocates, and bureaucrats alike—with debilitating consequences for reform.

# 3 "Storming Mad" but Staying Home: Depoliticizing the American Borrower

Mark Gregg[1] has a familiar story. In 2001, he could no longer work after having major surgery. As he explained to a *New York Times* reporter in 2003, finances were tight with only his Social Security disability check for support. Explaining that he "was really sick, so there were things going on that [he] wasn't really diligent about," Mr. Gregg admitted that he had overdrawn his bank account a few times. What he didn't know until the charges started showing up on his statement was that his bank—FirstMerit in Akron, Ohio—had automatically enrolled him in "overdraft protection" and was charging him a hefty fee for each overdraft.

Banks have long provided their best (i.e., wealthiest) customers with overdraft lines of credit. As with traditional loans, banks notify their eligible customers, who may choose whether to accept an overdraft loan. Customers are then able to overdraw their accounts by as much as several thousand dollars, repaying these loans at a relatively low annual interest rate. Mr. Gregg, however, was not the type of customer to qualify for such an exclusive loan. Instead, he was the "beneficiary" of a far more common—and costly—form of overdraft protection that has increasingly become the norm at U.S. banks.[2]

These overdraft protection programs, which typically cover personal checks, ATM withdrawals, automatic payments, and debit or check card purchases, allow customers to overdraw their accounts for a flat fee of, on average, thirty-five dollars for each overdraft—a fee equivalent to an annual interest rate of 1,000 percent or more (Berenson 2003). Unlike the more exclusive overdraft lines of credit, the overdraft limit for these new protection programs is much smaller, capped at a few hundred dollars, and the balance must be repaid in a matter of days. Until 2009, when regulations were implemented requiring upfront disclosure and affirmative consent for overdraft protection,[3] the vast majority of bank customers were automatically enrolled in protection programs; many, like Mr. Gregg, remained completely unaware of their participation until they received notice of the fee they were required to pay for overdrawing their account. Banks usually market overdraft protection as a courtesy service that "saves customers the embarrassment and cost of rejected payments" (CFPB 2013). In reality, however, overdraft fees are part of a growing number of charges that banks have implemented over the last few decades to boost their profits.[4]

Mr. Gregg accumulated around 1,000 dollars in overdraft fees following his surgery. When he couldn't pay them off, FirstMerit closed his account. Then they took the remaining fee balance—evidently without warning—from his mother, who had cosigned on her son's account. She was "storming mad" and thought the whole practice "should be illegal." But neither she nor her son did anything about it beyond talking with their bank. Mr. Gregg told the reporter he felt that banks like FirstMerit "have got you against a wall, and you just throw up your hands."

Stories like Mr. Gregg's, of people who suffer the effects of costly and deceptive lending practices yet fail to do something about it—particularly when that something involves politics—are common. Even in the midst of the 2008 financial crisis, borrowers like Mr. Gregg and his mother largely avoided political avenues to address their growing dissatisfaction with consumer financial protection. Political mobilization was elusive for those who were hit hardest by unscrupulous lending as well as for the millions of Americans whose finances were potentially threatened by weak consumer financial protection. In fact, observers called the inability to channel people's anxiety and anger over predatory financial practices toward demands for policy reform one of the most striking puzzles of the crisis (McCarty et al. 2013; Kirsch and Mayer 2013).

Political ambivalence in response to predatory lending is perplexing for a number of reasons. First, ordinary Americans have demonstrated their willingness to engage politically on issues that affect their financial security, like taxes, social program spending, and health care (e.g., Campbell 2002). (Imagine, for a moment, how Mr. Gregg might have responded if the problem had been with his Social Security check and not his checking account.) So why do Americans deviate from this pattern when it comes to fighting for consumer financial protections—a crucial pillar of so many households' finances? Second, financial reform was a federal legislative priority, making it a frequent topic of media coverage in the lead-up to and aftermath of the financial crisis. People were thus presented with an obvious opportunity to voice their concerns to lawmakers, yet most chose not to take it.

Perhaps the most puzzling part of the story, however, is that political inaction to address consumer financial protection is not indicative of a more general aversion to doing something in response to predatory financial practices. As will be discussed in this chapter and the next, evidence shows that many distressed borrowers have chosen to voice their significant displeasure directly to market-based actors like banks, lenders, and even trade associations. Similarly, groups of borrowers occasionally mobilized to protest predatory lending practices and demand reforms during the Great Recession; once again, however, protesters typically targeted big banks and financial trade groups instead of their elected representatives and federal financial regulators—even as public opinion indicated growing support for government regulation of the financial industry. Why have American borrowers been reluctant to act through political channels to secure greater consumer financial protection?

In this chapter, I argue that general theories of political engagement provide insufficient or incomplete answers to this puzzle of political inaction. Instead, I offer an alternative explanation: borrowers' strategies for engagement on financial protection have been shaped by their experiences with the policies at the heart of the political economy of credit. As the previous chapter details, the United States depends upon wide access to consumer finance to support a consumption-driven economy. In order to sustain this macroeconomic model, policymakers have relied on information disclosures as the primary form of consumer financial protection. I contend that the specific decisions policymakers have made with respect to the design and implementation of information disclosures shape people's preferences for action, or, in this case, for political inaction.

Drawing on the consumer credit policy dataset introduced in the previous chapter, I explain how existing consumer financial protections have the potential to both *privatize* and *personalize* the practice of consumer borrowing in the United States. Policies *privatize* consumer borrowing in two ways. First, Congress established a system wherein credit is provided to borrowers by government-backed market institutions, rather than directly from government agencies. This obscures the fact that federal policymakers not only were responsible for helping to create modern consumer credit, but also continue to play a key role promoting and regulating consumer finance. Second, relying on information disclosures as the primary policy remedy to protect borrowers further privatizes the use of consumer credit. These regulations are implemented by lenders in the form of lengthy contracts people receive in the course of normal financial transactions, thus masking government's role in the creation and enforcement of regulation. All of this means that the average American can open a bank account or apply for a loan and never "see" government play a role in protecting their finances during the process.

Information disclosures also *personalize* consumer borrowing in two ways. First, information disclosures—and the principal of caveat emptor they exemplify—convey a model of the borrower as a rational market actor, treating the procurement and usage of credit as a personal financial decision in which the onus is placed on the consumer to make appropriately informed—i.e., responsible—decisions. As I will demonstrate later in this chapter and the next, the result for most Americans is an assumption that people who experience problems with credit are probably to blame for their own financial misfortune. Second, these policies rarely offer protections based on membership in a particular constituency, instead basing them on participation in individual credit transactions. As a result, most credit protections fail to create distinctive constituency groups that could mobilize for political action.

I propose that the combination of privatizing and personalizing consumer borrowing encourages people to place more blame for credit problems on market actors—including both borrowers and lenders—than on political actors, even as people voice support for generic government regulation of the financial sector. Because financial protections teach borrowers to view credit purely as a personal financial matter, I argue that people are discouraged from engaging in political action to demand stronger government regulations. The following pages develop this theory in greater detail. I draw on public opinion data that captures consumer credit usage and attitudes about regulation compiled from a variety of sources, including an original survey of American borrowers, to explore how these policy experiences shape people's beliefs about and action on consumer financial protection.

This chapter ultimately demonstrates that the overwhelming majority of consumer financial regulations are designed and implemented in ways that implicitly discourage people from pursuing political reform. These trends illuminate an interesting finding regarding consumer financial protection policies in the United States. Consumer lending, particularly as a form of economic assistance, bears all of the hallmarks of what Suzanne Mettler (2011) calls a submerged policy. That is to say, despite government's role in generating and supporting consumer credit as a form of economic assistance, the provision of financing occurs almost entirely within the scope of the market, meaning that Americans increasingly view consumer financial protection as an apolitical issue. This pattern is also consistent with what Jacob Hacker (2006) dubs America's "personal responsibility crusade"—lawmakers' increasing predilection for policies that are characterized by market logic and that channel benefits through market structures. The chapter concludes by discussing the consequences of a policy regime that discourages borrower political action: the removal of people's most viable pathway to financial protection.

### *Are Borrowers Angry?*

There are many reasons why people might eschew political activism on behalf of financial issues, even in the aftermath of a major financial crisis. The most obvious is that, despite general outrage at Wall Street, most consumers may be satisfied with their own borrowing experiences and see no need for reform. But several indicators of consumer sentiment suggest this is not the case. Problems with financial products and services make up a significant proportion of the complaints that have been collected by Consumer Sentinel[5] in recent years. In 2018, for example, debt collection was second only to imposter scams in eliciting complaints, comprising 16 percent of all reports. Banks and lenders garnered another 5 percent of all consumer complaints. Similarly, problems with banks and lenders, credit bureaus, and debt collectors regularly rank in the top ten complaint categories in most states.

More evidence of growing consumer dissatisfaction with credit is reflected in the Fed's Survey of Consumer Finances. Figure 3.1 details people's specific problems with their own credit cards over the last decade and a half. For example, more than 90 percent of respondents in both 2000 and 2012 strongly agree that credit card interest rates are unreasonable. Relatedly, about three-quarters of respondents strongly agree that the common practice of sending out card solicitations with

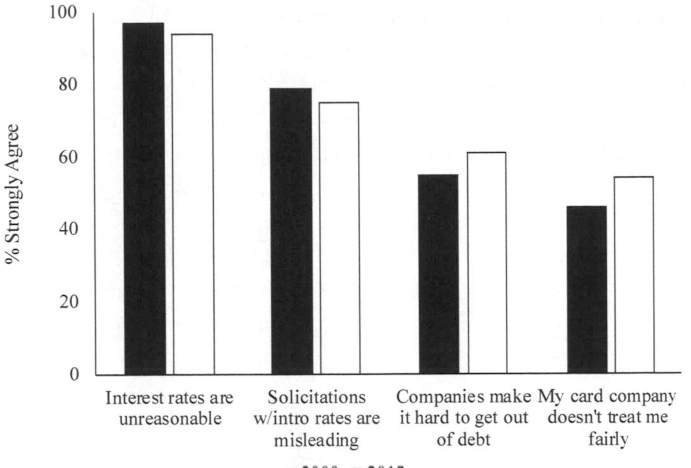


**FIGURE 3.1** Attitudes about Credit Cards, 2000 and 2012
Source: Board of Governors of the Federal Reserve System, Survey of Consumer Finances, 1970–2016

"teaser" introductory interest rates that later change is misleading. A majority of respondents (55 and 61 percent respectively) also strongly agree that credit card companies make it difficult for people to get out of debt. Perhaps most telling, however, is that about half of all respondents felt strongly that their own credit card companies failed to treat them fairly. And that number is on the rise, increasing eight percentage points between 2000 and 2012. These data make clear that a majority of Americans not only have negative views of many common financial practices, but that they also have significant complaints about their own lenders. When considered together, such indicators provide compelling evidence that a substantial number of Americans are dissatisfied with the state of consumer lending—feelings that were likely exacerbated by the 2008 financial crisis.

### *Explaining Consumer Inaction*

If consumers do indeed have grievances with the financial products and services they use, then perhaps their lack of political activism stems from other factors. One common refrain suggests that borrowers who suffer financially as a result of predatory lending and increased consumer debt must be lower income and, therefore, may not have the resources that have proven to be an integral contributor to political engagement.[6] This argument, however, underestimates the range of American borrowers who rely on credit and are subject to risky lending terms. While certain demographic groups are especially vulnerable to the harms of predatory lending, a reality described in chapter 1 and covered in greater depth in chapter 5, less affluent borrowers are neither the largest cohort of people who rely on credit nor the exclusive (or even primary) targets of risky loan practices that can ruin financial futures.

According to the Survey of Consumer Finances, a majority of Americans in every income quintile but the lowest use credit cards; the poorest Americans are considerably less likely to have access to mainstream sources of credit or traditional bank accounts (Bolton and Rosenthal 2005; Baradaran 2015). The growth in usage since credit cards became more widely available in the 1970s has similarly been skewed toward more affluent Americans. The lowest income quintile is the only group for whom the growth in card usage between 1970 and 2007 increased fewer than forty percentage points. By contrast, those in the middle-income quintiles experienced the greatest growth in usage during the last four decades. These trends suggest that middle- and upper-income Americans should be at least as likely, if not more so, to have a vested interest in protecting against risky lending practices—especially because these practices are not reserved for the least affluent borrowers.

As chapter 1 detailed, about four in ten non-mortgage consumer loans that originated on the eve of the 2008 financial crisis were subprime, meaning they were lent to borrowers with credit scores below 640 on a scale from one to 850 (Zibel and Andriotis 2015). While it is true that a larger percentage of low-income borrowers incurs costly finance charges, in terms of raw numbers, subprime consumer loans affect all socioeconomic groups—especially middle-income borrowers. Income[7] and credit score are correlated to a degree, with the most affluent Americans more likely to have higher credit scores and vice versa. However, the actual number of low-income borrowers is comparatively small such that in 2007, high-income people outnumbered low-income people in every single credit score decile, even doubling the number of low-income Americans in the lowest decile of credit scores (Board of Governors 2007). It is, in fact, middle-income borrowers who are the most evenly distributed across all credit score deciles and who represent the largest portion of each. This distribution means that middle- and even high-income borrowers held a substantial portion of those subprime loans, income groups predisposed toward greater political engagement. Furthermore, a 2007 report by the *Wall Street Journal* found that even borrowers with higher credit scores were frequently subjected to loans with subprime terms (Brooks and Simon 2007).

The idea that predatory lending is a problem for a wide swath of

Americans is reflected in this data. While low-income Americans may be least able to weather the financial burdens imposed by predatory loans, and we should certainly be concerned with the disproportionately harmful effects of such lending on the most vulnerable borrowers, the general stagnation in wages (Gould 2015) and relatively low rate of personal savings make costly credit and high fees dangerous even for more affluent borrowers. Most Americans are only one economic shock—perhaps in the form of a lost job or a serious illness—away from finding themselves in an inescapable cycle of debt. This reality helps to explain why Elizabeth Warren emphasized the relevance of consumer financial protection and reform for middle-class families in the lead-up to and aftermath of the 2008 crisis (Kirsch and Mayer 2013). It also suggests that resource deficiencies probably aren't to blame for people's lack of political action on credit issues.

If the actual financial toll taken by predatory lending isn't stalling political action, perhaps the psychological toll is. It's possible that financial stress itself—like that generated by mounting consumer debt or harassing debt collection practices—might limit civic participation. Recent work provides evidence to corroborate this theory. In a series of experiments designed to test how people respond to political appeals, Adam Seth Levine (2015) discovered that reminding people of their own economic insecurity makes them less likely to invest in related civic and political activity.

The problem in applying these explanations, and indeed each of the preceding accounts, to the current puzzle is that they would likely predict a general absence of engagement—whether targeted toward market or political actors—by affected borrowers. As will be discussed in greater detail later in this chapter and the next, this simply doesn't reflect the reality of people's engagement with consumer financial protection. While political activity has been virtually non-existent, it is fairly common for consumers to engage in market action, both to deal with their own credit grievances and, occasionally, to make broader demands of firms and trade associations for increased consumer financial protection. So, why are people unwilling to take political action to support stronger financial protection?

### *Does Government Have a Trust Problem?*

One explanation advocacy groups commonly cite for limited consumer political activity is that Americans ignore policymakers when trying to fix their financial problems because they have such a low opinion of government (Kirsch and Mayer 2013). It is, of course, true that the federal government—and especially Congress—has a poor reputation of late. Congressional approval ratings hovered in the teens and twenties for most of the period surrounding the 2008 financial crisis (Gallup 2016). But there are several reasons to question the idea that the dearth of political mobilization for financial protection is the result of general distrust in government.

First, the lack of political engagement on this issue isn't new. As will be demonstrated both later in this chapter and particularly in the next, this is a trend that dates back well into the 1960s, spanning times of both higher and lower trust in government. Second, the government's recent struggle with low approval ratings has not quashed political engagement for all issues. Nor, even, has it entirely done so for other financial issues generated in the wake of the crisis. In 2009, for example, when it was discovered that bonuses were paid to AIG executives using federal bailout funds, the public outcry aimed directly at political leaders was so great that it led to swift congressional hearings and a vote to tax those bonuses at 90 percent (McCarty et al. 2013).

Another indication that low trust in government is not solely responsible for pushing borrowers to pursue their grievances in the marketplace is that the banking and finance industry wasn't performing any better in the eyes of the public. As figure 3.2 illustrates, even at the best of times only a minority of Americans deem the financial industry honest and trustworthy. The banking industry also experienced a precipitous drop in public trust in the years prior to and immediately following the 2008 financial crisis.

According to a series of public opinion polls conducted by Harris Interactive between 2003 and 2010, the percent of respondents who agreed that banks were "honest and trustworthy" dropped by about ten points—from 40 percent to 30 percent—between 2004 and 2007. Between 2007 and 2009, during the onset of the crisis and the following recession, trust in banks plunged a further 18 percentage points, down to 12 percent. This drop was equally, if not more, precipitous than the decline in public approval of Congress for the same period, and it put public trust in financial institutions on par with or lower than trust in federal policymakers. Yet Americans still turned to banks and lenders to demand solutions to their problems with credit.

Finally, if people are convinced that government cannot be trusted to do what is right, we might expect that attitude to manifest in relative antipathy toward increased government regulation. Once again, however, this is not borne out in public opinion expressed during the crisis.

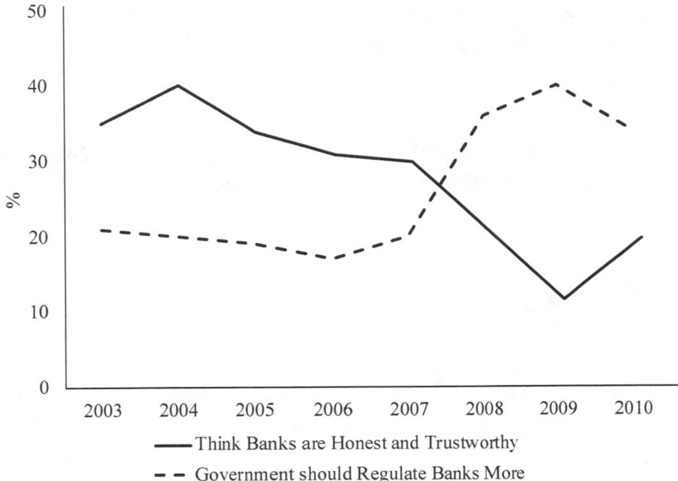


**FIGURE 3.2** Attitudes about Banks and Bank Regulation, 2003–2010
Source: Harris Interactive Poll, 2003–2010

As figure 3.2 also shows, respondents reported a substantial increase in their support for generic government regulation of the banking industry during the financial crisis. In fact, the percent of respondents voicing support for greater government regulation of banks actually doubled from 20 percent to 40 percent between 2007 and 2009. The growth in public support for government regulation of the financial industry is particularly noteworthy when compared to other industries that made headlines between 2003 and 2010. The auto industry, having undergone a similar collapse during the financial crisis, experienced only a modest two percentage point bump in the number of respondents supporting its further regulation during that period. People's desire for increased regulation of drug and health insurance companies, by contrast, actually dropped. Most notably, support for regulation of health insurance companies decreased about ten percentage points—from 52 percent of respondents (a slim majority) to 42 percent—between 2007 and 2010. These patterns are especially interesting because they reflect a decline in support for government regulation of health-care and related industries just as President Obama and Democrats in Congress were working to enact health-care reform.

If Americans were as satisfied with their own financial products and services as they often report being with their own health-care providers, we might have observed a similar public reaction to the banking industry when Congress considered financial reform. Of course, the banking industry contributed significantly to the financial crisis while the health-care industry was less obviously culpable, so support for greater regulation is no doubt driven in part by this fact. But if people completely distrusted government's ability to improve financial conditions, why were they so anxious for the government to regulate banks and lenders? Instead, public trust in banks declined while support for financial regulation increased. Despite these trends, people either stayed home or turned to market, and not political, actors to protest risky, high-cost consumer credit. Why?

### *How Credit Policies Shape Credit Politics*

I offer an alternative, policy-driven explanation for the lack of political action in response to predatory lending. People's strategies for engagement on consumer financial protection have been shaped by their experiences with the policies at the heart of the political economy of credit. By concerning themselves primarily with consumer credit as a way to bolster the national economy, policymakers have made specific, often path-dependent, decisions with respect to policy design and implementation of consumer financial regulations. I argue that these features generated regulatory feedback effects that have significantly influenced the behaviors of citizens in making demands for greater consumer financial protection.

Figure 3.3 illustrates the specific pathways identified in chapter 1 along which I argue regulatory feedback effects shape the social identity and civic status of consumers. Variables that align with these pathways are coded for each policy included in the consumer credit policy dataset from the previous chapter. With respect to social identity, I contend that consumer financial regulations that are designed to offer benefits in a transactional manner personalize the procurement and usage of financing while suppressing any sense of collective consumer identity. More traditionally targeted policies might activate collective consumer identi-

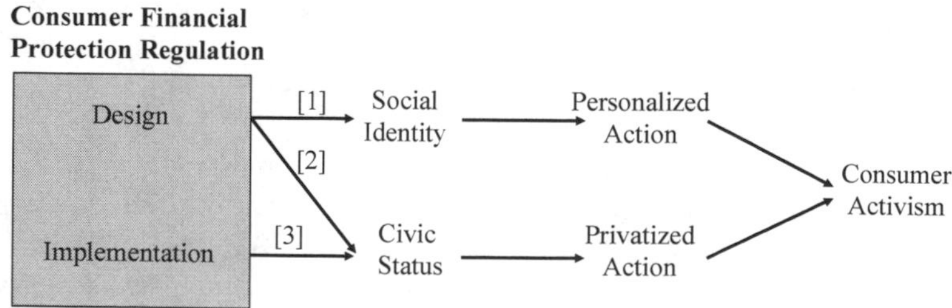


**FIGURE 3.3** Consumer Financial Protection Regulatory Feedback Effects for Individuals

ties. As chapter 1 explained, the creation of a discrete target population often enables beneficiaries, or in this case borrowers, to mobilize around that identity. When a policy treats beneficiaries as individuals, however, they may not be empowered to mobilize collectively.

The degree to which a policy constructs an individual or a collective social identity through policy design [1] is captured by a single dummy variable. Any policy that identifies a specific target population (e.g., elderly credit users, military borrowers) is coded as one. If the policy is broadly applicable to any individual who engages in a particular credit transaction (e.g., any person using a prepaid credit card), it is coded as zero. For example, the previous chapter discussed two policies that I coded as targeting a specific population: the CARD Act, which contains a section with specific regulations for young borrowers, and the Military Lending Act, which applies protections only to service members and their families. By contrast, the original Truth in Lending Act applied to all credit card users, an identity based on an individual transaction rather than an ascriptive or shared set of group characteristics.

I further identify two pathways along which policies can shape borrowers' civic status—the degree to which they view consumer financial protection as within the jurisdiction of the state. First, the remedy specified by a particular policy design can shape civic status [2]. If a policy provides remedies geared toward maintaining fair market competition rather than intervening in the function of supply and demand through a more restrictive measure, borrowers may learn that, as long as transactions are "fair" and borrowers are informed, they are accountable for their own financial affairs as responsible players in an increasingly complex market of financial products. By contrast, if policymakers design regulations to prohibit certain lending practices, like capping interest rates, borrowers may come to understand that the state also bears some responsibility for protecting consumers from harmful practices.

As discussed in the previous chapter, I employ two dummy variables to capture this aspect of policy design. The remedies for each policy are coded to distinguish between those designed to ensure fair market competition versus those that dictate specific terms and protective limits on the financial product or service. As previously discussed, information disclosures are the most prominent form of remedy used to bolster fair market competition across all types of consumer products (Beales et al. 1981; Hadfield et al. 1998), so a dummy variable is included to measure whether the policy establishes new information disclosures. A second dummy variable is constructed to measure whether a policy provides any restrictive remedy, for example, by outlawing certain types of practices or placing limits on the amount of interest charged for a transaction. These two types of remedies are included as separate dummy variables because policies may contain multiple remedies.

The degree to which government's role in consumer financial protection is evident in a policy's implementation can also shape a consumer's civic status through its effect on people's attributions of responsibility [3]. A dummy variable is included for each policy to identify whether the remedy is implemented in any way that makes government visible to borrowers—a conservative measure. Policies that are implemented entirely through the existing market transaction are coded as zero. By contrast, if government is evident in the implementation of a particular remedy, this variable is coded as one. For example, a policy that requires the disclosure of certain information on a credit card application might be implemented in one of two ways. The information might simply be included on the application a consumer receives directly from the credit card company, showing no indication that government mandated its provision. Alternately, a policy might require that each credit card application also include a specific pamphlet produced by a government agency that lists the terms that creditors are required by federal law to disclose and provides contact information for a federal agency that consumers can contact if the credit card company has not provided information on the required terms. Table 3.1 presents the results of each of these policy attributes for all policies in the dataset.

Do policymakers design and implement consumer financial protections that have the potential to personalize and privatize the use of finance as I hypothesize? The evidence suggests that they do.

### Personalizing Financial Protection

Figure 3.4 reports the degree to which U.S. consumer financial protections identify specific target populations versus providing benefits based on individual transactions. The overwhelming majority of financial protections enacted since 1934 provide benefits in the latter manner. About four of every five policies provide remedies to all borrowers of a particular type of credit, that is to say, based on an individual transaction. Only four consumer financial protection laws apply to a specific target group. Of those four, two are designed to extend access to credit to those who were absent from the ranks of borrowers at the time of passage: the Equal Credit Opportunity Act of 1974 and the Improving Access to Mainstream Financial Institutions Act of 2010. The ECOA, as will be discussed in chapter 5, helped expand access to women and minority borrowers by preventing credit discrimination. The Improving

**Table 3.1 Consumer Financial Protection Policy Attributes, 1934–2010**

| | | Social Identity | | Civic Status | |
|---|---|---|---|---|---|
| Year | Policy | *Transaction* | *Group* | *Market* | *Government* |
| 1934 | National Housing Act (Title I) | x | | x | |
| 1968 | Consumer Credit Protection Act | x | | x | |
| 1968 | Truth in Lending Act | x | | x | |
| 1970 | Fair Credit Reporting Act | x | | x | |
| 1970 | Provisions Relating to Credit Cards | x | | x | |
| 1974 | Equal Credit Opportunity Act | | Women | x | |
| 1974 | Fair Credit Billing Act | x | | x | |
| 1976 | Truth in Leasing Act | x | | x | |
| 1977 | Fair Debt Collection Practices Act | x | | x | |
| 1978 | Electronic Funds Transfers Act | x | | x | |
| 1980 | Truth in Lending Simplification and Reform Act | x | | x | |
| 1988 | Fair Credit and Charge Cards Disclosure Act | x | | x | |
| 1988 | Home Equity Loan Consumer Protection Act | x | | x | x |
| 1991 | Truth in Savings Act | x | | x | |
| 1996 | Omnibus Consolidated Appropriations Act | x | | x | |
| 1996 | Consumer Credit Reporting Reform Act | x | | x | |
| 1996 | Credit Repair Organizations Act | x | | x | x |
| 2003 | Fair and Accurate Credit Transactions Act | x | | x | x |
| 2006 | Military Lending Act | | Military | x | |
| 2009 | Credit CARD Act | x | Youth | x | |
| 2010 | Consumer Financial Protection Act of 2010 | x | | | x |
| 2010 | Improving Access to Financial Institutions Act | | Low-income | x | |
| | Total | 86% | 18% | 95% | 18% |

Access Act, which was not passed until after the most recent financial crisis, includes Treasury Department funds to support grants designed to stimulate credit access to unbanked low-income consumers.

Only two policies since 1934 have extended protections to a specific group of existing borrowers. The most significant of these was the Military Lending Act of 2006. This act, part of a larger defense appropriations bill for the 2007 fiscal year, authorized the Department of Defense to cap the interest rate on certain types of loans made to military mem-

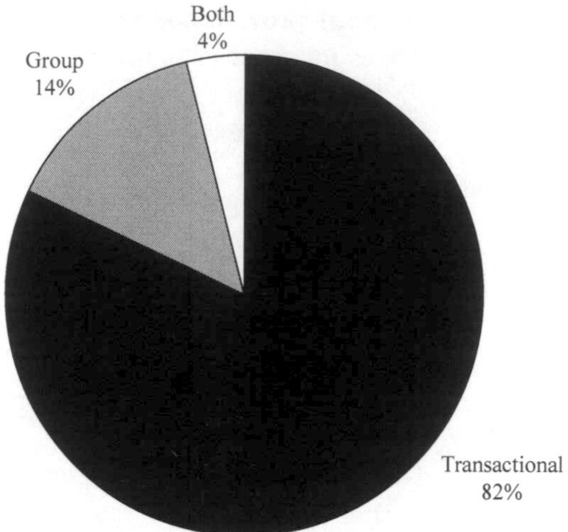


**FIGURE 3.4** Personalizing Attributes of Consumer Financial Protection, 1934–2010

bers and their families. The other policy providing some protective measures to a distinct group of potential borrowers is codified in Title III of the CARD Act of 2010. Passed after the financial crisis, this title sets forth rules for borrowers under twenty-one years of age that make it more difficult for them to access, and potentially abuse, credit cards. Despite these two exceptions, the overwhelming trend is that consumer credit policies are targeted toward individual transactions, potentially personalizing the use of consumer credit.

### Privatizing Financial Protection

To what extent do these policies treat borrowing as a political rather than a market issue, thus influencing the civic status of borrowers? As figure 3.5 shows, approximately one-third employ only a remedy based on the disclosure of information to consumers. In total, almost three-quarters of the policies rely on information disclosure as at least one type of remedy. By contrast, only one of every ten financial regulations relies exclusively on a restrictive remedy, with only half of all policies including any restrictions at all. And as chapter 2 detailed, many of these restrictive measures are minor provisions, ancillary to the overall disclosure mission of the law. For example, one such measure prohibits credit reporting agencies from including certain information in their credit reports. This evidence clearly suggests that the majority of consumer financial protections are designed with a preference for market remedies.

Perhaps even more important than the type of remedy adopted by these policies, however, is the way in which the remedy is implemented.

Only four policies (18 percent) provide consumers with an obvious indication that government is involved in the regulation of credit. Of those, just two—the Home Equity Loan Consumer Protection Act of 1988 and the Credit Repair Organizations Act of 1996—mandate that lenders provide consumers with specific information about their rights that includes contact information for federal government agencies. In each case, the allusion to government is still minimal. A third, the Fair and Accurate Credit Transactions Act, mandates a similarly minor indication of government involvement in credit. It requires the creation of a government-run website (MyMoney.gov) to distribute information on financial literacy, which illuminates the role of government in consumer financial protection only for people who choose to visit the site. Only one of the consumer protections enacted since 1934 provides a truly visible indication to borrowers that government is involved with the regulation of their financial affairs: the Consumer Financial Protection Act of 2010, which established the Consumer Financial Protection Bureau.

The result of these two dimensions of consumer financial protection regulation is that, while some policies provide limited remedies that extend beyond disclosure requirements designed to promote fair market competition, the tendency to bury these protective remedies within ordinary market transactions may well render them powerless to convince citizens that government is responsible for protecting borrowers' interests. Instead, the clear majority of policies obfuscate the role of government in consumer credit regulation, thus privatizing the use of credit for most borrowers.

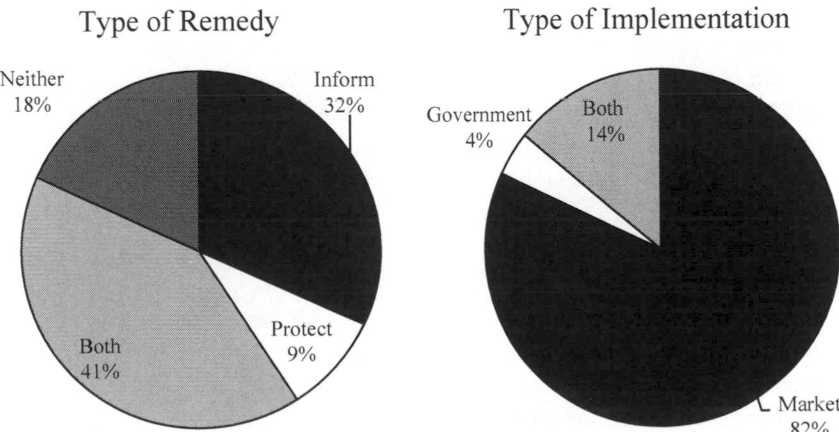


FIGURE 3.5 Privatizing Attributes of Consumer Financial Protection, 1934–2010

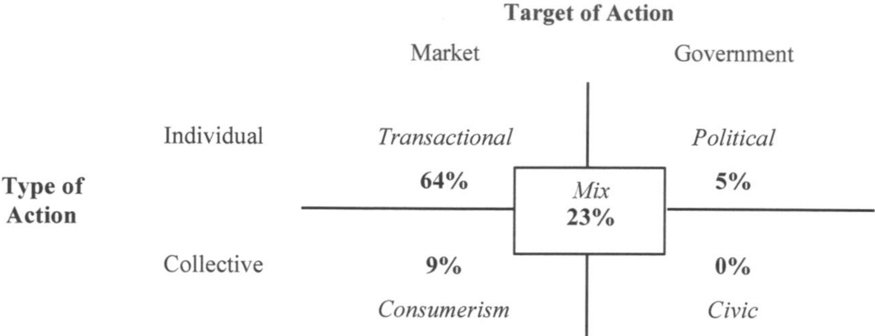


**FIGURE 3.6** Predicted Consumer Mobilization Strategies by Policy Attributes

I argue, as depicted in figure 3.3, that the way in which these policies shape social identity informs citizens' preferences for taking either individual or collective action in response to concerns about financial protection. Similarly, the way that policies shape the civic status of borrowers informs borrowers' preferences for the target of any action they take. The combination of these personalizing and privatizing elements of consumer financial protection design and implementation, illustrated in figure 3.6, shapes the landscape for borrower mobilization to address consumer financial protection in the United States.

Figure 3.6 illustrates how the various combinations of policy features described above are predicted to map onto potential strategies for consumer mobilization. About two-thirds of consumer financial regulations combine elements that I anticipate will generate personalized norms about borrowing with the privatization of policy remedies and implementation. I expect policies such as these to lead people to address both specific and systemic issues with consumer financing within the bounds of normal market behavior, for example, by calling their lender to complain about a problem or by moving their business to a different lender when they feel they are being treated unfairly. A further 9 percent of policies combine privatized policy designs with a group identity, potentially leading to collective mobilization within the market, or what I call consumerism. By contrast, only one policy—the Consumer Financial Protection Act of 2010, which created the CFPB—relies primarily on non-market design and implementation measures, potentially generating traditional self-interested forms of political engagement. About one in five policies (23 percent) include a mix of provisions, typically a combination of both information and minor safety disclosures. Only one mixed policy, the Military Lending Act of 2006, combines a prominent safety remedy with a collective target population. As a result, I predict that military predatory lending remains the one area likely to generate collective political mobilization to support consumer financial protections.

*Survey of Consumer Credit*

I argue that the specific design of consumer financial protection regulations teaches American borrowers to think of credit as a personal matter and to blame market actors—both themselves and their lenders—for problems they encounter with consumer finance. I expect that this will encourage people who decide to respond—either to specific problems with their own accounts or to broader concerns about predatory lending—to do so individually, and to target market, and not political, figures. To explore patterns of blame and corresponding action for consumer financial issues, I conducted an original survey[8] of 1,500 American adults representing all fifty states and the District of Columbia, hereafter referred to as the 2017 Survey of Consumer Credit.[9] The survey included questions about individuals' experiences with and opinions about consumer banking and credit. It also requested information about how borrowers respond, or might respond, to negative experiences with finance as well as how they participate in other forms of politics.

Survey respondents were asked to report what, if any, types of financial products and services they had used or made payments toward in the past year.[10] They were then asked whether they had been treated unfairly or experienced problems with any of these financial transactions. People who reported a negative experience were also asked to detail what type of problem they encountered.[11] Figure 3.7 presents the distribution of credit use for survey respondents, and the percent of borrowers who experienced problems for each type of financial service used.

Almost all respondents reported using at least one financial product or service in the past year, highlighting the importance of credit to the livelihood of the average American. The most common financial service used by respondents was, perhaps unsurprisingly, a bank account, which includes exposure to finance charges, like account fees and overdraft protection, associated with it. About eight in ten respondents had a checking account. Credit card usage was similarly high, with roughly three-quarters of respondents saying they had at least one. Finally, just under a quarter of survey respondents reported using a personal loan in the previous year. Twenty-nine percent of borrowers said they experienced at least one problem with the financing they used in the past year, and those rates were fairly consistent across different types of products

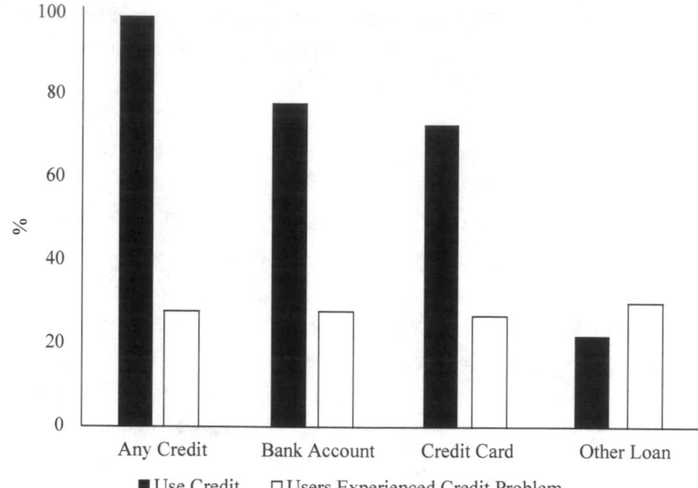


**FIGURE 3.7** Use of and Experience with Consumer Finance in the Past Year, 2017

and services. With almost a third of respondents reporting at least one recent negative credit experience, it's no wonder the Survey of Consumer Finances discussed earlier in the chapter found that nearly half of Americans feel their lenders are treating them unfairly.

## *Borrower Blame*

Whom do borrowers blame for these problems with financial products and services? I argue that most people, seeing almost no sign of government's role in protecting consumers' credit transactions, instead focus their ire on market actors—both borrowers and lenders. Figure 3.8 presents analysis of respondents' answers to a series of questions asking them to identify the degree to which each of these actors should be blamed for the "problems people experience with financial products and services like bank accounts, credit cards, and loans." The scores reflect the average (mean) blame assigned to each actor on a scale from one to five, where one equals no blame and five equals all of the blame. "Banks and lenders" and "consumers" received the greatest amount of blame from respondents at 3.2, falling between a moderate amount and a lot of blame. It is noteworthy that survey respondents placed equal blame on both lenders and consumers for problems with credit. This is consistent with the idea that information disclosures teach borrowers to hold themselves responsible for their own financial experiences.

Government actors, by contrast, were deemed less culpable. "The president" was accorded the least blame (2.7), with Congress and federal agencies receiving slightly more (2.9 each). Of particular interest is the gap that exists between the average blame borrowers assigned to market actors versus political actors. As figure 3.8 illustrates, the average blame people placed on market actors was about half a point higher than the blame assigned to political actors. These responses provide support for the notion that today's consumers are focused on the market, not the government, as the responsible party for financial grievances.

This blame gap—the extent to which respondents assign more blame to market actors than political actors—is not driven by a small group of respondents who are unusually likely to point the finger at financial institutions or borrowers. As figure 3.9 shows, just over half of all respondents place more blame for problems with credit on market actors than on political actors. Only 27 percent of respondents were likely to hold political actors more culpable, and about one in five respondents allocated equal blame to both groups.

But is the tendency to blame lenders and borrowers consistent across all respondents, or do people who use credit, and thus experience financial regulations, respond differently from those who do not? Figure 3.10 illustrates the average "blame gap"[12] by people's experiences with different types of financing. We have already ascertained that the average respondent placed greater blame for problems with credit on market actors than political actors. Across all three types of credit, however,

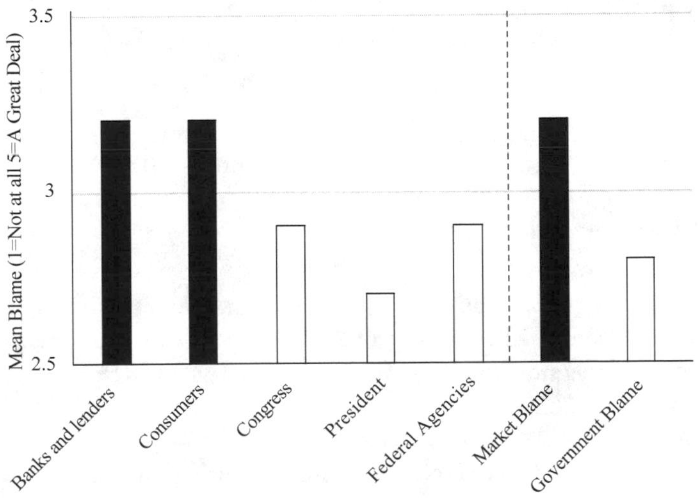


**FIGURE 3.8** Blame for Problems with Consumer Finance

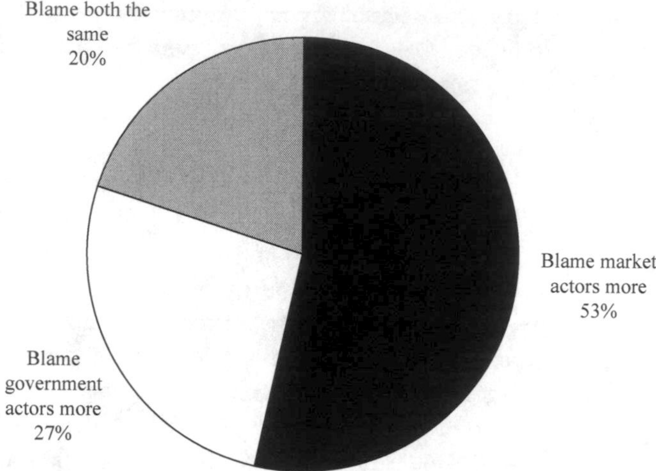


**FIGURE 3.9** Most Blame for Problems with Consumer Finance

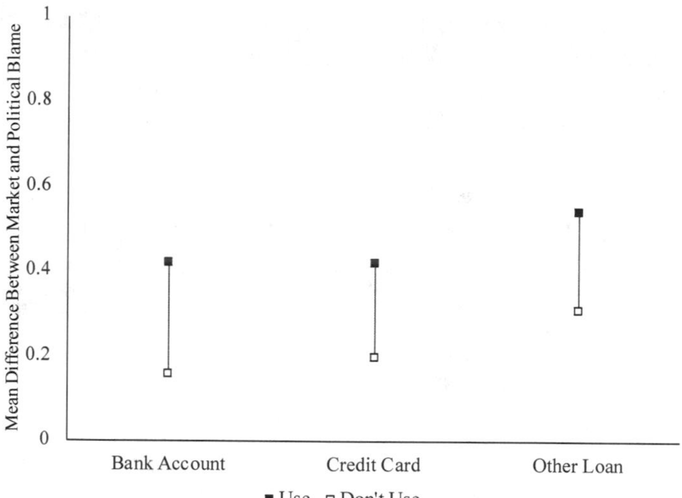


**FIGURE 3.10** Average Blame Gap between Market and Political Actors by Credit Usage
Note: The differences in the average blame gap for all product users are statistically significant at the p<.05 level.

respondents who used a specific financial product placed about 20 percent more blame on market actors relative to political actors than people who did not use the type of credit. And this isn't simply an artifact of demographic differences between credit users and non-users. These differences in the blame gap remain significant even when controlling for income, education, race, gender, and age.[13]

As figure 3.11 shows, the blame gap favoring market actors also extends to those respondents who have had specific negative experiences with banks and lenders. Unsurprisingly, respondents with at least one adverse credit experience placed more blame on actors across the board than people without a bad credit experience. It is important to note, however, that people who experienced problems with credit still report an equally large blame gap between market and political actors, focusing more of their ire on the former.

We might expect that people who place more blame for the negative consequences of consumer borrowing on one type of actor relative to another will have corresponding attitudes about what should be done to protect against those consequences in the future. To see whether people's opinions about reducing problems with borrowing reflect who they blame for those problems, respondents were asked whether they agreed with each of three statements about possible solutions: 1) people should be more responsible credit users, 2) banks and lenders should provide better information, and 3) government should more strictly regulate the financial industry. Figure 3.12 reports the results of those questions, separating respondents by which set of actors they blame more for problems with consumer credit. If the general measures of blame discussed previously correspond to people's opinions about more concrete solutions, we should expect people who focus their ire on market actors to agree more with market-based solutions, while those who point the finger at government actors should be more supportive of political solutions.

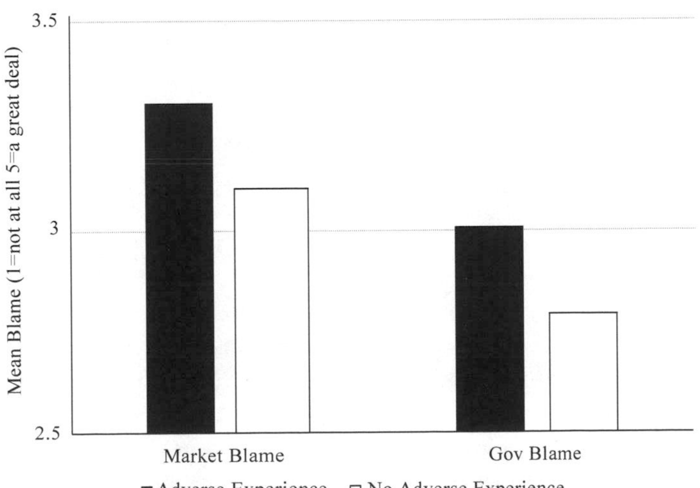


FIGURE 3.11 Market and Political Blame by Experience with Consumer Finance

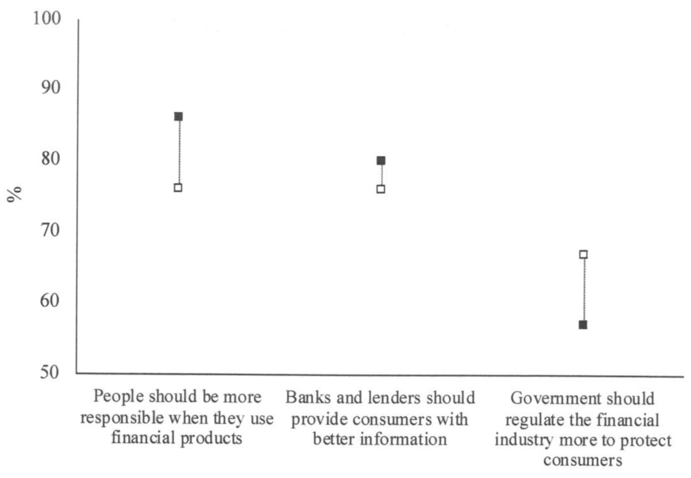


**FIGURE 3.12** Attitudes toward Financial Protection by Blame

Two noteworthy trends are illuminated by figure 3.12. First, each of these statements garnered support from a majority of respondents. Second, support for more government regulation was lower among all borrowers than support for either of the two market-based remedies, although the gap for people who placed greater blame on government was smaller. There are, however, key differences between the two groups of respondents. People who place greater blame on market actors for problems with credit are, unsurprisingly, about ten percentage points more supportive of the idea that consumers should be more responsible in their financial dealings and five percentage points more supportive of banks and lenders providing better information to their customers when compared to people who blame government actors more. By contrast, those who place greater blame on government actors are about ten percentage points more supportive of increasing government regulation of the financial industry than their market-focused peers.

Taken together, these results indicate that Americans—especially those who use and suffer adverse effects from financial products and services—are more likely to blame market actors for problems with consumer credit. They further suggest that questions of blame may translate to meaningful attitudes and preferences about how to solve people's consumer financial problems. The pattern of blame is consistent with the hypothesis that people's experiences with consumer financial protection regulations encourage them to view financial transactions, and their consequences, as influenced primarily by financial players rather than political forces. Blaming market actors, however, is only one piece of the puzzle.

*Borrower Action*

Whom do borrowers turn to when they experience problems with consumer financing? I argue that, once again, with little evidence of government intervention in the regulation of consumer banking and lending, people are more likely to seek solutions within the market. Because consumer financial regulations have consistently employed privatizing remedies and implementation strategies since their inception in 1968, I anticipate that people's incentives to target market actors will be as strong today as they were in the early years of government policymaking on consumer financial protection, even though the amount of federal financial regulation has grown considerably in the intervening decades.

Table 3.2 offers evidence that is consistent with this contention. The table presents responses to an identical set of questions about how Americans address credit problems that were administered in two different surveys forty years apart. The Fed's 1977 Survey of Consumer Finances included a battery of questions designed to test the efficacy of TILA's first consumer lending regulations one decade after their implementation. Borrowers were asked to detail any credit problems they encountered and what, if any, actions they took for each. I replicated these questions in the 2017 Survey of Consumer Credit to see how today's borrowers respond to their problems with consumer financial products and services.[14] The replies allow us address two important queries: First, do people primarily turn to market or political actors when faced with specific problems with financing? Second, has the growth of government policymaking on consumer financial protection between 1977 and 2017 increased people's willingness to acknowledge government as an appropriate target for action when complaints with financial products and services arise?

As the results in table 3.2 illustrate, a significant and growing majority of people who have adverse credit experiences do something in response. About two in three consumers in 1977 and four in five consumers in 2017 acted to address the problems they encountered. This confirms that people are not simply failing to engage when faced with the negative side effects of borrowing. It also suggests that borrowers today are not suffering from a greater level of apathy on this issue than their counterparts from the late seventies; if anything, the reverse is true. These responses further demonstrate that consumers in both periods

**Table 3.2 Borrower Action in Response to Problems with Consumer Finance, 1977 and 2017**

| | 1977 Survey of Consumer Finance | 2017 Survey of Consumer Credit |
|---|---|---|
| Experienced credit problem | 24% | 29% |
| Took action | 62% | 81% |
| Took market action | | |
| *Contact creditor* | 62% | 70% |
| *New source of credit* | 5% | 36% |
| *Contact trade association* | 3% | 10% |
| *Participated in boycott* | n/a | 7% |
| Took political action | | |
| *State or local agency* | 2% | 7% |
| *Federal agency* | 1% | 6% |
| *State or local elected official* | n/a | 6% |
| *Federal elected official* | 1% | 3% |

were far more likely to engage with market actors to address their grievances than to contact political actors. None of the political responses garnered even 10 percent of borrowers in either survey.

Figure 3.13 provides more detail on the patterns of action for 2017 respondents. Of those who reported doing something about an adverse financial experience, nearly all (97 percent) took at least one form of market action. Only 13 percent reported even a single political response, and only 3 percent exclusively took political action. This pattern fits with the predictions generated earlier in the chapter from evaluating U.S. credit regulations: most people exclusively target market actors with complaints, while a small number of consumers target a mix of market and political actors.

One interesting change does occur between 1977 and 2017. Respondents in 2017 reported engaging in a broader array of market actions than did respondents in 1977. While consumers in both periods were highly likely to address their complaints directly with lenders, 36 percent who experienced problems in the 2017 survey reported actively seeking new sources of credit compared with only 5 percent of borrowers in 1977. This could reflect the fact that more sources of credit are available today, or it could indicate that credit has become sufficiently important to people's economic livelihoods that going without is not a viable option.

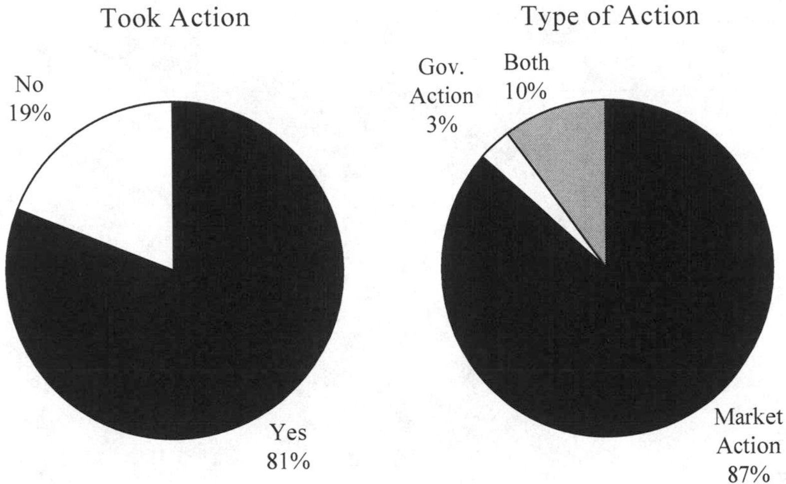


**FIGURE 3.13** Preferred Borrower Action for Reported Problems with Consumer Finance

Complaining to a creditor or seeking a better lending situation both seem like reasonable short-term methods for resolving specific problems with a financial product or service.[15] But requesting intervention from a state or federal agency is equally, if not more, likely to yield short-term resolution to the same type of problem,[16] yet American borrowers virtually ignore these alternatives. When people do submit complaints to someone other than their own lender, they are more likely to contact a trade association. Once again, the growing penchant for contacting a trade association (from 3 to 10 percent of borrowers between 1977 and 2017) rather than a comparable political agency is consistent with the prediction that borrowers, whether seeking a specific solution to a problem or voicing general concern about a lending practice, are more likely to look toward the market.

Perhaps these responses reflect something unique about people who are reacting to a specific negative experience. To what extent do these patterns carry over to the broader universe of borrowers? In order to gauge people's more general preferences for taking market versus political action to address issues of consumer financial protection, respondents were asked a series of questions about how likely they would be to engage in each specific action from table 3.2 in response to any hypothetical future problem they encountered with consumer finance. Their answers were then aggregated to create mean scores for the likelihood of taking future market action and future political action respectively, where one equals very unlikely and five equals very likely.[17]

Once again, respondents expressed a greater willingness to turn

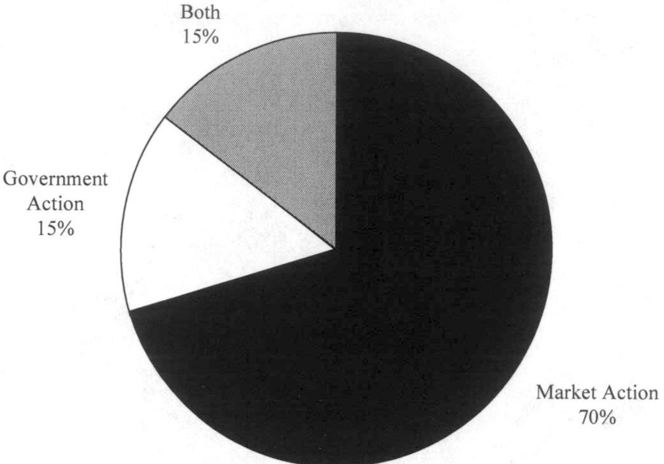


**FIGURE 3.14** Preferred Borrower Action for Future Problems with Consumer Finance

to market actors should they wish to pursue an issue with consumer credit in the future. About two-thirds of respondents (67 percent) said they would be willing to take at least one type of market action if they experienced a future problem with credit. By contrast, only one-third (32 percent) reported they would take political action. Put another way, the average respondent expressed a moderate willingness to take future market action and a moderate aversion to political action.[18]

As figure 3.14 shows, people's willingness to take market versus political action in response to future problems with credit also mirrors the real-world decisions of those who have already reacted to adverse borrowing experiences. Seven of ten respondents reported that they were more willing to engage within the market than within the political sphere if they experienced a future problem. A further 15 percent were equally interested in market and political avenues for pursuing potential grievances. Only 15 percent expressed greater willingness to take political action to address credit problems. All told, these responses provide further confirmation of the idea that borrowers are more likely to turn to the market when they are unhappy with consumer credit. They also suggest that people who have experienced problems with financing are not somehow distinctive from other borrowers in their actions and preferences.

These survey trends also reflect the real-world behavior of disgruntled borrowers during the aftermath of the financial crisis. While politicians and public interest groups lamented the lack of mass political mobilization to support Dodd-Frank's passage in 2010 (see Kirsch and

Mayer 2013), the same folks who ignored Congress occasionally took to the market to express their displeasure with credit practices. Thousands of consumers signed an online petition and threatened a boycott to oppose new debit card fees levied by Bank of America (Mayer 2012). Similarly, around 650,000 people opened accounts at credit unions as part of a widespread social media campaign encouraging people to transfer their funds out of big banks (Mincer 2011). And thousands turned out to protest the American Bankers Association and other financial institutions around the country (AFR 2009). Yet similar activities in the political sphere largely failed to launch.

### *Does Market Blame Generate Market Action?*

The previous two sections provide evidence that, having been exposed to several decades of privatizing consumer credit regulation, most Americans have learned to attribute more blame for their financial problems to market actors and are more likely to target banks, lenders, and trade associations when seeking redress for those problems. But are these two outcomes related to each other? Does market blame actually beget market action, as suggested by the theory of regulatory feedback effects outlined in this book? The following section looks at that connection in greater detail.

I begin by examining how blame for both market and political institutions correlates with a person's willingness to act within the financial realm. If blame for the market is driving, in part, the decision to address lending problems with financial actors, then we should expect to find an increased likelihood of pursuing market action as a person places increasing blame for consumer financial problems on banks, lenders, and consumers. The following section tests the effect of blame on both the actions of respondents who reported actual problems with credit as well as a respondent's likelihood of taking future market action. The degree to which a respondent blames market actors, in aggregate, for problems with credit serves as the measure of market blame; likewise for government actors and political blame. Additional measures are included to control for the individual characteristics of the respondent, including household income, education, age, gender, race, and partisan identification.[19]

Figure 3.15 illustrates the predicted effect of market and government blame respectively on taking market action when controlling for individual characteristics. It also includes a relative measure ("more market blame") to show how the increasing gap between market and

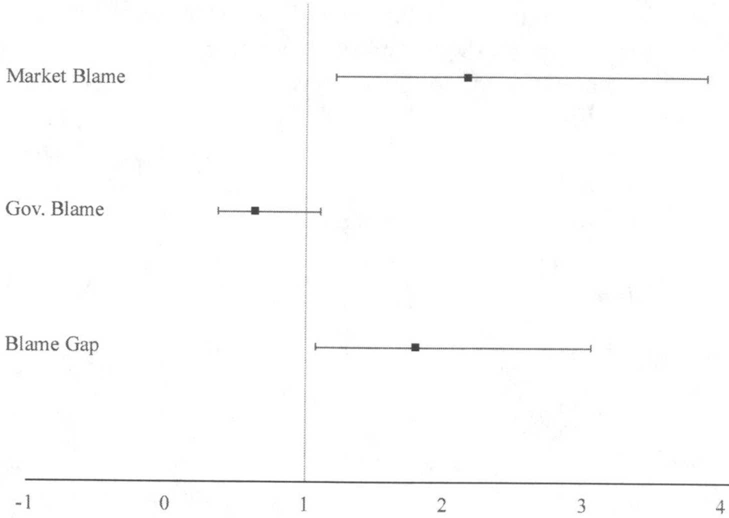


**FIGURE 3.15** Predicted Effect of Blame on Market Action

Notes: Points represent odds ratios from logistic regression with 95 percent confidence interval bars (n = 355). Full results for the model are available in the appendix.

government blame relates to a person's behavior. These results incorporate only people who reported doing something in response to an actual adverse credit experience. As respondents place more blame for problems with credit on market actors, they appear increasingly willing to engage in market action on behalf of those grievances. In fact, for the average respondent, each one-point increase in market blame doubles their likelihood of taking market action. Respondents who placed more blame on market actors relative to government actors experienced a similar result: for each one-point increase in the blame gap favoring market actors, the average respondent's likelihood of seeking a solution in the market was predicted to increase by 200 percent. By contrast, the amount of blame ascribed to political actors for problems with credit does not appear to affect a person's willingness to pursue redress within the financial arena.

These results support the idea that a direct relationship exists between market blame and market action: when borrowers blame banks and lenders more for problems with credit, then they are more likely to target those same actors if they decide to respond to their perceived problem. The cumulative effect of this trend is potentially large, given that about three in four respondents place more blame for lending problems on market rather than government institutions. But perhaps blaming market actors for credit problems simply increases the chance that someone will do anything at all—whether in the market or political sphere—to address their problem. To find out whether this is the case, I explore how the same measures of blame for market and political actors, and the gap between the two, correlate with respondents' willingness to take political action in response to an adverse credit experience, once again controlling for the characteristics of individual respondents. As figure 3.16 illustrates, the degree to which a respondent blames market actors for negative credit experiences does not appear to affect their willingness to engage in political action.

If anything, these results provide suggestive evidence that increased blame on banks and lenders may diminish a person's willingness to contact a political official or agency about credit issues. Similarly, respondents who allocated more blame to market actors relative to their governmental counterparts became increasingly less likely to take political action: each one-point increase in the blame gap diminished the likelihood of political action by about fifty percentage points for the average respondent. Unsurprisingly, increasing blame on government actors did correspond to an increased propensity to turn to political actors to address an adverse credit experience. This effect is on par with the relationship between market blame and market engagement presented in the figure 3.15.

Figure 3.17 presents similar evidence about the relationship between blame and action when it comes to hypothetical future problems one

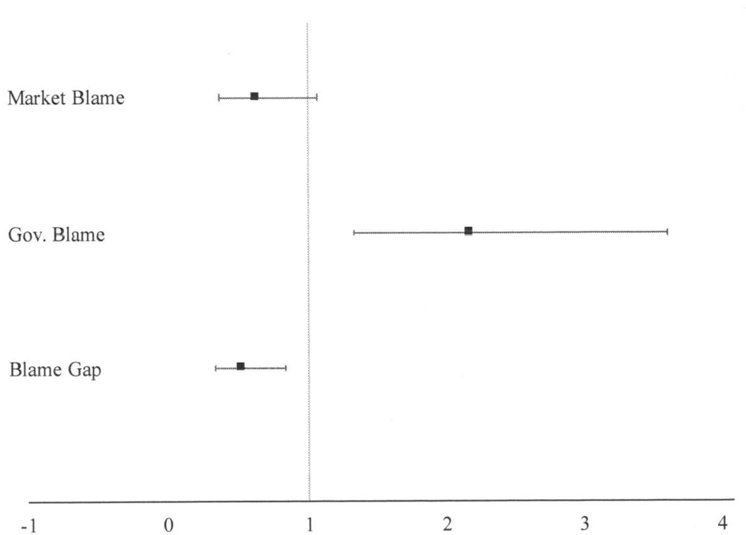


**FIGURE 3.16** Predicted Effect of Blame on Political Action

Notes: Points represent odds ratios from logistic regression with 95 percent confidence interval bars (n=355). Full results for the model are available in the Appendix.

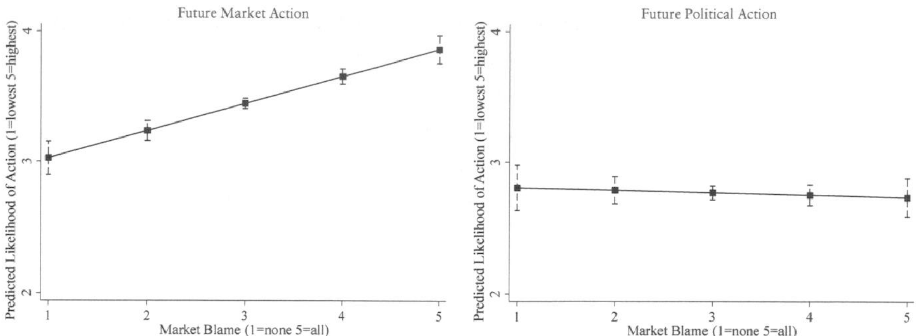


**FIGURE 3.17** Predicted Effect of Market Blame on Future Action
Notes: Points represent marginal effects from ordinary least squares (OLS) regression coefficients with 95 percent confidence intervals in dotted lines (n = 1,495). Full results for the models are available in the appendix.

might experience with credit. Once again, the predicted relationship between blame for market actors and willingness to take future action within the market if credit problems arise is strong and positive. For the average respondent, placing a great deal of blame on market actors versus not placing much blame on them at all corresponds with an increased willingness to take future market action of about three quarters of a point on a five-point scale. In practical terms, this is meaningful. It is the difference between being ambivalent versus being moderately likely to respond within the market. Once again, however, blaming banks, lenders, and borrowers does not produce the same incentive to take political action. As the second graph of figure 3.17 demonstrates, increasing blame for market actors does not correspond to a significant change in the average respondent's willingness to take political action for a future problem with credit.[20]

The previous sections focus on how people respond to real or hypothetical problems they encounter with banks and lenders. But perhaps asking people about how they respond to concrete experiences with their own banking and credit is a bad proxy for evaluating how angry borrowers react to a specific policy proposal to improve consumer financial protection more broadly. After all, we might think that how someone deals with a specific financial problem is quite different from how they would approach a systemic reform they support. To see whether people behave differently when considering a proposal to protect consumer finances, and whether their blame attribution maps on to those behaviors in different ways, the survey asked respondents to read a "press release describing a new proposal about overdraft fees." The press release, which is depicted in figure 3.18 and reflects real legislation, describes the problem of overdraft fees and outlines a solution.

After reading the proposal, respondents were asked whether they supported or opposed the reform on a scale from one to five, where one equals "strongly oppose" and five equals "strongly support." Perhaps unsurprisingly, seven in ten respondents (70 percent) signaled support for the measure. A further 15 percent indicated ambivalence, and only 14 percent opposed the plan. This is consistent with generally favorable opinions Americans voice for many lending reforms that have been introduced in recent years. It also offers further evidence that the lack of political engagement on behalf of consumer financial protection is not due to a lack of support for actual reform measures like this overdraft proposal.

Favoring a reform, however, does not mean a person is willing to do something on behalf of that approval. So, respondents who said they supported the proposal were asked how likely they would be to take different types of action to voice their support. Each respondent rated how likely they would be on a scale from one to five, where one equals "very unlikely" and five equals "very likely," to contact their member of Congress, to contact a federal agency "like the Federal Trade Commission," or to contact their bank. The average willingness to take each action for all pro-reform respondents is presented in figure 3.19.

The average supportive respondent reported being somewhat willing to contact their bank, but they expressed ambivalence toward contacting either their member of Congress or an agency like the FTC.[21] This outcome suggests that even proponents of a popular reform are reluctant to engage politically to see the proposal enacted. It also mirrors the patterns of behavior people reported with respect to specific financial experiences (either real or hypothetical). The prospects for political engagement look even dimmer when considering that people typically overreport their willingness to act on a survey.

If, like most Americans, you use a checking account, you are probably subject to "overdraft fees," which are basically high-interest, short-term loans. Here's how overdraft fees work. Banks charge a fee—usually about $34—each time you make a purchase that takes your account balance below zero. You won't be notified before you overdraw your account. If you make several purchases, even small ones, you end up paying multiple overdraft fees.

A proposal has been made to limit banks' use of overdraft fees by:

- Requiring ATMs to notify you if you are about to overdraw your account
- Limiting banks to only one overdraft fee charge per monthly statement
- Requiring banks to make overdraft fees proportional to the cost of the overdraft—usually much less than $34

**FIGURE 3.18** Overdraft Reform Proposal from 2017 Survey of Consumer Credit

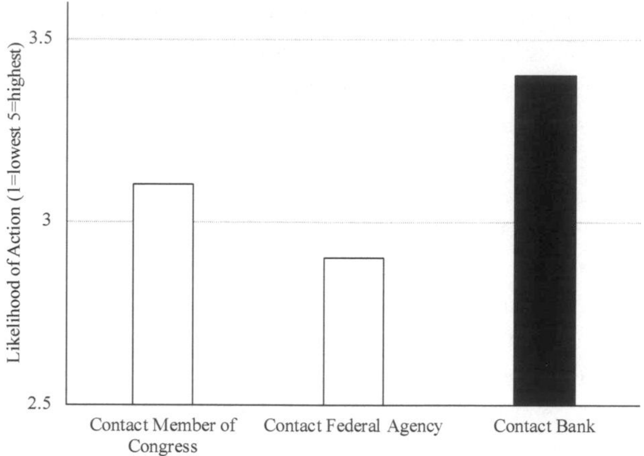


**FIGURE 3.19** Willingness to Act to Support Overdraft Reform Proposal by Type of Action

The previous pages indicate that borrowers' tendencies to place greater blame for lending problems on market actors translate to their preference for market-based action; likewise with respect to government blame and political action. Does the same link exist when people are confronted with a systemic proposal for reform? Figure 3.20 illustrates the relationship between both market and government blame and the respondents' willingness to contact their member of Congress or a federal agency in response to this overdraft proposal. The analysis includes only supporters of the reform, since we wouldn't expect those who oppose the plan to do something to see it come to fruition.

As the results show, there is a strong correlation between how much blame a respondent places on government for perceived problems with credit, and that person's willingness to contact either their member of Congress or a federal agency in response to the overdraft proposal. As blame for government increases, so too does that person's inclination to take these specific political actions. In fact, for the average proposal supporter, placing a moderate to a significant amount of blame for problems with banking and lending on government actors makes that person willing to voice their support to both political actors.

Market blame, by contrast, produces no such result. Blaming market actors does not appear to make someone more likely to contact either their member of Congress or a federal agency on behalf of the overdraft proposal, even when that person supports the reform. The problem with this, as we uncovered earlier, is that most Americans place more blame on market, and not political, actors for their problems with consumer finance. These results confirm that people's feelings about who bears responsibility for problems with consumer banking and lending influence not only how they deal with specific experiences with credit, but also how they respond to broader efforts to improve consumer financial protection.

Taken together, the evidence presented in this chapter helps to paint an increasingly clear picture of how borrowers think about consumer credit problems and how that thinking influences their decisions to act to protect their finances. Americans consistently attribute greater blame to market actors for problems with consumer financial products and services than they do to government actors. And that blame affects a wide range of activity surrounding consumer finances—from responses to individual problems with credit to action in support of systemic reform. The relationship is also strongest for those who actually use financial products and services, and thus, who experience firsthand the result of these regulatory policies (whether they know it or not). That these trends occur even though lawmakers play an increasing role in the creation and regulation of the consumer credit industry provides powerful evidence that government's responsibility has been effectively hidden

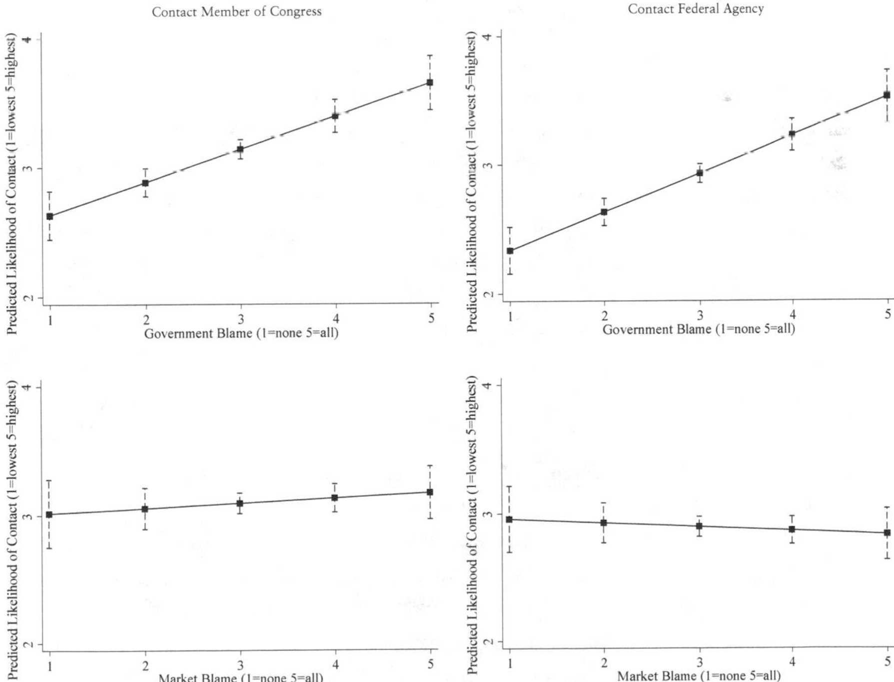


**FIGURE 3.20** Predicted Effect of Blame on Political Action for Overdraft Proposal
Notes: Points represent marginal effects from ordinary least squares (OLS) regression coefficients with 95 percent confidence intervals in dotted lines (n = 1,063). Full results for the models are available in the appendix.

from the millions of American borrowers. I argue that such a feat would not have been possible if consumer credit policies did not actively personalize and privatize the procurement and use of credit.

### *Reinforcing the Political Economy of Credit*

The consumer financial protection policy regime at the heart of this story bears all of the hallmarks of the submerged state—a network of policies providing benefits to ordinary Americans from within existing U.S. market institutions (Mettler 2011). Suzanne Mettler identifies three salient features of submerged policies that I argue match the design, implementation, and administration of consumer financial protections in the United States. First, submerged policies tend to provide benefits to individuals through market transactions, personalizing their use. Second, by providing benefits to individuals through market transactions they intentionally obscure government's role, ultimately encouraging beneficiaries to see only the free market and private enterprise at work. Finally, submerged policies tend to be upwardly redistributive, providing bigger benefits to more affluent citizens.

The previous discussion emphasizes the ways in which consumer financial regulations conform to the first two elements of the submerged state. Policymakers have clearly adopted policies that privatize the use of credit, and they are implemented with virtually no indication of government involvement in their creation. But consumer financial protections also mimic the upward redistribution of other submerged policies. Given the fixed administrative costs of lending combined with lenders' incentives to control for the riskiness of borrowers, consumer credit has always been regressive (Manning 2000; Trumbull 2014). While middle-class and affluent borrowers are not exempt from costly, and even predatory, lending terms, banks and lenders often grant wealthier borrowers more leeway than their less affluent peers—as Mr. Gregg's story ably demonstrated.

All of these features of the submerged state have been shown for other policies to correlate with two distinctive political outcomes. First, the privatized nature of submerged policies not only makes it difficult for citizens to form and express relevant policy preferences, but also fosters a sense that the market, not government, is responsible for the relevant issue. Relatedly, the governmental authority for submerged policies is often identifiable only to elite interests with the political knowledge and connections to interpret them. The result is that regular individuals are left unaware of the existence of relevant federal policy, thus removing any incentive to pursue government redress. Such is clearly the case for consumer financial protection.

This process of regulatory feedback reinforces the political economy of credit. By removing borrowers' incentives to agitate for political change, policymakers aren't held accountable for their continued embrace of weak financial protections. This pattern is also consistent with—and perhaps reinforced by—a larger turn in American social policymaking. Scholars have illuminated lawmakers' increasing fondness since the 1970s for policies that are characterized by market logic and that channel benefits and protections through market structures (Howard 1997; Hacker 2006; Soss et al. 2011; Mettler 2011). Joe Soss, Richard Fording, and Sanford Schram describe the trend as a broad neoliberal project "that turns citizens into prudent market actors who bear personal responsibility for their problems" (2011: 51). While Soss and his colleagues wrote this in the context of welfare retrenchment, it is an apt description for how exposure to consumer financial protections teaches citizens to look to Wall Street, not Washington.

### *The Problem of Political (In)action*

Does it really matter whether government policies lead consumers to blame, and subsequently to target, banks and lenders for both the individual and systemic problems they perceive with consumer credit and banking? In the last two decades, a growing cohort of scholars—led by historians and sociologists—has developed a narrative of consumption as an explicit form of politics in America.[22] Countering the existing wisdom that consumption and politics exist in entirely separate realms and with opposite motivations, their work argues that citizens throughout the nation's history have leveraged their consumptive power to bring about political change. From boycotting British goods prior to the Revolution to the "Don't Buy Where You Can't Work" civil rights campaigns of the 1930s and 1960s, these scholars emphasize that the explicitly political goals of certain consumer behavior ought to be considered another form of political activism—a thesis that has gained traction with the growth of "socially conscious" consumption in the last decade.[23]

In their insistence that citizens can leverage buying power toward political ends, scholars have treated market-based forms of consumer action as simply another expression of political will. But classifying consumer behavior as a form of political action on par with voting or writing a member of Congress overlooks some key ways in which market-based action may be fundamentally different from expressing consumer concerns through more traditional political channels. It is important to differentiate market from political consumer mobilization for two primary reasons. First, market actors and government actors are confronted with very different pressures and incentives—profit and electoral motivations respectively. Second, they possess different tools—both in form and scope—with which to address consumer complaints. As a result of these differences, the likelihood that borrower mobilization will be successful in securing specific remedies and broader reforms, the form that each will take, and the magnitude of each, will be shaped in large part by the target of the collective action—irrespective of whether consumers' underlying motivations are economic or political.

For millions of American borrowers who are potentially at risk from predatory lending, eschewing political action as a pathway to better consumer financial protection has serious consequences. It is possible that targeting market actors might be an effective way to resolve an individual problem with a consumer loan, although even that result is not guaranteed. But relying solely on market action is unlikely to bring about the more fundamental change to consumer financial regulation necessary to prevent the systemic damages wrought by uncurbed lending. Indeed, as a leading consumer advocate bluntly but accurately remarked when I mentioned examples of consumers making demands of banks and lenders, "And what did that accomplish?" (0312151 March 2015).

As we will see in the next chapter, the consequences of privatizing and personalizing consumer borrowing extend beyond their effects on individual consumers' predilections for market activism in lieu of political engagement. They also present a serious obstacle for public interest groups seeking to mobilize borrowers to demand regulatory change, thereby limiting the ability of these groups to wage a successful outside lobbying strategy in pursuit of reform. Without the political muscle provided by constituent support, federal lawmakers—even those who support more stringent consumer financial protections—are limited in their ability to enact fundamental policy changes.

# 4 The "Horseless Headmen": Consumer Groups and the Challenge of Political Mobilization

Representative Barney Frank (D-MA) had the unenviable task of chairing the House Financial Services Committee during the largest financial crisis since the Great Depression. While speaking at a community organizers' town hall in Boston in March 2008, he addressed an increasingly familiar topic: was Congress going to do anything to protect American borrowers and prevent another financial meltdown? Frank noted how difficult it would be for members of Congress to back robust financial reform without clear support from their constituents, and he chastised consumer interest groups for being "horseless headmen" (Byrnes 2008). In his own inimitable style, Frank identified a perceived weakness of the advocacy effort to tackle consumer financial protection: though stocked with a respected cadre of experts who wrote model laws and lobbied policymakers, these organizations failed to foment necessary grassroots political mobilization to reinforce their efforts. Consumer advocates, it turned out, thought so too.

At the very moment Frank faulted consumer groups for being horseless headmen, advocates were actively engaged in a year-old organizational effort specifically designed to mobilize borrowers toward political action to support lending reform. In 2007, with the specter of the financial crisis looming, several consumer advocacy groups coalesced to launch Americans for Fairness in Lending (AFFIL) as "a nonprofit organization dedicated to reforming the nation's lending industry to protect Americans' financial assets" (AFFIL 2018). Instead of relying on directly lobbying government officials, AFFIL attempted to grow a grassroots network of members who would share their stories of lender abuse with policymakers and mobilize to support reform. Despite the opportune moment for change and a healthy dose of early money, the organization struggled to gain traction with the public and finally shuttered its windows in 2010.

While observers might write off this result as a single case of organizational failure, or perhaps as the byproduct of a downswing in consumer mobilization more generally, neither answer is adequate. Frank's blunt assessment of the absence of mass mobilization efforts was not confined to a single organization, nor, as it happens, was it unique to the current historical moment. In fact, the Congressman's criticism echoed an earlier refrain from federal policymakers wrestling to pass consumer financial protections in the 1960s and 1970s during the heyday of the U.S. consumer movement.

At the 1967 Consumer Assembly, the first national meeting of its kind, prominent policymakers delivered a consistent message to consumer advocates—one that mirrors the sentiment Frank would express some forty years in the future: if you want us to pass good legislation to protect borrowers from lending abuses, you had better mobilize our constituents. President Johnson told the gathered advocates, "It has been said that the consumer lobby is the most widespread in our land, yet the least vociferous and the least powerful. . . . You can only wield the power that you have if you are willing to make yourselves heard" (Johnson 1967). The President's Special Assistant for Consumer Affairs, television personality-turned-political appointee Betty Furness, echoed his sentiments:

> I have found that the voice of the consumer is more apt to be a whimper than a roar. . . . We must convince him to . . . make himself heard on legislative issues that vitally affect him. . . . Senators and Representatives want satisfied voters just as industry wants satisfied customers . . . it is up to us to persuade the individual consumer to become directly involved in government–consumer relations. (Furness 1967)

Representative Leonor Sullivan, who was mired in a bitter committee battle to usher a Truth in Lending Bill through passage, was more blunt in her directive to consumer groups:

> As a Member of Congress deeply involved in many of the issues in which you are also concerned, I see much evidence of your interest—in your letters as officials of organizations or consumer groups. But I don't see much evidence of your effectiveness right now. You are not reaching your own people and enlisting their active help and support. . . . On the House Floor, we will lose—our efforts for a strong bill will be killed—unless the public is aroused, and that means that you people must get busy, really busy, in reaching the rank and file.[1] (Sullivan 1967)

Historians of the consumer movement, broadly construed, often speak of the 1960s and early 1970s as the halcyon days of consumer activism (Nadel 1971; Pertschuk 1982; Cohen 2010; Jacobs 2011). While consumers increasingly engaged around issues of car, product, and food safety regulation, grassroots political mobilization, as these speeches from the 1967 Consumer Assembly make clear, did not extend to the realm of consumer financial protection. Despite being taken to task by their legislative allies as early as the 1960s, consumer advocacy organizations either did not or could not manifest the requested political engagement from their members on issues of consumer financial protection, even at the height of the larger consumer movement. And once again, this problem is more puzzling because advocates have experienced some recent success engaging consumers in collective market action.

Why have public interest groups struggled—both historically and during the recent crisis—to mobilize angry borrowers to demand lending reform from policymakers? The previous chapter addressed the depoliticizing pressure that consumer financial protection regulations have exerted on the beliefs and actions of individual borrowers. This chapter continues the story by exploring the consequences of that policy legacy on the activities of consumer financial advocacy organizations, and specifically, on their attempts to instigate grassroots political action. I propose that consumer financial protections generate feedback effects that shape both the emergence of relevant public interest groups and the efficacy of those groups' campaigns to mobilize borrowers.

I begin by providing a brief narrative of the rise of consumer financial advocacy groups in the United States, revealing how the enactment of early consumer financial protections in the 1960s and 1970s corresponds with the emergence of new advocacy organizations and increased political activity among existing groups. Next, I explore the evolution of consumer advocates' efforts to mobilize consumers. I pay particular attention to the rise of two organizations—AFFIL and Americans for Financial Reform (AFR)—that were designed specifically to incite consumer political mobilization during and after the 2008 financial crisis, noting the difficulties each encountered fulfilling that mission. I argue that generating a successful message to appeal to borrowers proved a major stumbling block for these organizations.

In order for advocacy groups to mobilize people effectively toward a specific form of action, organizations need to create collective action frames that explicitly identify both a reason and a target for the requested action. Most importantly, the justification and target must resonate with the people being mobilized (Gamson and Lasch 1983; Gamson 1992; Folger 1986; Klandermans 1997). So, in order to get borrowers to turn to the state to address predatory lending problems, advocacy groups needed to find a way to appeal to borrowers as citizens in need of state protection from lender abuses. I contend that this was an exceptional challenge because of the personalizing and privatizing effects of policies central to the political economy of credit. How could advocacy organizations create a resonant call to political action when the public did not see consumer borrowing as a political issue but, instead, one of personal financial responsibility?

Drawing on archival research conducted at the Consumer Movement Archives and interviews with consumer advocates representing four advocacy organizations (including AFFIL and its partners), I find that, while advocates were aware of this messaging challenge, they did not overcome it. By exploring records of AFFIL's founding as well as transcripts of focus groups designed to test its messages to members, I conclude that leaders were mindful of the potential difficulty in getting borrowers to channel their ire toward political action. Through content analysis of AFFIL's major forms of communication—their blog and member emails—I identify the primary frames the group used in their political action appeals to members. As predicted, these appeals call on victims of predatory lending to seek help from government—not a frame I expect to resonate with borrowers who have been persistently exposed to personalizing and privatizing financial protections.

Did this mismatch between advocates' appeals and borrowers' beliefs about financial protection weaken efforts to mobilize consumers politically? If so, is there a realistic messaging alternative that consumer advocates could use to generate grassroots political action in support of lending reform? I administered an original survey experiment to explore these questions. Ultimately, I conclude that people's attitudes about personal responsibility in the use of credit do indeed discourage them from responding to organizational calls for political action in pursuit of more consumer-friendly financial protections. Furthermore, I find that the increasingly common strategy among consumer groups to liken credit to other consumer goods—remember Elizabeth Warren's toaster analogy—is also limited in its effectiveness. Instead, I demonstrate that reframing the issue of consumer financial protection in terms of government's responsibility to protect people's economic security—a task on par with Social Security or tax breaks—can increase people's penchant for related political action.

*Reshaping the Organizational Landscape*

Scholars note that new public policies can spawn new interest groups (Walker 1983; Skocpol 1992; Pierson 1993). As Paul Pierson explains, "The activity of interest groups often seems to follow rather than precede the adoption of public policies" (1993: 598). Jack Walker offered one reason for this phenomenon. Observing that many of the interest groups created in the postwar period emerged only after new public policies were enacted, Walker argued that when policies offer patronage benefits, groups have a greater incentive to form. I contend that the very presence or absence of policymaking in a particular arena may shape interest group behavior in other ways as well. If lawmakers are not engaged in policymaking for a particular issue, interest groups may still emerge but focus their energies on activity outside the political realm. By contrast, if an issue becomes subject to new governing activity, existing interest groups may be more likely to direct their efforts toward the political sphere. In the case of consumer financial protection, government policymaking—or the initial lack thereof—appears to have shaped the behavior of interest groups in both ways.

Figure 4.1 illustrates the timeline along which two types of public interest groups working to improve consumer financial protection were founded. The organizations above the timeline work almost exclusively on consumer lending issues. Those below the timeline engage in a broader consumer agenda, but they also dedicate substantial resources to consumer financial protection. The shaded area denotes the period after passage of TILA, the first major U.S. financial protection for consumer borrowing. While this figure does not include every public interest group ever active on the issue, it represents the major organizations working at the federal level.

Prior to passage of the Truth in Lending Act in 1968, the federal government was virtually absent from the regulation of consumer

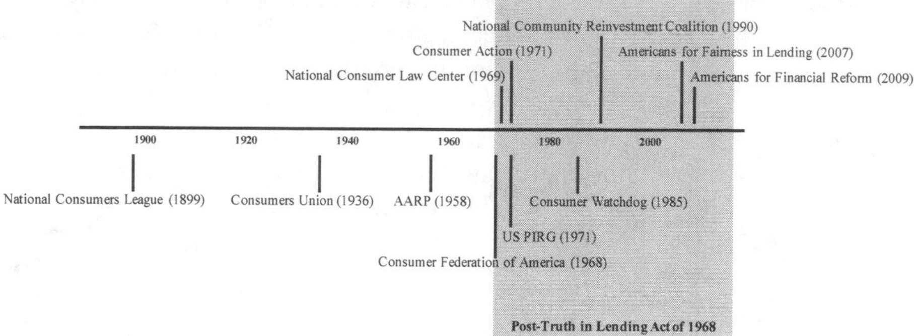


**FIGURE 4.1** Timeline of Consumer Financial Advocacy Group Emergence

credit. Also missing from the political landscape were interest groups solely dedicated to consumer financial protection. A few organizations engaged with consumer banking and lending as part of their larger consumer protection mission, but prior to the consideration of federal legislation, these organizations restricted their activities primarily to influencing market, and not political, behavior. As discussed in chapter 2, the early organizational effort came from Progressive reformers and labor[2] at the turn of the twentieth century who sought to partner with charitable organizations to combat the "loan shark evil." It was also during this period that, in the relative absence of federal regulation of consumer goods and services more broadly, organizations like Consumers' Research[3]—from which Consumers Union would emerge in 1936—decided that educating consumers about "good buys" could help to offset the overwhelming market power wielded by manufacturers.

Groups founded prior to the federal regulatory burst of the 1960s and 1970s typically maintained a model of consumer advocacy through education. As the postwar consumer economy grew, these organizations saw their memberships balloon (Morse 1963; Cohen 2003).[4] As more Americans began to use consumer financial products and services, these products were included in educational materials. But federal policymakers could not ignore mounting stories of wooly lending practices forever if they were to sustain a consumption economy fueled by credit, so legislative attempts to protect borrowers gained steam throughout the 1960s. As the federal government began to insert itself into the regulation of consumer financial protection, the organizational landscape around consumer financial protection changed as well.

Theda Skocpol (2003) has detailed the growth of Washington, DC-based, professionally staffed, elite-driven advocacy organizations that occurred beginning in the 1960s. This portrait is, in many ways, an accurate reflection of a new cohort of consumer financial advocacy groups that began to emerge at that time. Growing market segmentation ushered in an array of new consumer interest groups (Cohen 2003), but the appearance of a fragmented collection of organizations to speak up for the average consumer was also the result of progressive leadership. As one veteran consumer advocate explained, "The movement was just very fragmented. . . . There was a leader, Ralph Nader, who just believed in having a thousand organizations and letting them bloom" (1120141 November 2014).

Fragmented though they were, these new interest groups were fundamentally different from their predecessors in one important way: they were political. Emerging in the midst of the so-called "new social regulation" (see Derthick and Quirk 1985), these groups responded to the federal government's willingness to expand its authority over a whole range of consumer issues—including financial protection—by engaging in explicitly political behavior. In 1967, the newly minted Consumer Federation of America (CFA) set out to bring together the scattershot representatives of local, state, and national consumer organizations for the first time. Their goal was to coordinate diffuse political advocacy for a handful of important legislative efforts, chief among them the Truth in Lending Bill.

The resulting Consumer Assembly, held in Washington, DC, was a star-studded affair. The speakers for the event were a veritable who's who of the consumer movement. President Johnson kicked off the meeting and was followed in succession by leading political figures—from both the executive branch and Congress—who stood at the forefront of the crusade to enact consumer protections across an array of issues, in particular, the Truth in Lending bill being debated in Congress during the assembly. While lawmakers acknowledged the growing political presence of consumer groups, many speakers took the opportunity to chide advocates for failing to mobilize ordinary citizens to bolster their calls for lending reform. Representative Sullivan summarized the problem, noting "On the consumer credit bill . . . You good consumer leaders write us; your people don't" (Sullivan 1967). Representative Wright Patman, chairman of the House Banking and Currency Committee responsible for the bill, echoed his colleague's concerns and further articulated the consequences of consumer political inaction:

> While you are gaining growing recognition, I feel that there [are] some tremendous gaps . . . in consumer action. I must honestly say that I am gravely disappointed that there is so little mail, so

> little meaningful action from consumers. . . . As a result, there are not too many members who are willing to stick their necks out on controversial issues. Particularly when they know there isn't going to be any great outpouring . . . from consumers. . . . You and your organizations can do wonders to mobilize the forces on these important consumer issues. . . . This is the kind of action that is desperately needed in the area of monetary affairs. . . . If you want truth in lending—real truth in lending—then it is about time that each one of you let the House of Representatives know. (Patman 1967)

Unfortunately for consumer advocates, the fledgling organizations were not able to fully mobilize their members to take that political action. The Truth in Lending Act (TILA) was eventually signed into law the year following the assembly, but it did not contain the more stringent consumer protections that advocates hoped for. It did, however, set the expectation that regulating consumer lending was now within the government's jurisdiction.

As policymakers enacted more laws to regulate credit, new interest groups emerged that were dedicated specifically to supporting consumer financial protection policy. In fact, one of the most prominent borrower advocacy organizations to emerge from this period, the National Consumer Law Center (NCLC), was itself the product of public policy. It was established in 1969 with funding from the Office of Economic Opportunity specifically to train attorneys to better represent low-income Americans. One of NCLC's first programs was to prepare legal aid attorneys to use the new TILA requirements on behalf of their clients (Willier 1969).

Unlike their predecessors, who emerged in a world relatively devoid of federal policy activity on consumer financial protection, these new groups focused on political action instead of financial education as the most viable pathway to assisting borrowers. Advocates were determined that changing the law represented the best hope for protecting people from dangerous financial practices. But these organizations focused primarily on insider lobbying—communicating directly with policymakers—and, occasionally, on coalition building. They were not designed to mobilize consumers in meaningful ways. The annual reports from CFA provide evidence of this trend. The organization details its work on consumer financial issues in every annual report from 1975 through 2014,[5] but rarely were the listed activities intended to directly instigate grassroots political action. For example, in 1982, CFA earmarked interest rate caps as one of four priority policy issues. The report provides a list of the major actions CFA took at the federal level, which included generating press coverage, working with congressional staffs, helping to plan congressional hearings, delivering congressional testimony, submitting comments to federal regulators, and sending mailings to organizations to help build an interest rate coalition (CFA 1982). The direct mobilization of borrowers is notably absent from the list.

### *The Birth (and Death) of a "Unicorn"*

By 2004, many advocates were convinced that a new organizational approach was necessary to achieve any substantive policy reform to reverse the trend of growing consumer debt borrowed under increasingly risky lending terms. Staff from NCLC organized a conference in Cleveland, Ohio, to bring together more than one hundred representatives from major public interest groups around the country. Their goal was to figure out a new collaborative strategy to tackle the problem of predatory lending (AFFIL 2006). The idea to create an organization that could generate consumer political pressure to pair with the existing insider lobbying infrastructure found quick support among attendees. A staff attorney from NCLC clarified the need for such an organization, explaining, "We are going to have to fight a hard congressional battle in Washington. We cannot do this without grassroots support from across the country" (AFFIL 2004). A representative from one of the major faith-based organizations encapsulated what would become the mission of the new organization: "Three words come to mind after being here. . . . They are: Awareness, Action, and Change. We make people aware and give them some action to do to empower themselves so they can create the changed end result" (AFFIL 2004).

AFFIL emerged as the result of the Cleveland conference. It was officially established in 2006 and launched publicly in 2007. Headquartered at NCLC in Boston, AFFIL had a stated mission to "build a groundswell of support to put credit issues on the national agenda to lead to a return of fairness in lending and bring about the re-regulation of credit" (AFFIL 2006). As one of the advocates involved in AFFIL's founding explained, "We ended up identifying our niche as an . . . organizer. . . . We tried to get signatures on petitions . . . we tried to mobilize people to send in comments, to call their Senators, etc." (1120142 November 2014). Taking on the role of grassroots organizer was especially important because none of the existing national consumer groups could claim that mantle (Kelly 2009). According to another advocate, who was heavily involved in the legislative efforts to secure stronger credit protections for consumers, "AFFIL was—let's be clear—it wasn't just unusual, it was unheard of. It hadn't happened before, and it hasn't happened since. AFFIL was a unicorn" (0312151 March 2015).

The unicorn caught the attention of funders—both the Ford Foundation and Annie E. Casey Foundation provided financial support to AFFIL during its initial years of operation (AFFIL 2007a; 1120142 November 2014). In a move promoted by the Ford Foundation, one of the first things AFFIL did as a precursor to mobilizing consumers was to engage the services of a consultant, Benenson Janson, to launch a public awareness campaign about the need for federal credit regulation. Advertisements were created, and while only a limited number were placed in media outlets (1120142 November 2014), the campaign garnered its own press coverage in major newspapers including the *New York Times* (Elliott 2007).

AFFIL encountered some success with two early initiatives designed to raise awareness of the need for federal credit regulation. They collaborated in 2007 with filmmaker James Scurlock on a campaign to organize watch parties around the country for his film *Maxed Out*, a documentary on the growth of predatory lending in the United States. In what one advocate described as "the biggest sort of real-world organizing we did" (1120142 November 2014), more than 450 house parties were set up to screen the film in AFFIL's first year of action (AFFIL 2008a). In addition to the movie screenings, AFFIL worked to collect personal stories from those affected by predatory lending that the group might leverage for media and political mobilization efforts. While borrowers contributed to this archive, the most powerful narratives ultimately came from former customer service employees of financial institutions. For example, a customer service agent from a major national bank explained how she was "instructed to manipulate customers to take more money," and an account manager from another lender noted that she was expected to "encourage cardholders to max out existing cards" and sell "junk products" like "credit protection" (AFFIL 2008d). Their stories garnered quite a bit of media attention, but, as with the *Maxed Out* and ad campaigns, none of these activities directly mobilized consumers toward political action.

While these awareness-raising campaigns were underway, AFFIL dug in to the work of building up their membership base and mobilizing them to engage politically. The organization was particularly interested in trying to involve injured borrowers, citizen activists, members of community and civil rights groups, and people who were already politically active (AFFIL 2007a). One of their earliest attempts was designed to mobilize college students and young adults around the issue of predatory credit cards, but the campaign fell well short of its goals (AFFIL 2007b).

During 2008, AFFIL dedicated a tremendous amount of energy to turning out its members in support of the CARD Act under consideration in Congress. A summary of the organization's 2008 activities reports that, while nearly 10,000 people signed an online petition cosponsored by AFFIL asking the Fed to reform credit card lending, and about 300 people filed comments with the agency, only 300 people contacted their members of Congress in response to AFFIL's communication on the CARD Act (AFFIL 2008a). Another leading activist who was deeply involved in the federal lobbying effort for the CARD Act argued that even these successes could not be laid entirely at the feet of consumer interest groups: "I'm sure lots of people would like to take credit for [consumer comments], but I don't think we can" (0312151 March 2015). Instead, they pointed to the efforts of congressional staff that engaged in direct outreach to their constituents to drum up support for the bill, crediting their work for the unusual, though relatively small, outpouring of citizen support.

The fairly modest effect of AFFIL's mobilization efforts on consumer political engagement is reflected in the organization's own assessment of its work. AFFIL's director reported in a 2008 internal memo evaluating the year's activities that "it seems fair to say that this is, overall, a disappointing record of progress on the limited set of initiatives" (Campen 2008). Yet AFFIL struggled to figure out how to complete their mobilizing mission more successfully. They attempted a new campaign to rally their growing slate of members during the fight to pass financial reform in 2009, but their success was once again limited. Eventually, AFFIL's funders lost interest as the organization failed to achieve enough "measurable" success in mobilizing consumers (AFFIL 2008b).

As the end of 2009 approached, the staff could see the writing on the wall. The organization had enough money to run for one more year, but instead of continuing with its unproductive attempts at political mobilization, AFFIL decided to lend its remaining staff and expertise to a new coalition that was forming to represent consumer interests during the heated congressional debate over the Dodd-Frank Act: Americans for Financial Reform (AFR). As one of AFFIL's staff members explained, "Our board went to AFR and [said], 'we would like to donate our staff to you guys for next year, since this is such a critical year. Here, take us.' And that's what we did, and then we wound down" (1120142 November 2014). AFFIL's staff, a membership list of nearly 26,000 people, and a social media network nearing 20,000 followers rolled over into the newly formed AFR (AFFIL 2010).

### *A Second Attempt*

Americans for Financial Reform built on the coalition model that was, at least with respect to the issue of predatory lending, pioneered by AFFIL. But it was a different beast from the beginning. AFR was considerably larger in scale than its predecessor. It was led by a duo of experienced field organizers. Heather Booth, a progressive activist who cut her teeth during Freedom Summer in 1964, was tapped to be the executive director of the new coalition. Her deputy, Lisa Donner, was hired for both her field experience and her knowledge of consumer finance. While AFFIL's mission was primarily about generating grassroots political action, AFR planned to combine insider lobbying with mass mobilization efforts to achieve its goals for lending reform. To that end, AFR was built with three major departments: legislative, communication, and field mobilization (Kirsch and Mayer 2013).

AFR experienced considerable success from their insider lobbying efforts. Drawing on the resources and reputations of a diverse coalition of partners, AFR's legislative team played a key role at several critical moments during the debate over Dodd-Frank. Most notably, they helped ensure that the CFPB remained in the final legislation (Kirsch and Mayer 2013). In a steering committee meeting held the day before President Obama signed Dodd-Frank into law, a representative of one of the coalition partners summed up AFR's legislative efforts:

> From the experience of someone who has been part of many issue campaigns, this was a remarkable effort—outstanding. . . . What we had was a super-sophisticated inside game. We were involved deeply in the legislative process, and we leveraged the smarts of people inside and outside the Beltway. (AFR 2010)

AFR's attempts to mobilize consumers produced a far more mixed result. The organization sought to make the most of its resources by targeting specific districts for engaging citizens' political support for the bill. Rather than relying on their own outreach, AFR identified local political actors, like popular Illinois Attorney General Lisa Madigan, who could use their own contacts to encourage voters to express support to their members of Congress (Kirsch and Mayer 2013). To the limited extent that AFR succeeded in mobilizing borrowers politically, it was primarily the result of active outreach from established political leaders like Madigan.

But AFR did rally consumers in significant numbers to another type of action. With the help of local organizations and their national partners, AFR collaborated on a series of well-attended demonstrations and protests designed to target lenders themselves during 2009 and 2010. Consumer groups couldn't get citizens to take political action in large numbers, but they were able to mobilize more than 5,000 people to protest the 2009 annual meeting of the American Bankers Association at the so-called Showdown in Chicago. As Dodd-Frank neared a vote in Congress, additional well-attended showdowns were held outside of bank headquarters in Florida, Illinois, Indiana, Massachusetts, Missouri, Montana, New York, North Carolina, Ohio, Washington, and Washington, DC (AFR 2009). The largest of these drew as many as 8,000 protesters to Wall Street more than a year before Occupy Wall Street materialized (Kirsch and Mayer 2013). While these market-centered events demonstrated consumers' willingness to express their anger over predatory lending, they had little effect on either banking practices or the banks' efforts to weaken Dodd-Frank.

Dodd-Frank was signed into law on July 21, 2010. While the lobbying efforts by AFR and its allies helped to create a relatively independent Consumer Financial Protection Bureau (CFPB), a procedural victory for advocates, the law did not provide the more substantive reforms to consumer credit protections that groups like AFFIL and AFR had championed (McCarty et al. 2013; McGhee 2015). Ordinary voters simply were not motivated to demand those reforms from their representatives, even as they made similar demands of the very lenders who profited from the lack of more stringent regulation.

AFR's board gathered to dissect their efforts with Dodd-Frank on the verge of becoming the law of the land. The board summed up what they had set out to accomplish: "Our first goal was to pass this bill. The second goal was to help build a movement that could advance these efforts in order to win and sustain future victories and help build a broader movement for change" (AFR 2010). A member of the leadership team concluded that they had "achieved the first goal, beyond almost anyone's expectation." For the second, however, another member present conceded, "It would have been possible to do more Field [mobilizing]. Strategically, at the grassroots level, we failed to offset the real or perceived grassroots strength of the Tea Party." In their analysis of the financial reform lobbying effort, Larry Kirsch and Robert Mayer agreed, explaining, "Ultimately, AFR fell short in its ability to channel suffering and anger into political demands for strong regulatory reform" (2013: 153). Unlike its predecessor, AFR has remained a robust organization, but its work today mainly consists of coordinating its partners' inside lobbying efforts.

## *Why Political Mobilization Failed*

The previous chapter offered a policy-driven explanation for why consumers themselves are unlikely to initiate political action to address either specific borrowing problems or more general concerns with risky lending practices. One of the best tactics scholars have identified to get citizens to take political action is to be asked, or mobilized, by a political official or an organization in which one has membership (Rosenstone and Hansen 1993). Why, then, have consumer organizations struggled in their attempts to do just that? The question is especially perplexing because these groups have experienced modest success in getting borrowers to engage in collective action directed toward financial institutions.

### Organizational Capacity

Perhaps consumer interest groups had inadequate mobilizing structures with which to instigate political action among disgruntled borrowers. Organizational infrastructure, leadership, and money are all necessary to generate large-scale collective action of any type (McCarthy and Zald 1973; McAdam 1982). Did consumer groups possess these resources? As this chapter has described, a plethora of advocacy organizations—many with significant membership rolls—became increasingly active in their attempts to mobilize consumers in the lead-up to the financial crisis. With the creation of AFFIL in 2007 and AFR in 2009, the organizational structure was in place to mobilize grassroots political support among borrowers, and seasoned organizers staffed these new groups.

Consumers were also not without leadership in the form of a policy entrepreneur. Much like Harvey Wiley's mobilization efforts on behalf of the Pure Food and Drug Act in 1906 and Ralph Nader's publicly galvanizing pursuit of auto safety in the 1960s, Elizabeth Warren emerged as a vocal advocate for consumer financial protection prior to the crisis. Like both Wiley and Nader before her, Warren was well known to the public, particularly by the time legislative action reached its peak in 2010 (Kirsch and Mayer 2013). While Warren was already well regarded within the advocacy community, her public profile as an entrepreneur for consumer financial reform grew after she published "Unsafe at any Rate" in 2007, articulating a vision for a consumer financial product safety committee that became the blueprint for the CFPB. Warren was then tapped by Senate Majority Leader Harry Reid to serve as one of five outside experts on the Congressional Oversight Panel for the Troubled Asset Relief Program (TARP) enacted by Congress in 2008. Her reputation as a champion for lending reform continued to grow during debate over the creation of the CFPB and her subsequent election to the Senate.

The organizational infrastructure and leadership were both in place to support efforts at mass political mobilization among consumers, but did consumer advocates have sufficient resources to accomplish their goal? When asked, some leaders in the advocacy community have pointed to a relative lack of resources as one of the reasons their grassroots efforts may not have been successful. As one senior staff member of a consumer organization explained, "If you look across different sectors, the . . . resources . . . of consumer groups, compared to say, comparable groups elsewhere—environmental groups, health and safety groups, etc.—far more limited and it's always our major weakness" (0312151 March 2015). The director of another advocacy organization further illuminated the struggle for a group like AFFIL, which relied largely on foundation support, to secure funding for grassroots mobilization:

> A lot of grassroots lobbying, most foundations would never fund. Sometimes a fine line between grassroots activism and grassroots lobbying, but in the best of campaigns, grassroots organizing would morph into grassroots lobbying. Who's going to pay for that? (1119141 November 2014)

While consumer financial advocates may possess fewer resources than comparable public interest groups, this point should not be overstated. Consumers Union has an operating budget of nearly a quarter of a billion dollars annually, and Public Citizen, the National Consumer Law Center, and the Center for Responsible Lending each had annual budgets exceeding eight million dollars during the campaign (Mayer 2012). At least eight national groups dedicated in part or whole to consumer credit reform have annual budgets topping two million dollars, and foundations were initially supportive of AFFIL's grassroots mission. As one AFFIL staffer explained, funders were excited by the organization's prospects until they failed to deliver:

> It was two huge, huge grants. Huge grant from Ford—like $300,00 or $400,000. Ridiculous. And a grant from Casey, [$300,000]. They kept funding us for two, three years, whatever, and then finally they were like "we're not funding you anymore—you're not doing what we thought you were going to do." (1120142 November 2014)

Access to more resources would undoubtedly have increased the capacity of these groups to mobilize consumers, but their inability to generate citizen political action cannot be attributed solely to insufficient funds—especially when advocates were able to engage borrowers in large-scale market mobilization. If consumer groups possessed sufficient mobilizing structures to generate relatively successful lobbying efforts and to organize market protests, then perhaps the failure to engender mass political action can be attributed to the application of those resources.

## Collective Action Appeals

One of the most important tasks advocacy organizations must accomplish in order to persuade people to take a particular action is to create a successful collective action frame—a "set of action-oriented beliefs and meanings that inspire and legitimate social movement activities and campaigns" (Gamson 1992; McAdam et al. 1996). Simply put, people need a compelling reason to do something. A successful collective action frame typically meets three criteria: it taps into a sense of injustice or unequal treatment, it establishes a group identity, and it establishes an appropriate target for action (Gamson 1992; Folger 1986; Klandermans 1997). Each of these pieces must also resonate with the attitudes and experiences of the people being mobilized (Benford and Snow 2000). I argue that creating a resonant collective action frame proved to be a major stumbling block for consumer advocates' attempts to mobilize borrowers politically.

### *When Policies Preempt Political Mobilization*

For the purpose of borrower mobilization, a successful collective action frame would first need to capture people's existing discontent with financial products and services. Given the growing dissatisfaction with consumer banking and lending described in the previous chapters, tapping into borrower frustration shouldn't have provided much of a challenge. It is the other two elements—appealing to collective identity and pinpointing government as the target for action to rectify the problem of predatory lending—that I contend presented a problem. Chapter 3 argued that consumer credit policies have relied upon remedies and methods of implementation that both personalize and privatize people's relationship with consumer financing. As a result, borrowers are predisposed toward transactional methods of pursuing grievances with the consumer financial industry. That is to say, "responsible" consumers are more likely to engage in individual, market-based actions to solve their credit problems. For advocacy organizations to successfully employ a collective action frame that defines consumers as collective victims of corporate or capitalist abuse and encourages them to seek redress from government, these groups had to find a way to overcome the policy-induced preferences of borrowers—a tremendous messaging challenge.

Focusing on AFFIL as a case study, the following pages explore 1) whether a disconnect between borrower beliefs and organizational appeals existed and 2) whether it diminished the efficacy of AFFIL's mobilizing efforts. I begin by exploring AFFIL's own records, preserved at the Consumer Movement Archives, for evidence of such a messaging problem. I then used a mock action appeal, resembling those employed by AFFIL, to survey whether people's underlying attitudes about financial protection as an individual market issue inhibited their willingness to respond to organizational pleas for political action. Finally, I consider different strategies consumer groups might use in the future to overcome this messaging conundrum.

## *Identifying a Messaging Problem*

When consumer advocates gathered at that 2004 Cleveland conference to discuss the potential for a new organization designed explicitly to mobilize consumers toward political action, they acknowledged the need for a compelling message. One leading consumer advocate offered an incredibly prescient analysis of the problem they faced, lamenting:

> We're not going to change values, but you have to have a program that recognizes values and takes them over. Unfortunately, in the bankruptcy campaign, the industry took over "responsibility," predatory lenders took over "choice" and "freedom," [and] in the Fair Credit reporting campaign, [industry] took over "protection" of consumer credit. (AFFIL 2004)

The concerns voiced by attendees affirm the idea of the two-pronged collective action framing problem presented in this chapter. Advocates worried that people's inability to connect government regulation with consumer financial protection would inhibit their willingness to take political action, positing:

> People have forgotten that the government controls these corporations. Or at least used to. The average citizen looks at corporations and thinks it's only the bottom line that can govern them. So unless we teach people that they have the power to regulate, we won't get anywhere. (AFFIL 2004)

Attendees also noted the challenging prospect of balancing the impression that people are responsible borrowers with the need to convince them that they are also victims of predatory lenders. They admitted concerns about needing to make borrowers feel like part of a collective group as well. A representative from Consumers Union observed, "It's not just about personal responsibility and making it look like it's the consumer's fault. I think it's really important, whatever the ultimate message is, that it include the concept that this affects all of us" (AFFIL 2004).

Identifying a message that could overcome these obstacles became a priority for the new organization. Attendees saw presentations by two consulting groups—Spitfire and Benenson Jansen—that offered differing visions for what AFFIL could be. Ultimately, it was the latter group's focus on message testing that won over the consumer advocates (AFFIL 2004). As one attendee expressed, "I'm very excited about being part of research that tries to figure out, [do] we focus on victims, do we focus on bad guys, what's the key? So to me, message is what I'm most excited about" (AFFIL 2004).

Once AFFIL was officially launched, one of the first steps was to brainstorm and test potential messages designed to engage and mobilize consumers toward political action on lending reform. The firm Belden Russonello and Stewart Strategies was hired to conduct focus groups for several messaging campaigns that had been created by Benenson Jansen. Most of the campaigns focused on individual narratives about the consequences of predatory loans, relying on personal stories to draw people in. One, however, framed the consequences in terms of government deregulation. It creatively depicted families ravaged by debt and directly pointed the finger at government deregulation for the growth of predatory lending (and its potentially life-altering consequences).

Four separate focus groups were conducted in Chicago on June 12 and 13, 2006, to explore how people responded to the messages presented in each campaign. Participants included a multiethnic group of middle-income voters between the ages of 25 and 65 who were active in their communities. Each focus group was divided by age and gender, though not race or ethnicity. The first comprised women between the ages of 25 and 45, the second men ages 25 to 45, the third men ages 46 to 65, and the final women ages 46 to 65 (Beldon Russonello and Stewart Strategies 2006). Each group saw all of the campaigns, and the responses were remarkably consistent across all four cohorts.

The focus groups provide more evidence to support the theory proposed in this chapter. A summary of the sessions compiled by the moderators noted that participants were initially inclined to attribute any issues borrowers had to their own bad decisions, remarking frequently that people should be able to make responsible choices about credit (Beldon Russonello and Stewart Strategies 2006). As one young male participant described, "When we started out the conversation . . . everybody was saying these people are stupid enough to sign on the dotted line next to 375% [interest]." Another woman echoed this sentiment, explaining how it made her less willing to act in support of predatory lending reform. In response to a series of ads depicting victims of predatory lending she concluded, "Honestly, after reading all of these, I wouldn't [take action] because I think that you should be able to compute what you're going to be paying. . . . I think it's kind of on them for making that choice."

The moderators conclude that focus group participants' beliefs that credit problems were the consequence of people's bad decisions lessened their interest in responding to action appeals. But there was an exception. Messages that gave people a reason to blame government, and not borrowers, for credit problems made participants more likely to say they would follow up on the call to action. For example, in response to an ad that explicitly pointed a finger at federal deregulation of credit for the rise in risky lending terms, a male participant said, "I didn't know that since the 80s the lending laws or credit laws have been deregulated." An older woman also found this ad compelling, explaining, "The print that grabs my interest the most is the fact that consumer lending laws were deregulated in the 1980s. That's when all this stuff started happening. The deregulation of the laws allowed the finance and mortgage companies to do whatever they choose." The focus group summary concludes:

> Participants are also sometimes too quick to place blame on the victim. . . . Therefore . . . communications must . . . turn the

> message so that it clearly places the blame on laws that enable predatory lenders and shows the need for policy change. (Beldon Russonello and Stewart Strategies 2006: 5)

In summary, the focus groups' findings are in line with the idea that consumer groups like AFFIL needed to find a way to overcome a collective action framing problem. Ordinary Americans were predisposed to believe that problems with credit were largely the fault of individual borrowers. Appeals that referred to borrowers as victims and the government as the best source of protection simply did not resonate. The only way to overcome this problem, the moderators found, was to give people a reason to shift the blame for credit problems from individual borrowers and lenders to political actors.

### *AFFIL's Appeal Dilemma*

In reality, executing this task was easier said than done. It would not be enough simply to tell people they are victims of predatory lending and ask them to contact a policymaker to do something about it. Instead, appeals to action needed to provide recipients with a compelling reason to turn to government. Was the organization able to do this? To find out if and how AFFIL dealt with this framing obstacle, I conducted content analysis of 144 major action appeals emailed by AFFIL to its members over the entire course of the organization's existence. These emails were identified in AFFIL's archival material as representing all major action alerts. While this sample may not include the entire universe of communications sent by the organization, the fact that staff identified these emails as significant suggests that they are representative of how AFFIL tried to engage its members. The sample consists of an average of four emails per month sent between May 2007 and September 2010. Email was the primary form of communication with members, and AFFIL reported an average open rate of at least 25 percent and an average click-through rate of at least 35 percent—on par with or exceeding industry averages (AFFIL 2010). This is worth noting because it indicates that the lack of action wasn't the result of members ignoring AFFIL's messaging.

I began by analyzing whether each email asked members to take a specific action.[6] The email was considered to have an action appeal if it requested that the reader do something beyond looking at media or educational information about lending, for example, requesting that the reader sign a petition or contact a specific actor in a specific way. Next,

I identified the target of the requested action. Each email was coded as requesting political action if it directed the recipient to contact a government actor, including a candidate for office, legislator, executive, or governmental agency, in any way. If an email asked the recipient to contact a financial institution or trade association in some way, it was coded as requesting market action.[7] Emails received a separate code for market and political action because, while rare, a single request might direct recipients to contact both types of actors.[8]

Ninety percent of all emails contained an action appeal. Nearly three-quarters of appeals (73 percent) requested that members take at least one political action. Of those emails pushing political action, 85 percent asked the recipient to contact a member of the legislature and 15 percent asked them to submit a comment to a federal agency. One email requested that recipients contact the 2008 presidential candidates to encourage them to endorse AFFIL's fair lending principles. By contrast, only about one of every twenty emails (6 percent) asked people to take market action. One-third of the market action appeals asked the recipient to contact a bank. The remaining two-thirds encouraged the recipient to engage in protest activity directed at either an individual financial institution or the American Bankers Association at the so-called showdowns described earlier in this chapter.

The trend is clear: AFFIL was primarily concerned with getting its members to contact government officials to support consumer financial protections, despite the fact that consumers were not predisposed toward political action. How, then, did AFFIL try to convince its members to take the desired political action? In addition to the target of action, I also coded each email for the presence of five different frames—personal responsibility,[9] rights,[10] fairness,[11] protection,[12] and predatory lending[13]—used to talk about borrowers and lenders. Personal responsibility frames included language that provided information to consumers with the suggestion that they use it to make good choices about credit shopping. Rights frames stated that borrowers' rights were being violated by a lending practice or an existing law. For example, action appeals about mandatory arbitration—the practice employed by most lenders that forces borrowers to give up the ability to pursue court action over credit grievances—often spoke about people's "rights to trial." Fairness frames included those that suggested banks or policies were treating consumers unfairly in some way—for example, by suggesting that they were providing insufficient information about a credit product. Protection frames included any references to consumer safety, a government responsibility to protect consumers, or the idea that consumers were being victimized in some way by lenders. Finally, predatory frames captured any references to banks as predators or abusers, for example, by suggesting that banks were preying on young borrowers by peddling high-rate credit cards on college campuses. Once again, the presence of each of these frames was coded separately to account for the possibility that a single email might contain multiple themes.

Responsibility, rights, and fairness frames correspond more closely to an image of the borrower as a rational market actor. They are consistent with the idea that if people have enough information, or the ability to avail themselves of their property rights, they ought to be able to make responsible credit choices. By contrast, the protection and predatory frames suggest that borrowers are unable to protect themselves from financial abuse without assistance. The first group of frames better aligns with policy-generated attitudes about individual, responsible consumption, while the second suggests that consumers need government to intervene on their behalf. Figure 4.2 presents the distribution of each frame for all emails and for those specifically targeting market versus political action.

The most obvious trend is the frequency with which AFFIL's appeals emphasized the predatory nature of lenders and the need to protect consumer victims. Seventy-one percent of appeals talked about consumers as victims in need of protection, and almost as many (67 percent) made explicit reference to lenders as predators or abusive actors. These frames are antithetical to the idea that borrowers are simply rational market participants responsible for their own financial fortunes. In fact,

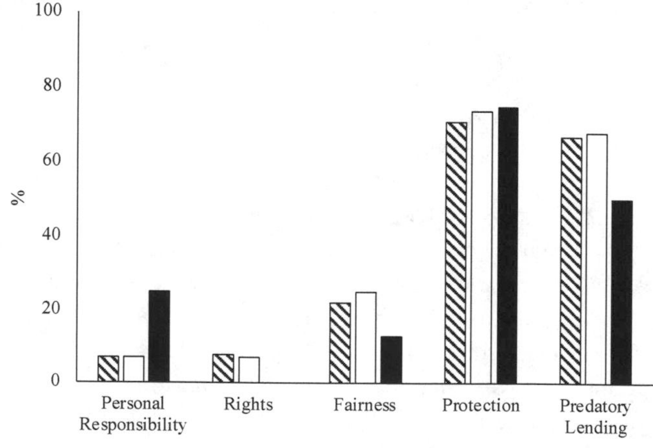


**FIGURE 4.2** Percent of AFFIL Action Appeals by Frame

fewer than 10 percent of AFFIL's appeals talked about borrowers in these terms, although a quarter of appeals calling for market action referred to the responsibility of individuals.[14] About a quarter of all appeals framed problems with consumer financing in terms of fairness, arguing that political action was necessary to ensure an equitable market. These frames fall more in line with the idea of rational market action, but they still represent a relatively small fraction of all emails. Finally, a small number of appeals (8 percent) discussed the need for action to secure legal rights, nearly all of which were designed to drum up support to eradicate mandatory arbitration clauses in credit contracts.

These results demonstrate that AFFIL was most likely to ask its members to engage in political action to secure protection from unscrupulous lenders, a frame at odds with borrowers' preexisting attitudes about consumer financial protection. But perhaps AFFIL employed distinctive language in appeals to members, who may have been more inclined than the average public to accept the idea that borrowers were victims of predatory lending in need of state protection. To determine whether the frames used to rally members were different from those used to generate action among the wider public, I conducted further content analysis of AFFIL's blog, its main interface with the public. The organization posted 431 items between February 2007 and September 2010, during which time the site had half a million visitors.

To demonstrate that the blog did in fact reach a wider audience than its membership base, figure 4.3 illustrates the effective number of page views[15] for the blog during AFFIL's first year of operation by the method people used to discover the site. While just over a quarter of AFFIL's web traffic was generated "direct" from member emails, the remaining three-quarters came to the webpage from other sources. About a quarter of all page views were generated from paid advertisements. Another 30 percent came either from search engines or media outlets. The variety in how people arrived at AFFIL's webpage suggests that the blog reached, and was designed to reach, an audience wider than just members.

I coded each of the 431 blog posts using the same criteria as the emails to determine whether it included an appeal to market action or an appeal to political action. Instead of coding the posts for all five types of frames, I collapsed the terms into two broad categories. Frames about predatory lending and protection were combined into one "victim" category, and frames about personal responsibility, rights, and fairness were combined into one "responsibility" category. For example, a post on March 1, 2010, titled "Call for Reform" began with the request, "Don't let the lobbyists drown you out: call your Senators and

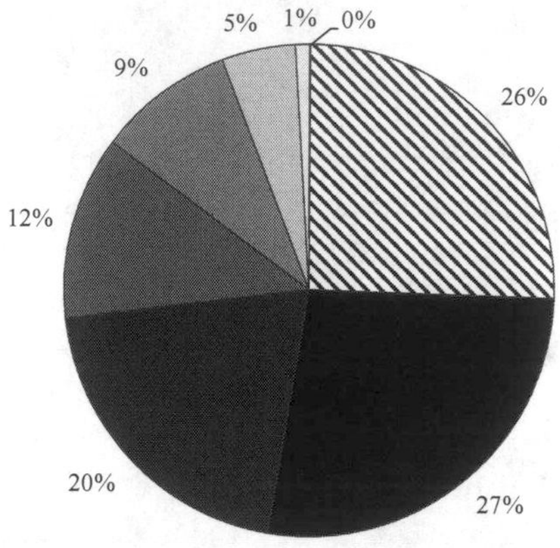


**FIGURE 4.3** AFFIL Website Effective Page Views by Source, 2007–2008

tell them that we need real financial reform that will hold big banks accountable." This was coded as a political action appeal. The post then went on to include the following reasoning: "Real reform will protect working families and small businesses by reining in the greedy, reckless behavior of big banks on Wall Street. Reform will crack down on the abuses committed by credit card companies and the mortgage lending industry." This post mentions both "protecting" working families and "greedy, reckless" banks that perpetuate "abuses" on borrowers. It was coded as a "victim" frame. The results of the blog post analysis are presented in figure 4.4.

As figure 4.4 demonstrates, the frames employed to appeal to a wider audience are nearly identical to those in the member emails with respect to the target of action they call for. Two-thirds of all appeals included a request to take political action, while only 2 percent of appeals requested market action. The gap between victim (40 percent) and personal responsibility (6 percent) frames is narrower in the blog posts than the emails, but there is still a 36-percentage point difference in usage of the two types of messages.

Taken together, these data suggest that AFFIL most frequently engaged collective action frames that called on borrowers as victims of predatory lending to engage in political action for reform—the combination I expect to be least likely to resonate with people's preexisting attitudes about consumer credit. And while a small subset of both the emails and blog posts appealing for political action attempted to justify that call with the deregulation framework employed in the ad cam-

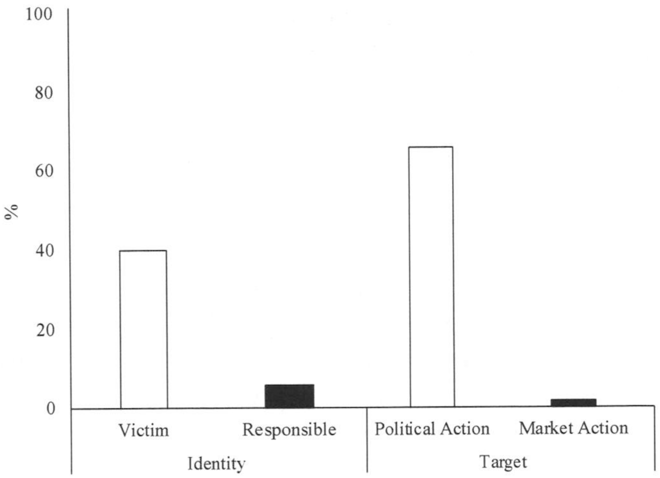


**FIGURE 4.4** Percent of AFFIL Blog Posts by Frame

paign, most did not, leaving consumers without a compelling reason to take the requested action. Even consumer advocates acknowledged the potential shortcoming of AFFIL's approach. One admitted, "It didn't resonate with me. Personally, I always felt like [the victim frame] was kind of a threat, because you know the main retort was always that people just have to take personal responsibility, and I don't actually feel like we ever sufficiently addressed that question" (1120142 November 2014). Another conceded the difficulty of presenting government action as a credible solution, commenting, "You know, 'I'm from the government, I'm here to help' doesn't ring true" (0312151 March 2015).

### *Did Preferences Demobilize Borrowers?*

The preceding sections provide evidence consistent with the idea that AFFIL's struggles to mobilize consumers toward political action were obstructed, at least in part, by the organization's challenges in generating appeals that resonated with people. But the analysis of archival evidence does not give us enough insight into how consumers reacted to those messages. How do we know what people were thinking when they read these appeals, and can we be sure that priming predatory lending doesn't resonate with people enough to make them want to take political action to reform an unpopular lending practice? I return to the 2017 Survey of Consumer Credit to answer these questions.

The previous chapter introduced the mock proposal for overdraft reform presented to survey takers. Respondents were asked to read the proposal and report their opinion of it. Recall that support for the proposal was generally high, but while the average respondent was willing to contact their bank to voice that support, they were not willing to do the same for their member of Congress or a federal agency. These results are especially important when considering that most of AFFIL's political action appeals asked their members to contact either a legislator or a regulator—actions that survey respondents were unlikely to take, even for a popular reform. While these results shed some light on the potential reactions to advocacy groups' political appeals for lending reform, they do not help us to untangle how people's attitudes toward credit correspond with their responses, or how priming predatory lending and consumer protection might alter that response.

One way to uncover whether the frames AFFIL relied on were likely to resonate with borrowers is to find out more about what people were thinking when presented with the mock overdraft appeal—an appeal that was designed using language consistent with (and in places directly from) AFFIL's action alerts. Immediately following the question gauging respondents' support for the overdraft proposal, I included a retrospective probe to capture people's reasoning for their answers. Scholars have used retrospective probes to uncover the specific considerations a person accounts for when responding to an opinion question (Hochschild 1981; Zaller and Feldman 1992). The probe, which allowed for an open-ended response, asked: "Still thinking about the previous questions you just answered, I'd like you to tell me what ideas came to mind as you were answering the questions. Exactly what things went through your mind?"

I conducted content analysis of the open-ended responses, coding them for the presence of three distinct types of reasoning. First, I recorded whether a respondent mentioned either a government or a financial institution, and whether the tone they associated with the institution was positive, neutral, or negative. I expected respondents to mention banks—whether positively or negatively—more frequently than government, consistent with the argument that consumers think of financial rather than political actors when contemplating lending reform. Second, I captured whether each respondent made mention of any of five major frames to talk about the reform: predatory lenders, consumer protection, fairness, information, and personal responsibility. I expected more people to mention fairness, information, and personal responsibility because these ideas are in concert with the model of borrowers as rational market actors described in the previous chapter.[16] Finally, I made note of whether respondents mentioned a personal experience with overdraft fees. Figure 4.5 presents the results of the open-ended responses.[17]

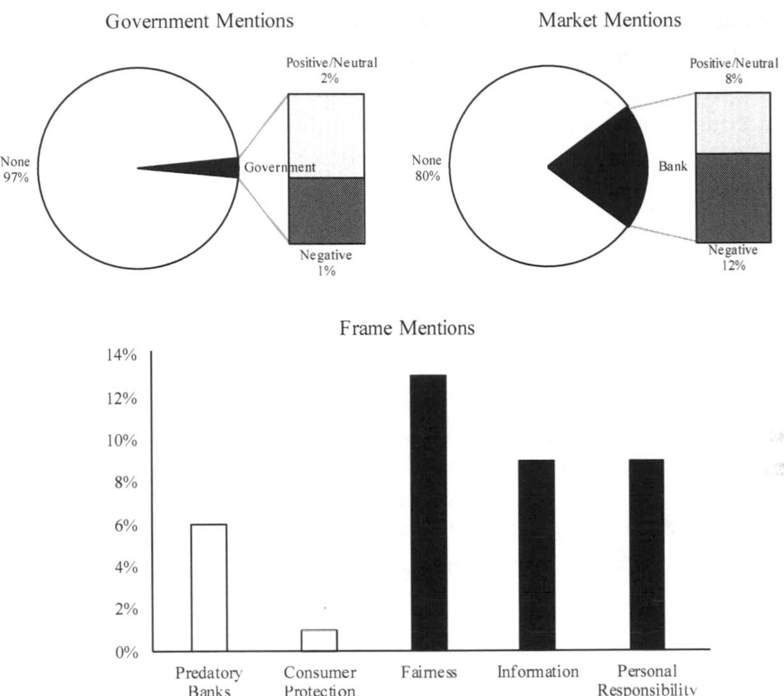


**FIGURE 4.5** Content of Open-Ended Responses to Overdraft Proposal

Twenty percent of respondents mentioned banks or financial institutions in their open-ended response, compared with only 3 percent who singled out government in their thinking. This conforms to the notion that people's beliefs about lending reform focus more on market actors than the political sphere. It is also notable that people were more negative when describing banks than the government, providing further evidence that American borrowers don't choose to engage with banks and lenders instead of politicians simply because they view market institutions more positively.

When it comes to the specific frames people employed to talk about the proposal, responses were consistent with my expectations. The idea of fairness was the most popular, with 13 percent of respondents mentioning the term. The role of information and the personal responsibility of borrowers were the next most frequently mentioned frames, with about 10 percent of respondents discussing each. By contrast, only 6 percent of people talked about banks as predatory or abusive entities, and only 1 percent of respondents specifically voiced the idea that consumers should be protected. These response rates offer further confirmation that, when presented with an action appeal for a specific lending reform, the average consumer thinks more about market institutions, market remedies, and responsible market behavior than they do about government institutions and consumer protections.

Evidence from the open-ended probe demonstrates that people's preconceived attitudes about consumer finance are rooted in the market and not the political arena. The ideas mentioned by consumers are a reverse image of the types of beliefs that AFFIL appeals tried to prime. These results suggest that when presented with an appeal for political action that talks about banks as predators and consumers as victims, no part of that frame is likely to resonate with the average person's existing beliefs about consumer credit. This should weaken the efficacy of the most common types of messages consumer advocates have historically employed.

A short experiment embedded in the survey confirms this expectation. A group of 240 respondents were randomly assigned to receive an additional message at the end of the overdraft proposal. Designed to mirror the language in AFFIL's email alerts, the message stated, "This proposal would help make sure that *people like you are protected from predatory lending practices* when you use financial services like bank accounts and ATM cards." People who received this frame about banks as predatory lenders did not mention either predatory practices or the need for consumer protection at higher rates than those who received the appeal without the additional text. Nor did receiving this additional language—which reflects the most common strategy AFFIL used to generate political action—produce any increase in their willingness to take action in support of the reform.[18]

From this experiment, we now know that the average American thinks about market actors, market fairness, and responsible borrowing behavior when confronted with a popular proposed lending reform—even in the presence of messages telling them they are victims of predatory lending. But how does the presence of these attitudes correspond with people's willingness to engage in political action to support consumer financial protections? I conducted statistical analysis of the survey responses to find out, capturing the relationship between the attitudes respondents expressed in their open-ended responses[19] and their willingness to take each of the three requested political actions to voice that support—contacting their member of Congress, contacting a federal agency, and contacting their bank. I also controlled for several individual attributes that are believed to influence political preferences and participation, including education, income, age, gender, race, and party identification.[20] The results of this analysis are presented in figure 4.6.

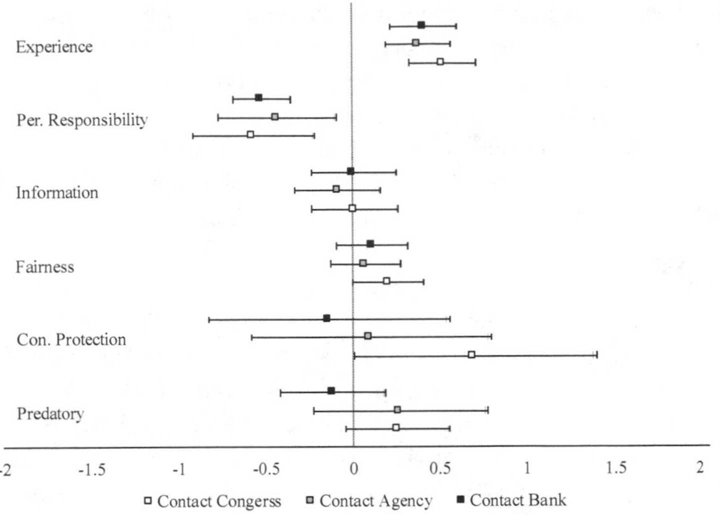


**FIGURE 4.6** Predicted Effect of Attitudes on Willingness to Take Political Action

Notes: Points represent ordinary least squares (OLS) coefficients with 95 percent confidence interval bars (n = 1,045). Full results for the models are available in the appendix.

Perhaps unsurprisingly, mentioning a personal experience with overdraft loans corresponds with an increase of between a third and half of a point (on a five-point scale) in the average respondent's willingness to take each of the three actions. What about the attitudes people drew on when processing the proposal? Were respondents who thought about the predatory behavior of banks or the need for consumer protection—frames employed most heavily by groups like AFFIL—more willing to turn to political action to support the proposal?

The results are mixed. Respondents who explicitly mentioned consumer protection were, on average, about two-thirds of a point more willing to contact their member of Congress to support the overdraft reform. That is a substantively meaningful bump in potential political mobilization. A somewhat similar, if only marginally significant, pattern holds for respondents who thought about predatory lending practices when reading the appeal. Thinking about predatory financial behavior correlated with a quarter point increase in the average respondent's likelihood of contacting Congress to support the proposal. However, the mobilizing effect of thinking about predatory banks and the need for consumer protection is limited; holding these attitudes did not correlate with a similar uptick in the likelihood of contacting a federal agency. These findings suggest that, for people who believe that banks are predatory institutions or that consumers warrant protection, appeals to political action might be moderately influential. The problem, however, is that so few people hold those beliefs about consumer financing.

What about the more commonly referenced attitudes that conform to a market approach to consumer financial protection? Figure 4.6 illustrates the relationship between referencing three such attitudes—fairness, the need for information, and the personal responsibility of borrowers—and a person's willingness to take each of three actions. As expected, thinking about the overdraft reform in terms of the information it would provide to consumers does not correspond with an increase in either form of political action to support the overdraft proposal. Referencing fairness correlates with a minimal bump in a person's willingness to contact their member of Congress—about one fifth of a point, but that increase vanishes when people are asked to contact a federal agency. Given that these were two of the most popular attitudes respondents drew on when processing the proposed reform, we can conclude that thinking about market dimensions of banking and finance is not likely to encourage political action.

The most serious problem for consumer groups, however, is that thinking about borrowers' personal responsibility when processing a proposed reform corresponds with a strong reaction in the opposite direction. For the median respondent, thinking about personal responsibility correlates with a sizeable decrease in their willingness to engage in each of the three actions by about a half of a point (on a five-point scale), and the most sizeable decrease is reserved for contacting a member of Congress. By way of comparison, thinking about personal responsibility corresponds with an equally sized movement in taking action as having a personal experience with overdrafts does, but instead of relating to an increased likelihood of voicing support, it does the opposite. In fact, mentioning personal responsibility correlates with the largest shift in either direction on the average respondent's willingness to take all three actions, including other factors like race, income, and even party identification. This is especially notable because the analysis is restricted to people who already support the proposal. Given that the average respondent was already predisposed against engaging in AFFIL's two most requested types of action—contacting a legislator or governmental agency—this result is ominous.

### *A Viable Alternative*

From archival records to survey results, there is ample evidence to suggest that consumer interest groups like AFFIL were hamstrung in their attempts to mobilize borrowers toward political action. It seems clear that the average American is much more likely to think of credit and banking in market terms, the product of their interactions with financial protections that privatize and personalize the use of credit. Even when confronted with a proposal they support and an explicit request to mobilize, borrowers who draw on these market-centered attitudes are reluctant to take political action. Consumer groups did not seem to find a viable way to bridge the gap between people's preexisting preferences for a transactional approach to credit with calls for political participation to protect victims of predatory lending. Could advocates have done something, or do something in the future, to overcome this messaging problem?

Scholars expect that people's political preferences can be influenced by attempts to frame an issue in a specific way (Tversky and Kahneman 1981; Zaller 1992; Nelson et al. 1997; Sniderman and Theriault 2004; see Chong and Druckman 2007). Framing occurs when a particular subset of considerations is highlighted to lead a person to emphasize those specific considerations over others when reporting a preference (Gamson and Modigliani 1989; Entman 1993; Druckman 2004; Chong and Druckman 2007). While framing effects may be fleeting, for the purpose of consumer groups, even a short-term nudge might incentivize people to make the immediate decision to take political action in response to an appeal.

Of course, consumer groups like AFFIL tried to engage in framing by emphasizing the predatory behavior of banks and the need for government protections for consumers. The problem, as I have demonstrated, is that these frames did not resonate with people's preexisting beliefs about consumer financial protection. What are the viable alternatives? Interestingly, consumer groups themselves give us a few possibilities. The 2006 focus groups AFFIL held to test potential messages suggested one possible answer to this problem: find a way to make people—at least temporarily—blame government for the plight of borrowers.

### Priming Government's Role

In the case of consumer finance, can reminding people that government is responsible for the regulation of credit overcome their tendency to attribute blame to market actors—both borrowers and lenders—enough to drive them to political action? I conducted an experiment as part of the 2017 Survey of Consumer Credit to explore this possibility.[21] After reading the overdraft proposal and responding to questions about their support and their thought process (the retrospective probe), par-

**Table 4.1 Priming Government for Action to Support Overdraft Reform**

| | |
|---|---|
| Control | "Still thinking about the proposal to change overdraft fees from the previous page, if a consumer organization asked you to take any of the following actions to voice your support for this proposal to change overdraft fees, how likely would you be to do each?" |
| Government Frame | "Still thinking about the proposal to change overdraft fees from the previous page, **supporters of this proposal argue that policymakers in Congress and in federal government agencies are responsible for passing laws to protect people like you when you use financial services like bank accounts and ATM cards.** If a consumer organization asked you to take any of the following actions to voice your support for this proposal to change overdraft fees, how likely would you be to do each?" |
| Competitive Rebuttal | "Still thinking about the proposal to change overdraft fees from the previous page, **supporters of this proposal argue that policymakers in Congress and in federal government agencies are responsible for passing laws to protect people like you when you use financial services like bank accounts and ATM cards. Critics of this proposal argue that people like you are responsible for making smart decisions when you use financial services like bank accounts and ATM cards.** If a consumer organization asked you to take any of the following actions to voice your support for this proposal to change overdraft fees, how likely would you be to do each?" |
| Competitive Reframing | "Still thinking about the proposal to change overdraft fees from the previous page, **critics of this proposal argue that people like you are responsible for making smart decisions when you use financial services like bank accounts and ATM cards. Supporters of this proposal actually agree, but they argue that people like you can't make smart financial decisions unless government policymakers in Congress and in federal agencies pass laws that require banks to give you clear, accurate, and easy to understand information about financial products and services.** If a consumer organization asked you to take any of the following actions to voice your support for this proposal to change overdraft fees, how likely would you be to do each?" |

ticipants were randomly assigned to one of four groups.[22] Participants in each group were asked how willing they would be to contact their bank, member of Congress, and a federal agency in support of the proposed reform, but those requests were framed in distinct ways, each designed to highlight government's policymaking responsibility in different terms. Table 4.1 displays the different frames employed in the control and treatment groups.

The first treatment primes the notion that government is responsible for enacting policy to protect consumer finances. The goal of this treatment is to see if simply reminding people of government's regulatory responsibility—as the AFFIL focus groups suggest—is sufficient to increase their willingness to engage in political action. It's rare, however, for people to be exposed to a single frame for any issue. Scholars have demonstrated, therefore, that to maximize the external validity of information-based experiments like this one, both sides of an argument should be presented. In many cases, this so-called competitive framing reduces or eliminates the effect of the initial information treatment under consideration—here, the role government plays protecting consumer finances—because it no longer promotes the salience of only one belief or opinion (Sniderman and Theriault 2004; Chong and Druckman 2007).

In accordance with this logic, the second treatment introduces an element of competitive framing. Beyond receiving information that primes government's responsibility to protect people's finances, participants in the second treatment group were also told that some disagree with that responsibility, instead believing that borrowers are responsible for protecting their own finances. Personal responsibility was chosen as the rebuttal, or competitive, frame because the theory and evidence presented thus far suggest it is the most commonly held attitude about consumer financial protection.

Finally, a third treatment employs a different type of competitive framing. Rather than trying to rebut the notion of personal responsibility, this treatment attempts to use the personal responsibility frame as a justification for government regulation. It allows us to see whether personal responsibility can be co-opted by consumer advocates as a reason to support greater government intervention, if that intervention is framed as facilitating borrower's ability to be responsible market actors. Such an approach might be more consistent with the lessons people learn from their experiences with existing consumer financial protection regulations.

The survey experiment allows me to isolate the effects of each frame on participants' responses to advocacy appeals requesting political action in support of overdraft reform, thereby testing the causal effect of that frame (Iyengar 1990; Chong and Druckman 2007). Recall that after receiving their respective treatments, all participants were asked how willing they would be to contact their member of Congress, contact a federal agency, and contact their bank in support of the proposed reform. Once again, willingness to take each specified action was measured on a scale from one to five, with one equating to "very unlikely" and five equating to "very likely." Contacting their bank was included to explore whether any effect produced by priming government's role in consumer financial protection was restricted only to political action, rather than generating a broader uptick in people's willingness to act. Figure 4.7 depicts the difference in participants' mean willingness to contact their member of Congress and their bank for each treatment.[23]

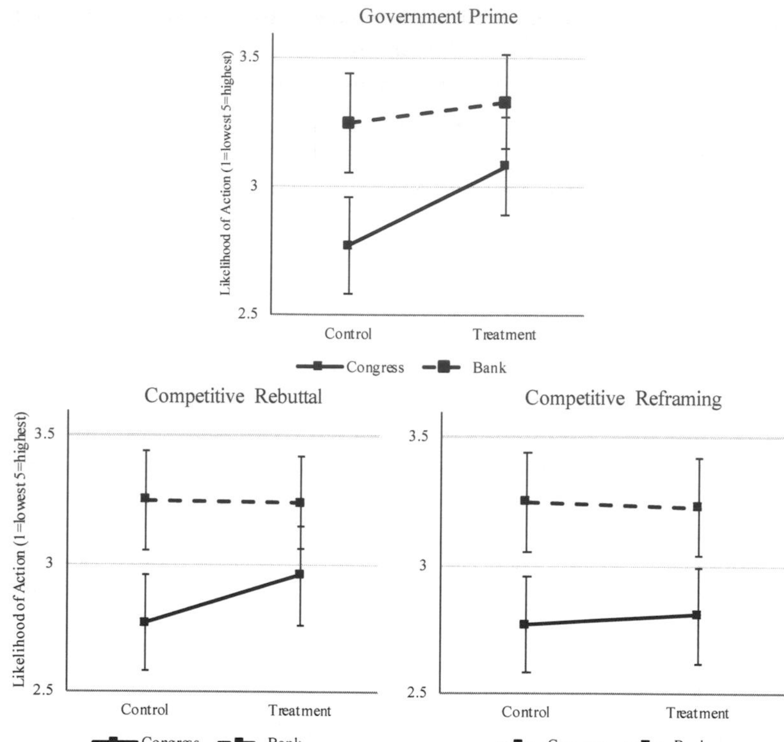


**FIGURE 4.7** Effect of Government Primes on Likelihood of Action
Notes: Points represent means with 95 percent confidence interval bars. Full results for the models are available in the appendix.

The first notable takeaway from these results is that, on average, people were more willing to contact their bank than their member of Congress to support the proposal. The baseline response from the control group suggests that the average respondent would reach out to their financial institution, but not their elected representative, to voice their approval for the overdraft reform. This is consistent with all of the evidence presented thus far about how people favor the market when reacting to either specific credit problems or systemic proposals for lending reform.

Reminding people of the role government plays in protecting their finances, however, produced a meaningful increase in participants' willingness to contact their member of Congress to support the overdraft reform. Receiving the treatment corresponded with a third of a point increase in their likelihood of taking action, which moved people above the threshold at which they become more likely to act than not. Receiving the government frame does not result in a significant difference in people's willingness to contact their bank, confirming that the treatment is specifically encouraging a political response. The positive effect of the government frame on political action persists even when controlling for participants' individual characteristics.[24] This is consistent with findings from the AFFIL focus group that priming government deregulation made people more seriously consider political action to combat predatory lending.

The problem, however, is that the participatory boost that comes from priming government's role in consumer financial protection disappears when placed in the more realistic competitive context. Participants who were exposed to the rebuttal treatment reported a marginally significant increase in their willingness to contact their member of Congress to support the overdraft proposal, but the increase was not large enough to be substantively meaningful. Put simply, the boost this treatment generated still left the average respondent at best ambivalent toward political action. The final treatment, which attempted to reframe government's role in consumer financial protection in terms that already resonate with borrowers—improving the ability to be responsible consumers—was the least effective. Participants did not respond to this attempt. The result is, perhaps, unsurprising in light of the evidence from the open-ended probes discussed previously. It seems clear that personal responsibility is a poison pill when it comes to political action on consumer financial protection: when people think about borrowers' responsibility for their financial affairs, it depresses political mobilization.

### Shifting the Focus

The previous experimental results tell us that simply reminding people that government has a role to play in regulating consumer finance can only do so much to boost borrower political engagement on behalf of lending reform. Even when priming government does lead to a boost in people's willingness to take political action, their likelihood of doing so remains lower than contacting a bank. So, what other strategies exist to mobilize ordinary Americans to support consumer financial protection? Rhetoric from consumer advocates offers another possibility: perhaps drawing a parallel between consumer finance and other consumer goods might help make the case for political action to support regulation.

Elizabeth Warren's toaster analogy, described in the introduction, provides one example of this strategy. Ironically, AFFIL's own talking points also highlight this method. In a 2007 internal memo, the organization describes the need for consumer financial regulation using the following logic:

> We need regulation to protect us from dangerous lending products just like we are protected from poison in our food, unsafe cars and dangerous medicine. (Detail: analogies on toasters and cereal aisle and side effects of drugs analogies) . . . We as a society have come to expect that the products for sale in our country are safe—we know the FDA is out there monitoring our food and drugs, for example. What people don't know is that there is no one looking after financial products like that. (AFFIL 2007c)

While this did not become a common refrain in the organization's action appeals, it has emerged as an increasingly popular way to talk about lending reform in the aftermath of the 2008 financial crisis. For example, AFR uses this type of reference not only in some of their appeals for political action, but also in their own opinion surveys gauging public support for banking regulation and the CFPB. Is this an effective way to mobilize people politically on behalf of lending reform?

On the one hand, drawing similarities between the regulation of goods like food and drugs and the regulation of credit makes sense. Agencies like the Food and Drug Administration (FDA) are quite popular among the public, and most people consistently support the safety regulations they enforce (see, for example, Pew 2012). But there are also reasons to be cautious. If borrowers have been exposed to depoliticizing regulations in the realm of consumer finance, the opposite is true of food and drug regulation. Anyone who has shopped for meat in their local grocery store or a pain reliever in the pharmacy aisle knows to expect the seal of governmental approval on the packaging. Consumers are thus conditioned to see government's role in the regulation of these goods. Without that same conditioning, how likely are Americans to accept the comparison of something like food and drugs with consumer credit? It is also worth noting that the ubiquity of these messages has not, so far, generated a wave of political engagement.

The logic of the comparative approach is sound, but perhaps a better comparison exists. If, as many scholars argue, consumer financing is not so much a good as it is an alternative form of financial support, or a substitute form of welfare, then framing consumer financial protection as akin to other popular policies governments implement to insulate us from economic shocks might be a better approach. Once again, I turn to an experiment embedded in the Survey of Consumer Credit to test the efficacy of each of these two similarity scenarios.

Those survey respondents who did not get one of the previous statements about government's role in financial regulation were randomly

**Table 4.2 Similarity Scenarios for Action to Support Overdraft Reform**

| | |
|---|---|
| Consumer Similarity | "Still thinking about the proposal to change overdraft fees from the previous page, **supporters of this proposal argue that shopping for financial products and services, like bank accounts and ATM cards, is very similar to shopping for other goods and services. That's why supporters argue that government policymakers in Congress and in federal agencies are responsible for passing laws to protect us from unsafe and deceptive financial practices too.** If a consumer organization asked you to take any of the following actions to voice your support for this proposal to change overdraft fees, how likely would you be to do each?" |
| Economic Security Similarity | "Still thinking about the proposal to change overdraft fees from the previous page, **supporters of this proposal argue that using financial products and services, like bank accounts and ATM cards, can affect people's financial security too. That's why supporters argue that government policymakers in Congress and in federal agencies are responsible for passing laws to help us be financially secure by limiting risky banking practices too.** If a consumer organization asked you to take any of the following actions to voice your support for this proposal to change overdraft fees, how likely would you be to do each?" |

assigned to one of two additional groups, each receiving one of the similarity scenarios detailed in table 4.2. The first treatment likens consumer credit to other consumer goods and services, a strategy popularized by Warren's toaster analogy. The second treatment takes an alternative approach, drawing parallels between consumer financial protection and other public measures to reduce economic insecurity. Of course, different participants will not give equal credence to the idea that consumer goods should be regulated or that government should enact policies to protect against economic insecurity.

We should expect the treatments to be successful only for people who accept each of these underlying premises. Presumably, comparing consumer credit to a toaster, for example, will fail to motivate someone who does not agree that government should regulate toasters in the first place. As such, prior to receiving the treatment question, participants were asked how much they agreed with one of the following statements depending on their respective treatment: "Policymakers in Congress and in federal agencies are responsible for passing laws to protect people like you from deceptive sales practices and unsafe products when you shop for things like food, drugs, and all sorts of other goods and services" or "Policymakers in Congress and in federal agencies are responsible for passing laws to help people like you be financially secure by providing things like tax breaks or social security benefits."[25] About two-thirds of respondents expressed agreement with each statement (68 and

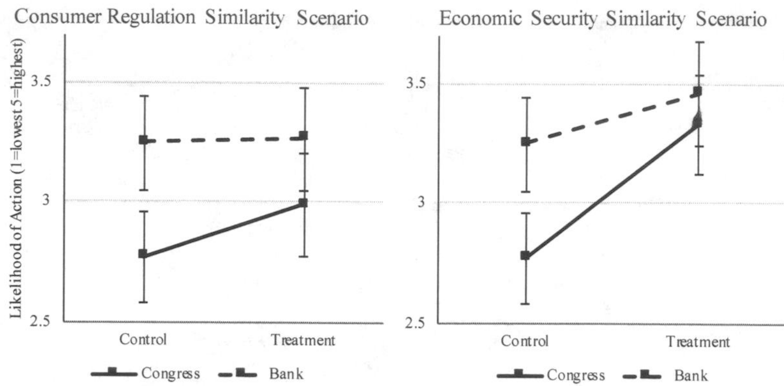


**FIGURE 4.8** Effect of Similarity Scenarios on Likelihood of Action

Note: Points represent means with 95 percent confidence interval bars. Full results for the models are available in the appendix.

63 percent for consumer regulation and protection against economic insecurity respectively).

Figure 4.8 presents the effects of the similarity scenarios for those who agreed with the underlying logics of government intervention. The consumer similarity scenario produces a marginally significant boost in the likelihood that a person will contact their member of Congress to support the overdraft proposal; however, the fifth of a point increase is not large enough to make a meaningful shift in behavior. The average respondent is still unlikely to act after encountering this frame. Unsurprisingly, likening consumer credit to the regulation of other goods does not change how willing a person is to contact their bank to voice support for the measure.

Comparing consumer financial protection to policies that protect us from economic risk more broadly is a different story. Across all of the alternative approaches I tested, this frame is the most successful at generating political action. The likelihood of contacting a member of Congress to support the overdraft proposal rose by more than half a point for the average participant exposed to the economic security frame. Not only is this a large enough increase to make consumers more likely than not to take political action, but it is also the only treatment that makes people as likely to contact a political official as their financial institution. While not presented in figure 4.8, the economic security scenario is also the only frame that corresponds with an increased likelihood of contacting a federal agency—producing a significant increase of about a third of a point on participants' willingness to do so.

We can learn a few important lessons from these experimental results. Most importantly, consumer advocacy groups should consider drawing parallels between financial regulations and the broader network of public policies that are designed to bolster our financial security in their appeals for political action. While likening credit to the regulation of other goods has a modest effect on people's willingness to engage politically, and it might be the most intuitive approach, it may not be as powerful. In addition, reminding people that government is responsible for legislating on the issue of consumer credit protection might be sufficient to increase their likelihood of responding positively to an appeal for political action, but the effect is weakened in the presence of conflicting arguments. This should give advocates pause in relying on the narrative of financial deregulation as sufficient fuel for political mobilization. Finally, attempting to tap into people's preconceived beliefs about credit as an issue of personal responsibility is not a productive way to politically mobilize borrowers. If anything, the reverse appears to be true.

There are, of course, limitations to the extent to which these results should be generalized from the survey context to the real world. As mentioned earlier, people often overreport their willingness to take a hypothetical action. But there is no theoretical reason to believe that the tendency to overreport is greater for members of the control versus the treatment groups in these experiments. Potentially more concerning, the effects of attempts like these to reframe an issue are notoriously short-lived. It is unlikely that any of these methods will permanently reshape people's underlying beliefs about consumer financial protection. Even a temporary shift, however, might be enough to instigate political action in response to a discrete request. In the absence of a major sea change in the design and implementation of consumer financial protections, it is these short-term remedies that could provide the best path forward for public interest groups who want to build grassroots political mobilization to support lending reform.

### *The Importance of Political Mobilization*

This chapter has explored the consequences of the political economy of credit for advocacy group efforts to incite political action among borrowers, arguing that regulatory feedback effects can shape the prospects for a successful campaign. While groups like AFFIL and AFR were occasionally able to engage the public in collective market action, the only significant examples of political action—comments submitted during passage of the CARD Act and targeted engagement during the debates over Dodd-Frank—were initiated by direct appeals for participation from political officials themselves. In such cases, the connection between financial protection and politics was made explicit to people by the very fact that it was a governmental actor asking for their engagement. When consumer organizations were responsible for doing the mobilizing, however, the chapter presents several pieces of evidence to show that they struggled in large part because they were unable to overcome a messaging problem—one created by the political economy of credit. Organizations used appeals that simply did not resonate with people's preexisting beliefs about who was to blame for problems with credit, or who was responsible for solving those problems. The chapter also suggests some stopgap fixes to this problem.

But is it really necessary to mobilize consumers toward political action on credit issues? Even without hearing from their constituents in large numbers, federal policymakers have, after all, passed legislation when their hands have been forced. For elected officials like Barney Frank, Leonor Sullivan, and Wright Patman, the problem is not in getting a new regulation enacted; it is getting support for a bill that introduces meaningful reform. As chapter 2 makes clear, policymakers are constrained by the political economy of credit. Left to their own devices, most will continue to rely on information disclosures in order to maintain broad access to consumer financing to support the consumption economy, even as those disclosures become less effective. Without considerable pressure from voters themselves, the small contingent of policymakers willing to pursue different approaches have not been able to convince their colleagues to embrace more meaningful reforms like the "vanilla" loan products introduced during the debate over Dodd-Frank.

Advocates themselves lament the consequences of failed attempts to mobilize consumers politically. As one former AFFIL staff member acknowledged, "There's no other way we're going to have change. The inside-the-Beltway strategy is weak and small" (1120142 November 2014). Another leading consumer advocate imagined the tantalizing promise collective political action by borrowers has to change the game:

> I think that currently, it is mostly a battle among the experts and a battle among the special interests. But, if the consumers were mobilized . . . I think they'd have immense influence and would be more powerful on the consumer side than what we have now. . . . That would be so much more influential if you could rally the public. (1119141 November 2014)

The failure to mobilize ordinary Americans to support stronger consumer financial protections has diminished lawmakers' receptivity to public interest group lobbying efforts. But the problems for consumer advocates don't end with attempts to mobilize consumers. As chapter 6 will demonstrate, the political economy of credit created an administrative arrangement for consumer financial protection that stymies public interest group lobbying in the regulatory arena as well. These obstacles further dim the prospects for lending reform, generating serious consequences for borrowers, especially marginalized borrowers, as the next chapter explores in detail.

# 5 Democratization and Its Discontents: Demobilizing Marginalized Borrowers

On Sunday, May 25, 1969, the National Conference on Social Welfare convened its annual forum in New York City with an atmosphere described by conference organizers as rife with "confrontation and dissent" (Branscombe 1969: ix). What followed was "the most tumultuous conference in NCSW history" (Kidneigh 1969: 178)—a dubious distinction for an organization that had been gathering annually for almost a century. The National Welfare Rights Organization (NWRO)[1]—a social action group mobilizing on behalf of welfare recipients across the United States—figured prominently in that tumult. In the middle of the conference, about 300 attendees walked out to join NWRO members at a local Sears department store to protest the retail giant's lending policies, which prohibited welfare beneficiaries from securing store credit. The protest began with attendees destroying their own Sears credit cards before marching inside to stage a "shop-in." NWRO members and conference attendees flooded the store and attempted either to purchase large appliances and other goods on credit or to apply for store credit (Kornbluh 2007). Protesters then demanded that Sears reverse their discriminatory lending policies by providing 150 dollars in store credit to welfare recipients (Nadasen 2005).

The protest was not a stand-alone event but rather part of a series of similar efforts by NWRO chapters across the country that began the previous summer. In 1968, the Philadelphia NWRO, led by Roxanne Jones, instigated a string of demonstrations at local department stores to demand access to credit for their members, who were denied because of their status as welfare recipients even when they possessed credit histories that otherwise would have qualified them for store credit. Jones and her fellow members called for 50 dollars of store credit for welfare beneficiaries, and they were able to successfully negotiate credit agreements with several major retailers in town (Nadasen 2005; Kornbluh 2007). The tactic spread across the country, leading to a sequence of sit-ins, shop-ins, pickets, and other protests—frequently carried out on the busiest shopping days of the year—to demand access to credit for welfare recipients.

The direct action was designed to achieve one of the NWRO's major goals: securing equal access to credit to support full participation in the U.S. consumer economy. As welfare rights activist Etta Horn justified, "This whole society is run on credit . . . so why can't we have it?" (Kornbluh 2007: 126). Horn's argument, which would be echoed by a growing number of women's and civil rights groups in the late 1960s and 1970s, resonates with the logic underpinning the political economy of credit. Policymakers proved increasingly supportive of the idea that credit should be made more widely available to previously excluded groups.

Federal lawmakers began to pursue the so-called democratization of credit[2] in the 1970s as a means of expanding the purchasing power of women, people of color, and low-income consumers, while sidestepping contentious political battles over taxation and the expansion of more traditional public welfare programs (Krippner 2005, 2011). These efforts were bolstered by women's and civil rights groups, who lobbied both private lenders and government policymakers to grant them access to the growing supply of consumer credit in its various forms (Kornbluh 1997; Hyman 2011; Thurston 2015, 2018). This first phase of credit democratization included attempts to expand financing to creditworthy borrowers who were excluded primarily because of their race or gender. With passage of the Equal Credit Opportunity Act of 1974 (ECOA) and its 1976 amendments, Congress ensured that access to consumer financing would not be denied based on people's gender, marital status, race, religion, national origin, age, or receipt of public benefits.

Over the next several decades, federal policymakers engaged in a second phase of credit democratization designed to expand the lending market to less affluent Americans. While ECOA made lending discrimination illegal if borrowers were otherwise "creditworthy," it did little to incentivize financial institutions to extend credit to borrowers who might pose a higher risk of default. Making generous use of preemption,[3] Congress (aided by the Supreme Court) began to chip away at state regulations that limited high-interest, high-fee banking and lending practices. By eliminating these restrictions, financial institutions could increase the interest rates and fees they charged on certain loans, improving their potential profit and making it desirable to extend their services to lower-income, "riskier" borrowers.

With these policy choices, federal lawmakers facilitated the dramatic expansion of access to consumer financing, especially for Americans who might otherwise have relied upon traditional social welfare programs for support. Their actions promulgated what some scholars have dubbed an American "credit-welfare state" (Prasad 2012). The privatization of social service provision in the U.S. is a defining feature of the modern American welfare state, but most accounts of welfare privatization overlook the increasing reliance on consumer credit as an ersatz form of welfare. In so doing, they also fail to examine how the democratization of credit—and its subsequent expansion of consumer financing to women, communities of color, and lower-income Americans—affects the politics of borrowers who have become increasingly reliant on the economic support it provides.

I argue that policymakers, by democratizing consumer financing, expanded the political economy of credit to incorporate new groups of borrowers and, paradoxically, heightened the need for consumer regulations to protect these uniquely vulnerable groups. The process ushered in an array of risky, potentially predatory credit products and terms, like subprime loans and high-interest, high-fee credit, that helped contribute to the deleveraging of American borrowers by the eve of the 2008 financial crisis. Despite the negative effects of these new lending practices—effects that were compounded, as chapter 1 demonstrates, because more and more households relied on credit in lieu of savings, rising wages, or traditional forms of redistribution[4]—these new borrowers fell into the same trap as their more affluent peers: they largely failed to engage in political action either to pursue specific problems with lenders or to support more systemic policy reform to protect their finances. For women, communities of color, and lower-income borrowers who lobbied hard for the democratization of credit mere decades earlier, this lack of political mobilization marked a consequential shift—one worthy of further inquiry.

This chapter explores the evolution of credit's democratization and its consequences for the political behavior of historically marginalized borrowers. I contend that the democratization of consumer financing is a natural outgrowth of the political economy of credit, and it produces feedback effects for marginalized borrowers similar to those that have de-politicized their mainstream peers. Despite their early activism—both market and political—to support the expansion of credit, marginalized borrowers subsequently have experienced the privatizing and personalizing effects of consumer financial protections. I once again turn to the 2017 Survey of Consumer Credit to demonstrate how this phenomenon results in diminished political engagement among those who rely on credit in lieu of more traditional forms of public support. While all groups of borrowers are beset by these demobilizing effects, I argue that they are especially consequential for folks whose race, gender, and/or socioeconomic status puts them at greater risk of predatory lending practices in the first place. I find, however, that the gap between blaming government versus market actors may be narrower for many marginalized borrowers, increasing the chance that these groups will respond to messages promoting government action. I explore this possibility through the same survey experiments introduced in the previous chapter, finding that some marginalized borrowers—most notably people of color—are more receptive to a broader range of advocacy appeals for political action.

## *Democratizing Credit in the United States*

The postwar American economy saw consumer spending skyrocket for a host of new products (Cohen 2003). In order to pay for these goods, consumers, including white, male, and more affluent Americans, increasingly utilized new forms of credit like the novel Charga-Plate and credit card systems described in chapter 2 that were facilitated by technological advancements in finance. But not everyone benefited from access to these credit market innovations. Women, people of color, and lower-income Americans—groups I refer to as marginalized borrowers—were largely excluded from accessing the growing supply of mainstream credit, limiting their ability to participate in the new consumer's republic that characterized the postwar political economy. When marginalized groups were able to borrow, they were confined to high-cost, predatory installment loans peddled within poor communities (Hyman 2011; Baradaran 2015). Louis Hyman paints a concerning picture of credit inequalities in the postwar United States:

> By the mid-1960s, a two-tier credit system had emerged in the United States. . . . For middle-class Americans, credit had become an entitlement. . . . To be denied credit went beyond an economic inconvenience; credit access cut to the core of what it meant to be an affluent, responsible adult in postwar America. . . . Even as poor Americans evinced consumer desires of the 1960s, their credit experiences remained more akin to the world of the 1920s. For poor African Americans in the cities . . . credit relations toxically stagnated. . . . Affluent white women, despite their greater access to retailers, confronted inequalities in credit as well. (2011: 173)

### Expanding Access to "Creditworthy" Marginalized Borrowers

What I describe as a first phase of credit's democratization included attempts to expand access to mainstream financing to creditworthy borrowers who were excluded primarily because of their race or gender. The potential problem created by insufficient credit for marginalized borrowers came into sharper focus in the 1960s. Sparked by social upheaval and an outbreak of race riots that ignited urban enclaves across the country, from the Watts neighborhood in Los Angeles to the Bronx in New York City, scholars and government agencies began to examine the economic and social conditions of minority communities in cities throughout the United States.

In his breakthrough 1963 study of black and Latinx low-income residents in New York City, *The Poor Pay More*, sociologist David Caplovitz documented what he called the "poverty penalty." Caplovitz described how low-income families incurred additional costs, often for shoddier goods, because they were unable to get credit from mainstream retailers. This forced low-income folks to rely on high-fee installment loans offered from less reputable door-to-door salesmen. A 1968 report from the Federal Trade Commission came to similar conclusions, noting that 93 percent of the durable goods sold to low-income residents of Washington, DC, were purchased on installment credit with annual interest rates averaging 23 percent. Ironically, the highly predatory nature of these loans meant that borrowers frequently defaulted on their payments, so retailers rarely made a profit. It was a no-win situation: low-income consumers got poor quality goods for exorbitant prices, and merchants failed to capitalize on their sales.

Insufficient access to consumer financing was a serious threat to the political economy of credit, and it increasingly became tied in the minds of policymakers to a variety of concerns associated with the condition of low-income communities in the United States, most notably the race riots. President Lyndon Johnson convened an eleven-member commission to investigate the causes of the unrest. The National Advisory Commission on Civil Disorders, known colloquially as the Kerner Commission after its chairperson, Illinois Governor Otto Kerner, argued that urban turmoil could be traced in part to "discriminatory consumer and credit practices" in low-income communities (Kerner Commission 1968).

Federal policymakers had long been convinced that access to consumer financing could fuel consumption by middle-class Americans and maintain national economic stability. In the aftermath of the race riots and the subsequent conclusions from the Kerner Report and the Office of Economic Opportunity, Congress began to consider whether access to credit was also essential for the stability of low-income minority communities.[5] Anecdotal observations noting that many of the retailers hardest hit by rioters were those who sold on credit bolstered this conclusion (Hyman 2011). Politicians and advocates alike became enamored of the possibility that expanding access to "ghetto credit" might be a good way to solve a number of pressing concerns about the volatility of the inner city.

Senator William Proxmire, once again in his role as chair of the Senate Subcommittee on Financial Institutions, argued for the importance of closing the "credit gap" in the nation's urban core (Congressional Record 1969: 12252). Over four days in 1968, Proxmire's subcommittee held hearings on "Private Investment in the Inner City." In his opening statement, the Senator articulated concerns over the state of the "inner core area, or ghetto area" of American cities, posing to witnesses the following question: "What is the proper role of government and private financial institutions in meeting urban problems?" (U.S. Senate 1968: 2) Those asking the questions, as is often the case, largely predetermined the answer. In his opening introduction, Proxmire noted:

> The purpose of the hearings is to determine what financial institutions are doing now to help meet the investment and credit needs of the ghetto, and to explore what additional steps can be taken to channel more private investment into the inner city. We are interested in credit across the board, including consumer credit, mortgage credit, and business credit. (U.S. Senate 1968: 1)[6]

Others echoed Proxmire's enthusiasm for integrating marginalized inner-city borrowers into the larger consumer marketplace. John Jacob, acting executive director of the Washington, DC, chapter of the National Urban League, encouraged the committee to "consider a concept that would extend the consumer credit system available now to most Americans—to all Americans . . . to consider a credit card for the poor—a credit card for ghetto residents" (U.S. Senate 1968: 233). Jacob went on to embrace the logic of the political economy of credit, arguing that Congress should "extend that great American tradition of 'buy now-pay later' to the ghetto consumer as well" (U.S. Senate 1968: 234).

While Proxmire didn't embrace Jacob's proposal for a "ghetto credit card," he supported the underlying idea. The hearings led Proxmire, along with five cosponsors, to propose the Community Credit Expansion Act to "increase the availability of consumer credit, mortgage credit, and business credit in urban and rural poverty areas" (Congressional Record 1969: 12251). The Act included a number of new programs to expand financing to economically depressed areas. It called for the creation of National Development Banks—private financial institutions required to devote at least 80 percent of their loans and investments to benefit people in high-poverty areas. The bill also returned to the New Deal playbook that produced the Title 1 home modernization loans. Proxmire and his colleagues sought to use government securitization to entice banks to lend to previously overlooked clients—in this case, marginalized inner-city borrowers rather than the middle-class suburbanites targeted by policymakers during the 1930s. Title VIII of the Act called for the Department of Housing and Urban Development to insure private banks for up to 80 percent of their loan volume on credit extended to low-income neighborhoods, capping the interest on these loans at one percent per month.

Lawmakers participating in the 1968 hearings that led to this bill were quite explicit in their references to New Deal innovations in government-backed private credit, offering them as models for once again harnessing government policy to stimulate private lending to boost the urban economy. Notably, their logic for engaging private capital in lieu of larger tax-funded public programs also reflected the economic and political arguments espoused by New Deal policymakers like Eccles, Hopkins, and Fahey described in chapter 2. Senator Walter Mondale, for example, testified during the hearings:

> Our task as a nation is to bring about a reallocation of resources—to channel more capital into the ghetto. . . . The government can . . . tax the necessary funds away from the economy at large and invest them in areas of high social yield. . . .

> Yet there are limits to public action. The consensus of today is that we must shift still farther toward a true partnership of the public with the private sector. Public policy must develop new methods for inducing the private sector of the economy to bring their resources and funds into the inner city. . . . How can the Federal Government induce the private financial community to play a greater role in meeting urban problems? (U.S. Senate 1968: 4–5)

Similarly, Senator Gaylord Nelson expounded upon the need to leverage private credit, explicitly referencing problems of cost and the potential burden on taxpayers:

> Of course, government taxation and expenditure is one way of directing the resources needed for economic and social development into these areas. . . . On the other hand, when one considers that estimates for the rehabilitation of our urban areas have run as high as $1 trillion, one realizes the absolutely crucial role our productive free enterprise system . . . will have to play in this battle. . . . I believe that, given the proper incentives to offset unwarranted risks, our free enterprise system will respond. (U.S. Senate 1968: 86)

Proxmire's bill didn't pass, but the idea that access to credit should be expanded to help bring marginalized borrowers into the mainstream consumer marketplace lingered. The legislative focus shifted away from creating "ghetto credit" and turned instead to ensuring that marginalized communities weren't unfairly discriminated against when they applied for existing forms of mainstream consumer financing. The new battle centered specifically on the issue of discrimination in lending, and it was fueled in part by two distinct campaigns calling for expanded access to consumer financing.

One, waged predominantly by white, professional women with support from groups like the National Organization for Women (NOW), mobilized against the prevailing practice of denying credit to American women who, were they men, would qualify for financing. As part of a larger movement to secure economic and political rights for women, activists framed access to credit as a civil rights issue and lobbied state legislatures and Congress to outlaw discrimination in the extension of credit based on sex and marital status. Local chapters of NOW formed credit task forces to lobby local politicians, and they succeeded in persuading about half of the states to outlaw credit discrimination against women by 1974 (Hyman 2011). These groups were careful to frame credit as a privilege that should be enjoyed by all those who were creditworthy; they simply argued that women should be judged on the same economic considerations as their white male counterparts. Representative Leonor Sullivan encapsulated this logic during 1974 hearings held before the House Banking and Currency Subcommittee on Consumer Affairs, stating, "The overall problem" is "making consumer credit available to all creditworthy Americans."

Members of the National Welfare Rights Organization composed a second group demanding access to credit. Unlike their more affluent, predominantly white peers from women's organizations, however, NWRO members argued that credit was a core aspect of economic citizenship in the United States, making access to financing a social right that should be enjoyed by every American (Nadasen 2005; Kornbluh 2007; Trumbull 2014). NWRO members embraced the campaign slogan "Give us credit for being American" (Kornbluh 2007). They argued that existing lending practices largely excluded them from participating in the consumer society of the postwar era, and NWRO groups in cities across the country staged protests, sit-ins, and shop-ins—like the one described earlier in the chapter—at local department stores and national chain retailers like Sears and Montgomery Ward to protest discriminatory lending policies.

Initially, the advocacy efforts of the more affluent, white women's groups convinced members of Congress that gender-based discrimination should, and could, be expunged. Congress enacted the Equal Credit Opportunity Act in 1974 (P.L. 93–495). The law prohibited discrimination specifically on the basis of gender and marital status.[7] The bill passed the House by a vote of 282 to 94. Seventy-eight percent of House Democrats supported the bill along with 51 percent of House Republicans. The Senate adopted the measure by a vote of 89 to zero (Congressional Record 1974a, 1974b). The large, generally bipartisan, support garnered by the bill is another testament to the importance policymakers placed on access to consumer credit. Despite the use by women's groups of civil rights rhetoric regarding ECOA, the justification for the bill was again framed in terms of the national economy:

> The Congress finds that there is need to insure that the various financial institutions and other firms engaged in the extensions of credit exercise their responsibility to make credit available

> with fairness, impartiality, and without discrimination on the basis of sex or marital status. Economic stabilization would be enhanced and competition among the various financial institutions and other firms engaged in the extension of credit would be strengthened by an absence of discrimination. (P.L. 93–495 § 502)

While affluent white women were the first beneficiaries of congressional attempts to expand access to credit, concerns over the economic security and stability of minority communities persisted. Within two years of ECOA's passage, policymakers recognized calls from groups like the NWRO. In 1976, Congress amended ECOA to expand provisions against discrimination to include race, national origin, religion, and receipt of public benefits. These new anti-discrimination measures were codified by the Federal Reserve through Regulation B. The law did not require banks to lend to people if they were deemed too risky; it simply mandated that demographic factors alone could not be used to determine one's creditworthiness.[8]

The expansion of credit to women and racial minorities relied heavily on advances in credit scoring technology. Underlying ECOA was the assumption that lenders had the ability to "objectively" determine a person's creditworthiness without considering demographic characteristics like race or gender. The Fair Credit Reporting Act of 1970 established national guidelines for the type of information credit bureaus could collect, to whom they could report it, and how consumers could access and amend that information. Proprietary industry models were used to determine whether a prospective borrower represented a good risk along two dimensions: how likely the borrower was to default on her loan (lowering a lender's profit margin) and how likely the borrower was to revolve[9] her credit (raising the lender's profit margin).

Scholars who replicated these models discovered that the expansion of credit, particularly to minority borrowers, was a potential boon for lenders. Studies found that more affluent borrowers, while less liable to default on loans, were also considerably less likely to revolve their credit from month to month, lowering the potential profit their accounts generated. By contrast, less affluent and minority borrowers—whose wages and savings were typically smaller—relied more heavily on credit to purchase large goods (Sullivan and Johnson 1980). They also paid them off more slowly, revolving their credit and boosting the profits of financial institutions. The Survey of Consumer Finances data described in the first chapter confirms this pattern. Expanding mainstream credit to marginalized borrowers, it turned out, could be considerably more profitable than lending to affluent Americans.

### From Creditworthy Borrowers to Subprime Lending

The first phase of democratization, driven by women's and civil rights groups, resulted in new federal policies to reduce gender and racial discrimination in lending, thus expanding access to consumer financing to women and racial minorities who still represented safe credit risks. But low-income Americans who lacked good credit histories were largely left behind when it came to mainstream credit access. In the postwar period, states still had usury caps that limited the amount of interest and fees lenders could charge, making it less profitable for financial institutions to extend credit to borrowers they deemed too risky. The second phase of credit's democratization—carried out largely on the initiative of federal policymakers—would resolve this dilemma, expanding the pool of borrowers to include increasingly "risky" but no less profitable targets.

Chapter 2 described how the Supreme Court in 1978 opened the door for the preemption of state usury laws by ruling in *Marquette National Bank of Minneapolis v. First of Omaha Service Corp* that banks could export nationwide the interest rate from the state in which they were headquartered. Two years later, Congress expanded this policy to include any state bank insured by the FDIC with the adoption of the Depository Institutions Deregulation and Monetary Control Act of 1980. The elimination of state consumer financial protections was furthered by two additional federal laws: the Riegle-Neal Interstate Banking and Branching Efficiency Act of 1994 and §731 of the Gramm-Leach-Bliley Financial Modernization Act of 1999. Each expanded the population of banks allowed to export most-favorable national rates for credit contracts. Finally, the Supreme Court's 1996 *Smiley v. Citibank* decision, which extended the logic of *Marquette* (and effectively the DIDMCA, Riegle-Neal, and Gramm-Leach-Bliley Acts) to non-interest finance charges and fees, completed the elimination of state restrictions not only on interest rates but on fees as well.

The result was the virtual elimination of regulations that capped the profit that lenders could make on loan terms and fees. Now, borrowers who had previously been deemed too risky suddenly held the potential to generate profit. Financial institutions simply had to find the right balance of interest rates and fees to cushion their potential risk should these borrowers default on their loans. As Louis Hyman describes, this shift couldn't have come at a better time for lenders. By the 1990s, the prime credit market was relatively saturated. There were few traditionally creditworthy Americans remaining who didn't already have access to consumer financing (Hyman 2011). With the restrictions on usury caps and fees all but lifted, companies began to explore whether it might be profitable after all to make loans to riskier, subprime borrowers. Subprime lending now held the potential to be a money-making endeavor—potential that was quickly and enthusiastically realized.

Once again, policymakers' predilection for removing consumer financial protections to expand access to credit to marginalized borrowers was all part and parcel of ensuring the continued growth of the political economy of credit. It was a way to boost purchasing power through government-backed private sources of capital, rather than enacting policies to ensure higher wages or expand forms of welfare support. These moves to democratize credit took place as welfare state retrenchment was in full swing (Hacker 2006; Soss et al. 2011). Instead, federal policymakers embraced newly expanded credit as a substitute for redistribution (Krippner 2011; Prasad 2012). Matthew Hilton explains, "The mobilization of the state around issues of consumption created opportunities for those who saw in the consumer a citizen around whom modern welfare regimes could be built" (2007: 69). The 1980s and 1990s saw lawmakers embrace the idea that the market, aided and abetted by federal policy, could provide support for low-income Americans just as easily as government itself could—a fundamental pillar of what would become the "third way" politics in the 1990s (Ramsay 2007; Krippner 2011).

Beginning in the 1970s, the democratization of credit in the United States facilitated a dramatic rise in consumer borrowing. Figure 5.1 illustrates how that expansion was distributed across the income spectrum. The chart on the left shows the growth in the number of Americans per income bracket who had at least one credit card between 1970 and 2007. While upper income groups experienced the largest boost in the percentage with credit cards—no doubt fueled in part by the expansion of credit to middle class and affluent women and racial minorities—and they still comprise the majority of American borrowers, the bottom two income quintiles experienced considerable growth in credit card usage as well. These groups also saw increases in the number of cardholders carrying a balance from month to month. As the second chart in figure 5.1 demonstrates, the number of card holders in the lowest income quintile carrying a revolving balance grew by 31 percentage points between 1970 and 2007—the largest increase for any income group.

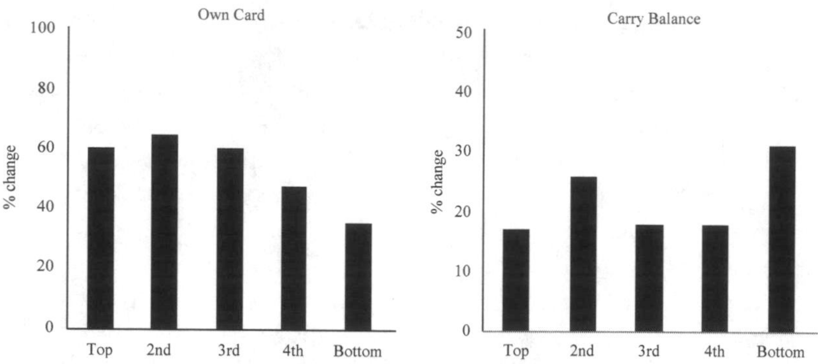


**FIGURE 5.1** Change in Credit Card Use and Balance by Income Quintile, 1970–2007
Source: Board of Governors of the Federal Reserve System, Survey of Consumer Finances, 1970–2016

## *Democratization, Political Mobilization, and Marginalized Borrowers*

The economic consequences of the democratization of consumer financing have garnered increased attention from scholars in recent years, particularly in the wake of the 2008 financial crisis. Once again, however, little notice has been paid to the political effects, if any, of expanding consumer financing to marginalized borrowers. This scholarly gap is remarkable for two reasons. First, the precarity of marginalized borrowers' finances—and their increasing reliance on credit to weather financial shocks—makes consumer financial protection an especially salient political issue for these groups. Their responses should inform the work of activists and scholars. Second, given the compelling argument scholars have made that federal policymakers democratized credit as part of the larger privatization of social welfare provision in the United States, ignoring the politics of consumer financial protection gives us an incomplete picture of the politics of the U.S. welfare state. The following pages explore how marginalized borrowers, once embraced by the modern consumer finance system, came to engage with the issue of consumer financial protection. I expect that marginalized borrowers' patterns of engagement have been shaped by their experiences with the policies at the heart of the political economy of credit.

By pursuing access to private credit in lieu of alternative forms of financial support—from wages to welfare—policymakers expanded the privatization of risk protection in the United States. While broad access to credit has been possible only because of the explicit decisions of government actors, marginalized borrowers, like their mainstream counterparts, experience transactions only with market actors when they use credit, thus obscuring government's role in the process. Policymakers have further hidden their influence over credit by consistently choosing to regulate credit through information disclosure, which leaves no indication to borrowers that government is playing a role in the process. Recall that 95 percent of federal policies regulating credit that were enacted between 1934 and 2010 employ information disclosures that completely hide government's role in their implementation. By contrast, only 15 percent of credit regulations highlight government's role in the provision and regulation of credit.

In chapter 3, I argued that the privatizing and personalizing nature of consumer financial protections taught mainstream American borrowers to think of credit primarily as an individual market transaction and to blame market actors—both themselves and their lenders—for problems they encounter with consumer financing. I further demonstrated that borrowers who place greater blame on market actors are more likely to pursue both specific problems with credit and broader preferences for lending reform within the market, rather than the political sphere. I expect that these same patterns are at work for borrowers who "benefited" from the democratization of credit. Despite the examples of marginalized borrowers agitating both politically and within the market to get access to financing, I expect that gaining access to credit—and the experiences with consumer financial protections that follow—will similarly teach marginalized borrowers to think of consumer finance as a market issue with market solutions, diminishing their political engagement despite the increasingly steep consequences these groups face from predatory loans.

### *Whom Marginalized Borrowers Blame for Credit Problems*

Whom do marginalized borrowers blame for problems with credit? I argue that most people, seeing very little evidence of government's role in protecting consumers' financial transactions, instead focus their ire on market actors. I turn once again to the 2017 Survey of Consumer Credit to explore this possibility for marginalized borrowers.

Figure 5.2 presents the average marginalized borrower's response to a question asking them to identify the degree to which each of these actors should be blamed for the "problems people experience with financial products and services like bank accounts, credit cards, and loans."[10] "Banks and lenders" and "consumers" once again received the greatest amount of blame from respondents at between 3.2 and 3.1, respectively, depending on the group. "The president" received the least blame from respondents, with scores between 2.7 and 2.9 across groups. It is notable that the distribution of blame for each actor varied little across

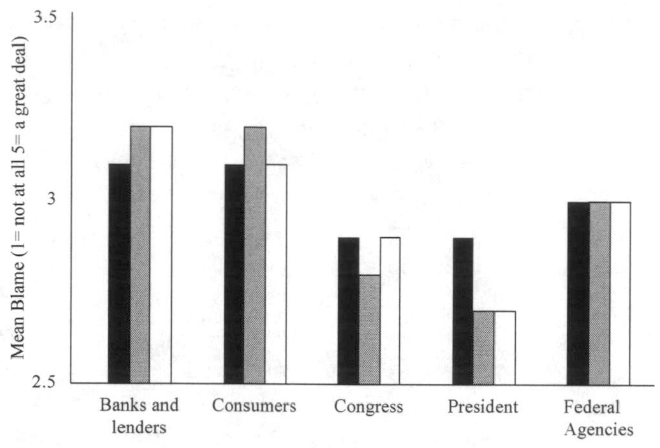


FIGURE 5.2 Blame for Problems with Consumer Finance by Demographic Group

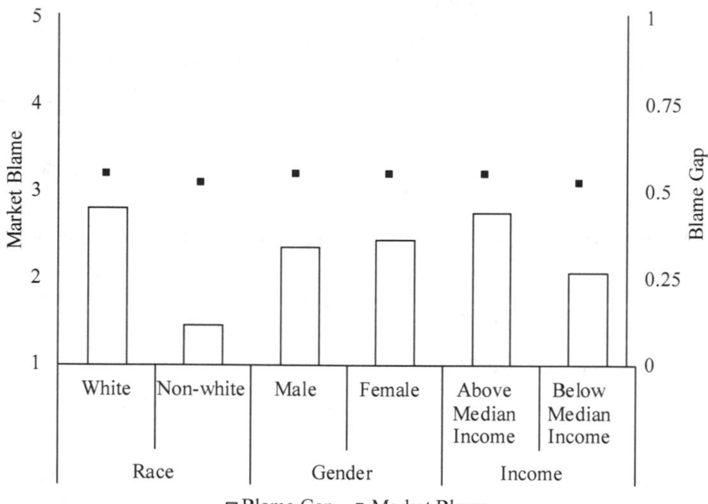


FIGURE 5.3 Blame Gap for Problems with Consumer Finance by Demographic Group

the three demographic groups. These responses provide some support for the contention that marginalized borrowers are focused to a greater degree on the market than the government as the responsible party for problems with credit. But how do these patterns compare to mainstream borrowers?

Figure 5.3 illustrates both the average blame for problems with credit that each group places on market actors (the points) and the size of the gap between their level of blame for market actors relative to political actors (the bars). As figure 5.3 shows, the average blame placed on market actors (including banks and lenders and consumers) by both mainstream and marginalized groups is roughly equivalent, ranging between 3.1 and 3.2. However, the gap that exists between how much mainstream versus marginalized respondents blame market actors relative to political actors (including Congress, the president, and federal agencies) varies more dramatically.[11] Men and women place similarly greater blame on market relative to political actors, with gaps of .35 and .37 points respectively. White and affluent respondents, however, exhibit a much larger blame gap than their non-white and less-affluent peers. White (.46) and more affluent respondents (.45) blame market actors for problems with credit on average almost half a point more than they blame political actors. By contrast, non-white respondents only blame market actors more by about a tenth of a point (.13), and low-income respondents blame market actors more by about a quarter point (.28). These differences suggest that, while men and women assign blame in similar ways, both non-white and lower-income Americans place a greater deal of blame on political actors for problems with consumer finance than do their white and affluent counterparts, though still not as much blame as they place on market actors.

These results initially suggest that non-white and lower-income borrowers might be less susceptible to the privatizing effects of using consumer credit, but a closer look at blame for respondents who actually report using credit versus those who do not complicates the story. Figure 5.4 illustrates the extent to which people assign greater blame to market actors than political actors by their experiences as borrowers. It reports the blame gap for marginalized borrowers by their use of different financial products, including bank accounts, credit cards, and personal loans.

As the results demonstrate, across all three categories of financial products, marginalized borrowers who use the specific type of credit report a larger gap in blame between market and political actors than do respondents from their demographic cohort who do not use that type of credit. In short, even among those groups who appeared predisposed to place greater blame on government actors for credit problems, credit users look more toward the market than do non-users. These results hold when controlling for other demographic characteristics within group. They are also consistent with the findings for mainstream borrowers discussed in chapter 3.

Taken together, these results indicate that marginalized borrowers place greater blame for the problems they experience with consumer

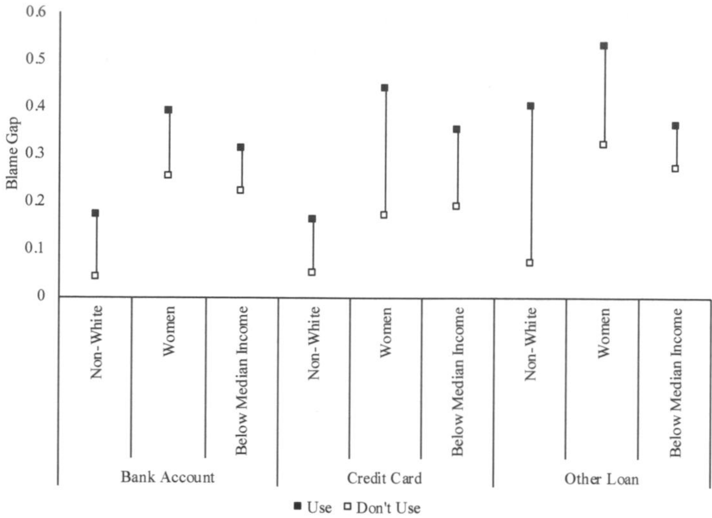


**FIGURE 5.4** Blame Gap by Credit Usage and Demographic Group
Note: The differences in mean blame for credit users versus non-users are statistically significant at the $p<.05$ level.

credit on market actors than they assign to political actors. The pattern of blame is consistent with the idea that, despite any government-supported welfare function credit serves, people's experiences with consumer financial protection policies encourage them to view credit transactions, and the consequences of those transactions, as influenced primarily by market rather than political forces. Once again, however, blame is only one piece of the puzzle.

## *How Do Marginalized Borrowers Act?*

Whom do marginalized borrowers turn to when they experience problems with consumer credit? I argue that, once again, with little evidence of government intervention in the regulation of financial protection, they are more likely to turn to market actors to pursue their grievances. Table 5.1 offers evidence that is consistent with this contention. The table presents responses to the same set of questions described in chapter 3[12] about how borrowers address financial problems. Marginalized borrowers were asked to detail any credit problems they encountered and what, if any, actions they took in response to those problems. As the results illustrate, between a quarter and a third of respondents from each group reported that they had experienced a problem with credit, with lower-income borrowers reporting a slightly higher rate of adverse credit experiences.[13]

Interestingly, white and non-white borrowers reported similar rates of adverse credit experiences, with 30 percent of white borrowers and 28 percent of non-white borrowers reporting problems. The gap between men and women is similarly small, with 30 percent of men reporting at least one problem with credit compared to 28 percent of women. The gap between more and less affluent borrowers, however, is larger. Twenty-seven percent of borrowers making at least 50 to 75 thousand dollars annually reported having at least one adverse credit experience. By contrast, 32 percent of borrowers making less than that experienced problems with credit—a five percentage point gap.

Significant majorities of marginalized borrowers who reported adverse credit experiences also chose to act.[14] Figure 5.5 provides more detail on the patterns of market versus political action among respondents with adverse credit experiences, comparing marginalized with mainstream borrowers. While all groups exhibited a high rate of action, there are differences. Non-white borrowers were slightly more likely to do something in response to adverse credit experiences than their white counterparts were. By contrast, women and lower-income borrowers were respectively 11 and 14 percentage points less likely to act on behalf of their credit problems compared with male and affluent borrowers.

When it comes to the type of action people took, marginalized and

**Table 5.1 Marginalized Borrower Action in Response to Problems with Consumer Finance**

| | Non-white | Women | Low Income |
|---|---|---|---|
| Experienced credit problem | 28% | 28% | 32% |
| Took action | 83% | 76% | 76% |
| Took market action | | | |
| *Contact creditor* | 56% | 75% | 73% |
| *New source of credit* | 31% | 42% | 34% |
| *Contact trade association* | 8% | 11% | 13% |
| *Participated in boycott* | 6% | 6% | 8% |
| Took political action | | | |
| *State or local agency* | 8% | 7% | 7% |
| *Federal agency* | 5% | 4% | 5% |
| *State or local elected official* | 5% | 4% | 6% |
| *Federal elected official* | 2% | 2% | 3% |

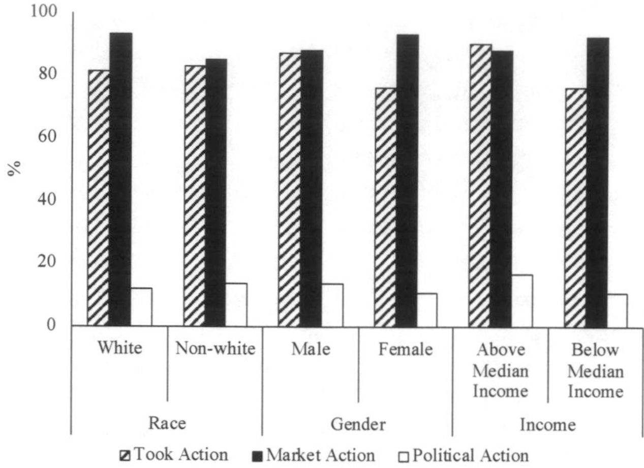


**FIGURE 5.5** Preferred Borrower Action for Reported Problems with Consumer Finance by Demographic Group

mainstream borrowers look very similar. Of those who reported doing something to respond to an adverse credit experience, nearly all (between 85 and 93 percent) took a form of market action. Only between 11 and 17 percent of each group reported taking at least one political action. Contacting a lender about the problem or switching their business to a new company were the most common reactions. A smaller percentage of borrowers from each group reached out to a trade association to voice their concerns. What is particularly striking is that only 1 percent of respondents—a rate consistent across both marginalized and mainstream borrowers—indicated that they took a political action without also taking market action. This data confirms that marginalized borrowers are not simply failing to act when faced with the consequences of predatory lending. But they focus that activity primarily within the market.

Perhaps the tendency to prefer market action reflects something unique about marginalized borrowers who experience problems with banking and lending. To what extent do these patterns of preferred action carry over to the broader universe of marginalized borrowers? In order to gauge their more general inclinations for taking market versus political action on credit issues, respondents were asked how likely they might be to take each specific action included in table 5.1 in response to a hypothetical future problem with consumer credit. Their answers were then aggregated to create a mean likelihood score for engaging in market action and one for political action, where one equals very unlikely and five equals very likely.[15] Figure 5.6 reports the average likelihood

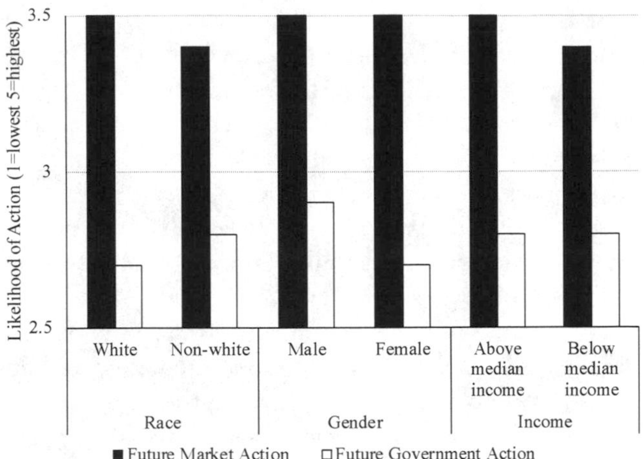


**FIGURE 5.6** Preferred Borrower Action for Future Problems with Consumer Finance by Demographic Group

of taking both future market and political action by mainstream and marginalized borrowers.

Once again, all cohorts expressed a greater willingness to turn to market actors should they wish to pursue an issue with consumer credit in the future. Indeed, three marks the mid-point where respondents were "neither likely nor unlikely" to take a specific action, so respondents expressed, on average, a willingness to engage with financial institutions while remaining unwilling to reach out to policymakers to address future issues of consumer financial protection. These results provide further confirmation of the idea that marginalized borrowers are more likely to turn to market actors when they are unhappy with consumer credit.

### *Does Market Blame Drive Market Action for Marginalized Borrowers?*

The previous two sections provide evidence that, having been exposed to federal consumer financial protections after the democratization of credit, most marginalized borrowers have learned to place greater blame for their consumer financial problems on market actors and are more likely to target market actors when seeking redress for those problems. The following section employs statistical analysis to explore whether those patterns of blame and action are related to one another.

As in chapter 3, I begin by examining the relationship between blame for market actors relative to political actors and a person's willingness to take market and political action, focusing on non-white, female, and less-affluent borrowers respectively. If placing more blame on the market influences a person's decision to engage in market action, then we should expect to find an increase in the likelihood of pursuing market action as a person places increasing relative blame for consumer financial problems on market actors. By contrast, placing greater relative blame on market actors should decrease a marginalized borrower's willingness to take political action—or at least have no positive effect. The following section considers that relationship for respondents who reported actual problems with credit.[16]

There are a few downsides to this approach. First, restricting the analysis to only marginalized borrowers who reported credit problems provides a small sample to analyze—ranging from 109 to 175 respondents per group. Second, respondents, as we have seen, tend to place greater relative blame on market actors. As figure 5.7 demonstrates, while the blame gap for marginalized borrowers approximates a normal distribution, it is skewed toward a greater level of relative blame accorded to market actors. Both of these dynamics increase the difficulty of capturing statistically significant patterns between blame and action. Despite this, exploring the results for those marginalized borrowers who reported credit problems is instructive.

Figure 5.8 illustrates the predicted relationship between a person's blame gap and their likelihood of taking both market-based and political action in response to real adverse credit experiences. As expected, the comparably low numbers of respondents in each group who place more blame on political actors relative to market actors results in more statistical uncertainty when predicting the relationship between blame and action at the lower end of the scale. Despite this, the patterns appear consistent.

For each cohort of marginalized borrowers, an increasing blame gap toward market actors suggests an increased propensity for market action. The relationship is statistically strongest for non-white borrowers. By contrast, increasing the relative blame marginalized borrowers attribute to market actors appears to diminish the chances they take political action in response to a problem with consumer financing. These results are more robust, with a marginally significant relationship for non-white borrowers and women. In both cases, the results appear weakest between blame and action for low-income borrowers. In combination, these results are consistent with—though not sufficient to confirm—the theory that market blame drives, to a degree, market but not political action for credit grievances.

In an effort to widen the scope of inquiry beyond marginalized

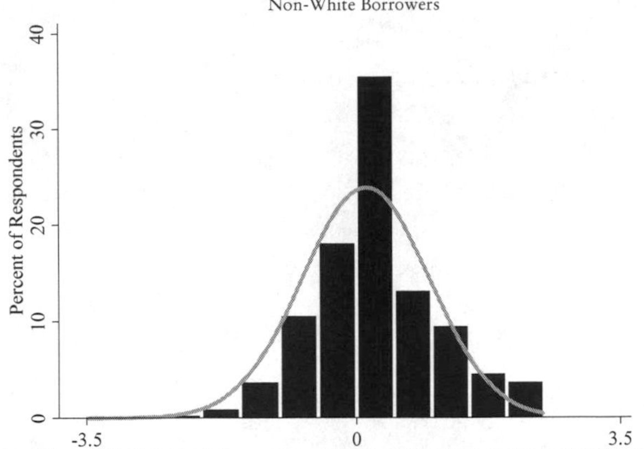


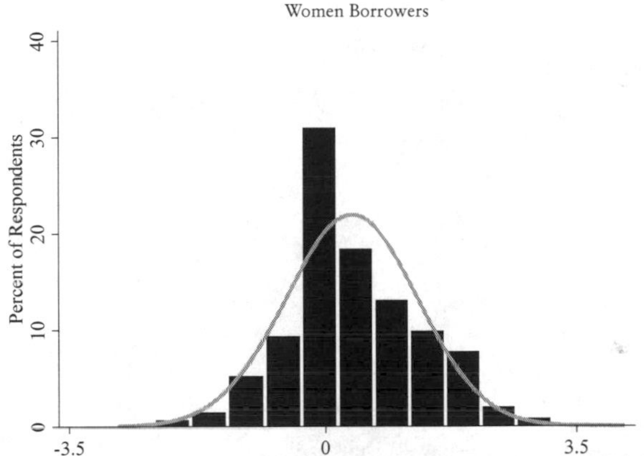


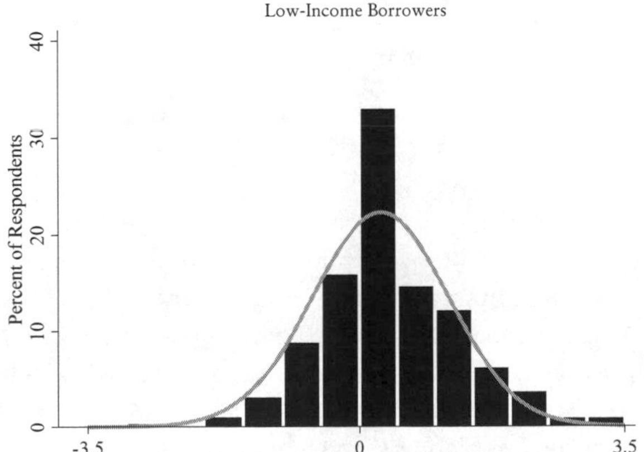


**FIGURE 5.7** Distribution of Blame Gap for Marginalized Borrowers

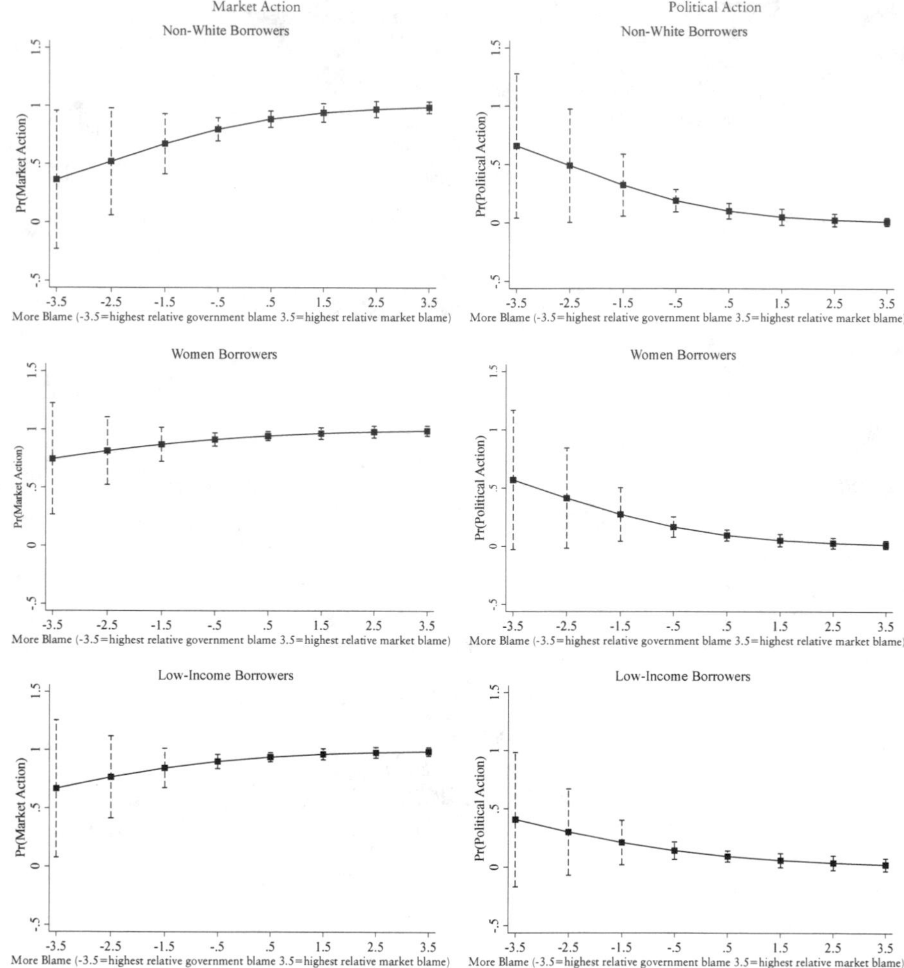


**FIGURE 5.8** Effect of Blame Gap on Action for Marginalized Borrowers

Notes: Points represent marginal effects from logistic regression with 95 percent confidence interval bars (n = 109, 161, and 175 respectively). Full results for the model are available in the appendix.

borrowers with specific grievances, figure 5.9 illustrates the predicted effect of market blame on future market and political action when controlling for political blame and individual characteristics. For each cohort, as a respondent places more blame on market actors for credit problems, they are predicted to be increasingly willing to engage in market action on behalf of those grievances. For the median respondent, placing a great deal of blame on market actors versus not placing much blame on them at all is predicted to increase their willingness to take future action between half a point and a full point on a five-point scale.

These results are especially notable because they move respondents in all three marginalized groups from being unwilling to being likely to take future market action in response to credit grievances. By contrast, increasing market blame generates no significant uptick in borrowers' willingness to take political action.

As in chapter 3, it seems prudent to consider whether the way a marginalized borrower responds to a discrete problem with consumer financing—real or hypothetical—is similar to their potential support

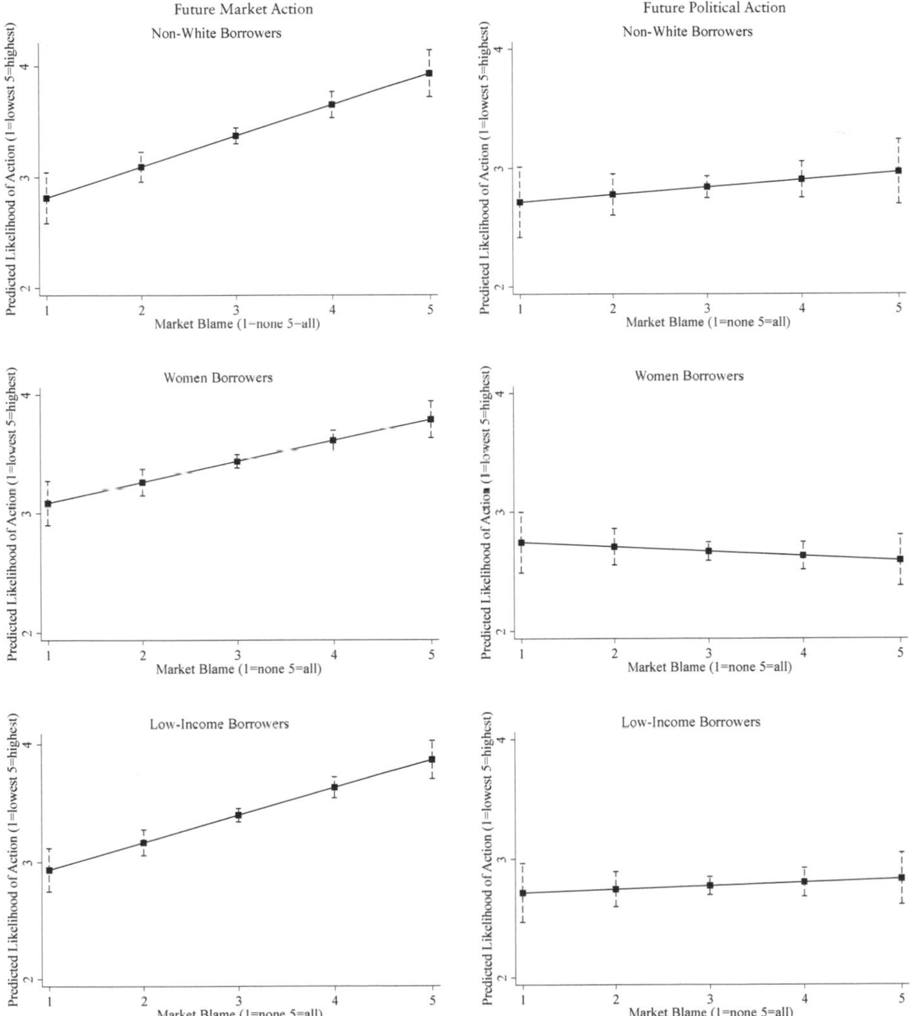


**FIGURE 5.9** Effect of Market Blame on Future Action for Marginalized Borrowers

Notes: Points represent marginal effects from ordinary least squares (OLS) coefficients with 95 percent confidence intervals in dotted lines (n = 463, 744, and 718 respectively). Full results for the models are available in the appendix.

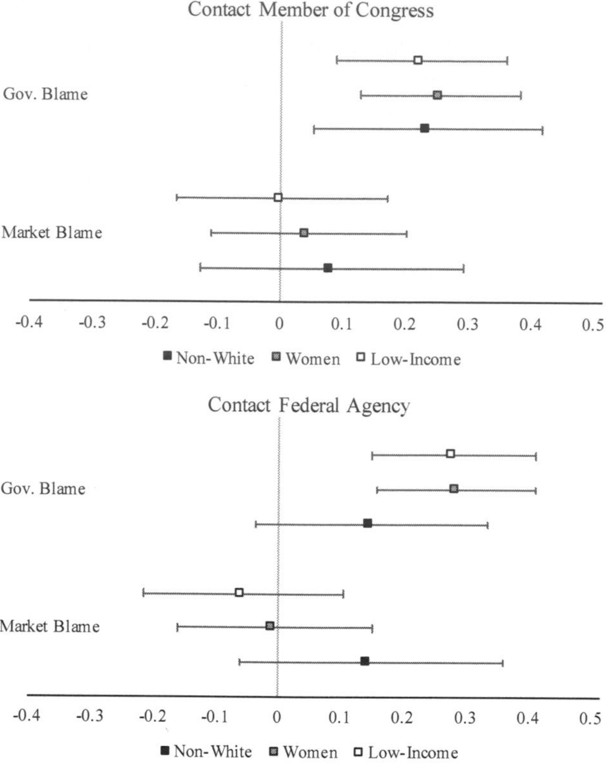


**FIGURE 5.10** Predicted Effect of Blame on Political Action for Overdraft Proposal for Marginalized Borrowers

Note: Points represent coefficients from ordinary least squares (OLS) regression with 95 percent confidence interval bars.

for a policy proposal to improve consumer financial protection more broadly. Figure 5.10 explores how market versus political blame maps on to marginalized borrowers' willingness to voice their support of the same proposal for overdraft reform described in chapters 3 and 4. Once again, the results parallel people's propensity for blame to affect action in response to actual or hypothetical negative experiences with their own sources of finance.

There is a fairly consistent correlation between blaming government actors and the likelihood that a marginalized borrower is willing to contact their member of Congress or a federal agency to support the overdraft reform. For all three groups, each one-point increase in government blame on a scale from one to five corresponds with a quarter-point increase in their willingness to contact a member of Congress. A similar relationship exists for low-income borrowers and women when it comes to contacting a federal agency, but it does not extend to non-white borrowers. On the other hand, increasing market blame—the more commonly held attitude about problems for consumer financing—does not produce an uptick in borrowers' willingness to contact either Congress or a federal agency.

These results all confirm that people's opinions about who is responsible for problems with consumer banking and lending influence not only how they respond to specific experiences with credit, but also how they respond to broader proposals to improve consumer financial protection. They demonstrate that the commonly held belief that market actors are more to blame for consumer lending problems results in a diminished willingness to make demands for greater consumer financial protection from political actors and institutions. Chapter 4 uncovered the potential for certain types of messages to, at least temporarily, improve mainstream borrowers' willingness to take political action on behalf of reform. Do the same measures work for marginalized borrowers?

### *Mobilizing Marginalized Borrowers*

In the previous chapter we explored whether reminding people that government is indeed responsible for consumer financial protection can help overcome their aversion to placing blame for problems with credit on political actors, and thus their lack of political action. A framing experiment was administered to see whether two different types of information treatments might shift people's attributions for consumer financial protection sufficiently to encourage them to reach out to policymakers in support of the overdraft proposal: reminding people about government's responsibility for lending regulation or drawing parallels between government's role in regulating other policy issues and their role in consumer financial protection. While priming government's regulatory responsibility and likening financial protection to the regulation of other consumer goods each produced marginal gains in borrower political action, drawing a parallel between consumer financial protection and other federal policies designed to promote people's economic security generated the most robust effect on people's willingness to engage with policymakers to support the overdraft reform. Should we expect marginalized borrowers to respond differently? Perhaps.

One of the most important contributors to preference formation is the weight a person assigns to an attitude or belief—in this case, that government is a responsible party with respect to consumer financing. If we think that marginalized borrowers might give different weight to that underlying consideration compared to their mainstream peers, we might expect that they will be more responsive to frames that highlight government's role in financial regulation. Earlier in this chapter we noted that non-white and low-income borrowers attributed greater blame for problems with consumer banking and lending to government actors than their mainstream counterparts—even as those same borrowers still placed more emphasis on the responsibility of market actors. By contrast, men and women exhibited relatively consistent attributions of blame.

One takeaway is that non-white and low-income borrowers may place more weight on the consideration that government has a role in protecting consumers' finances, and so they may be more able to incorporate messages that highlight that argument.[17] We can further explore potential differences in the thoughts of marginalized versus mainstream borrowers by returning to the open-end probes described in the previous chapter. Recall that respondents were asked to describe their thought process after reading the overdraft proposal and indicating their level of support for it. This opportunity to explain their thinking came immediately before borrowers were asked about their likelihood of acting to support the proposal, and thus before receiving the different messages designed to encourage their political engagement. Did marginalized borrowers cite different rationales when considering the overdraft reform than their mainstream counterparts? Figure 5.11 sheds some light on this question.

In general, as figure 5.11 shows, marginalized and mainstream borrowers rarely mentioned consumer protection in their comments—only 1 percent of each group did so. They were similarly unlikely to mention predatory banks, with only 5 to 7 percent of each group doing so. References to the more market-oriented concepts—fairness, information, and especially personal responsibility, however, begin to show differences in thinking between marginalized and mainstream borrowers—especially for people of color and less affluent borrowers. Most notably, white (11 percent) and wealthier (13 percent) borrowers were considerably more likely to reference personal responsibility than their non-white (4 percent) and lower-income (6 percent) peers. This evidence suggests that, while marginalized borrowers still place greater blame on market actors for problems with banking and lending, they may be less likely to consider these problems the fault of borrowers, perhaps making these borrowers more open to the idea of government intervention.

The following sections consider the mobilizing effect of the three most promising frames from the previous chapter's analysis—the com-

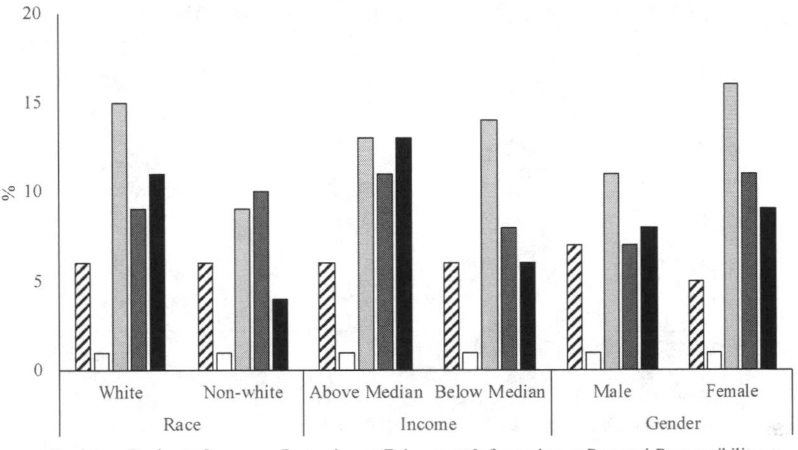


**FIGURE 5.11** Open-Ended Responses to Overdraft Reform by Demographic Group

petitive government prime, the consumer similarity scenario, and the economic similarity scenario—on non-white and low-income participants' willingness to contact their member of Congress or a federal agency to support the overdraft proposal.[18] Figure 5.12 reports the effect of the competitive government prime on supporters' willingness to take political action on behalf of the reform. Recall that after receiving their respective treatments, all participants reported how willing they would be to contact their member of Congress and contact a federal agency in support of the proposal, with responses measured on a scale from one to five, where one equals "very unlikely" and five equals "very likely."

As the results show, receiving the competitive government prime increased the likelihood that non-white participants would contact both their member of Congress and a federal agency by about half a point. This is a statistically significant and a substantively meaningful result, moving borrowers across the threshold for political action. Recall that mainstream borrowers did not react so positively to the competitive framing scenario, which pitted the argument that government is responsible for consumer financial protection against the counter that people are responsible for their own finances. This result is especially notable in light of white and non-white borrowers' divergent rates of reference to personal responsibility. One obvious hypothesis is that non-white borrowers are more likely to react to a reminder of government's involvement in protecting consumer finances, even when that reminder is presented with a rebuttal priming personal responsibility, because

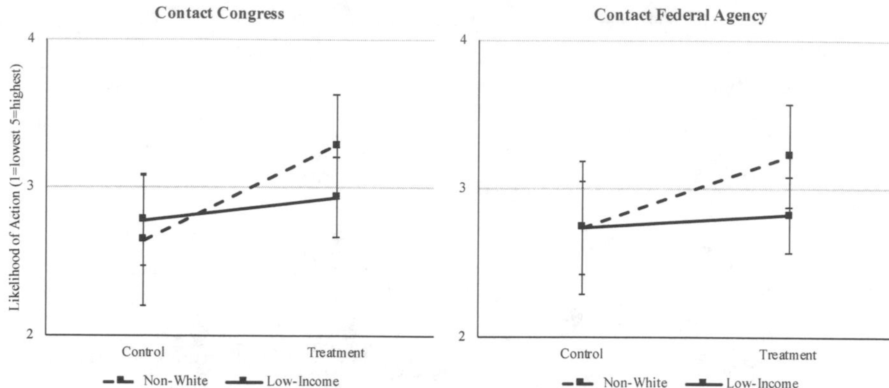


**FIGURE 5.12** Effect of Competitive Government Frame on Political Action
Notes: Points represent means with 95 percent confidence interval bars. Full results for the models are available in the appendix.

personal responsibility holds less weight in these borrowers' evaluations of credit. Interestingly, however, the treatment does not produce a similar effect among low-income participants.

Figure 5.13 presents the results of the two similarity scenarios on participants' willingness to take political action to support the overdraft proposal. Remember that the consumer goods similarity scenario failed to produce a meaningful boost in reported political engagement for all participants. A different story emerges for some marginalized borrowers. Likening consumer credit to the regulation of other goods increased how willing a person is to contact their member of Congress to voice support for the measure for both non-white and low-income borrowers. The boost is significant and substantive for each group, increasing political action by one-third of a point for low-income participants and about three-quarters of a point for non-white borrowers. The treatment also produces a significant and substantive increase in non-white borrowers' willingness to contact a federal agency about the proposal; it did not improve the same measure for low-income borrowers. Once again, the consumer similarity scenario produces more robust effects on political engagement for these groups of marginalized borrowers than it did for the larger population of survey participants. Is the same true for the economic similarity scenario?

Drawing a parallel between consumer financial protection and other policies designed to protect our economic security produced the biggest improvement in mainstream borrowers' willingness to contact a political actor about the overdraft reform. The likelihood of contacting a member of Congress to support the overdraft proposal rose by more

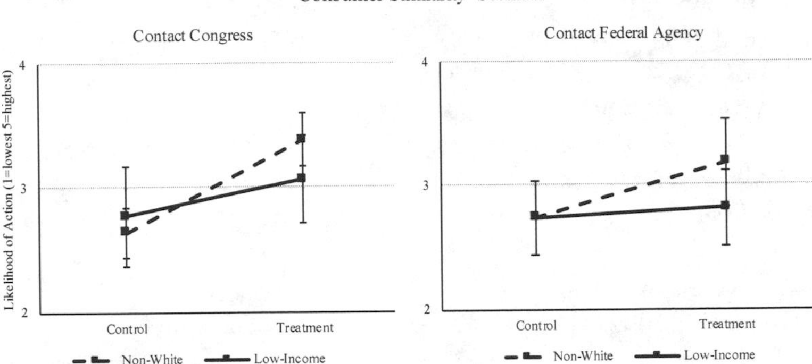


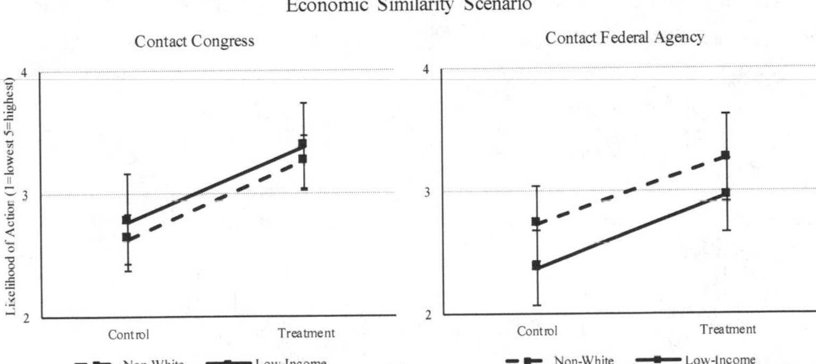


**FIGURE 5.13** Effect of Similarity Scenarios on Political Action
Notes: Points represent means with 95 percent confidence interval bars. Full results for the models are available in the appendix.

than half a point for the average participant exposed to the economic security frame. The effect is even larger for these two groups of marginalized borrowers. Low-income and non-white participants both reported an average increase in their willingness to contact their member of Congress of about three-fifths of a point. This was a big enough increase to move each group over the participation threshold. Exposure to the economic similarity scenario also produced a meaningful increase in the likelihood that non-white borrowers would contact a federal agency about the proposal. While low-income borrowers experienced a significant increase in their willingness to do the same, it was not large enough to induce them to act.

## *Marginalized Borrowers and Political Mobilization*

Taken together, the evidence presented in this chapter helps to paint a picture of how marginalized borrowers think about consumer credit problems and how that thinking influences their decisions to act on an increasingly significant piece of U.S. political economy. In many ways, the democratization of credit to marginalized borrowers mirrors the same logic that jumpstarted the political economy of credit in the aftermath of the New Deal. Policymakers turned to government-backed but privately generated loans to boost consumption among new segments of the citizenry in order to maintain and grow the nation's economy. The political consequences of inclusion in the ranks of American borrowers were similar as well.

Marginalized borrowers, like their mainstream counterparts, consistently place more blame on market actors for problems with consumer financial products and services than they do on political actors, although the gap between the two is smaller. Not only are these borrowers more likely to blame market actors for credit grievances, but it also appears that market blame drives them toward market action when they choose to do something in response to those grievances. That this occurs even though lawmakers have played a significant role in the democratization and subsequent regulation of the consumer credit made available to marginalized borrowers provides powerful evidence that government's fingerprints have been effectively obscured from consumer financial protections. I argue that such a feat was possible because the democratization of credit actively personalized and privatized the procurement and use of consumer financing for a new group of borrowers.

These results are particularly striking for two reasons. First, they demonstrate that the democratization of consumer financing depoliticized groups that, prior to having credit access, were quite politically active in this policy arena. Women's groups, civil rights groups, and intersectional groups like the National Welfare Rights Organization were active political and market participants during the push for expanded access to credit. It was only after securing consumer financing that these groups became less politically mobilized on the issue, despite growing concerns about unequal debt burdens, predatory lending, and the effects of the financial crisis.

Second, this pattern runs counter to existing scholarship on the role of resources and participation. It might be easy to assume that marginalized borrowers are less likely to pursue political action over problems with credit because they may lack the resources we typically consider necessary for political participation (Brady et al. 1995; Leighley and Nagler 2013). But the evidence presented in this chapter complicates that narrative. Among marginalized groups, those who have access to credit represent better resourced members of the group, yet it is exactly these better resourced members who are less likely to politicize credit than their peers who lack access.

The consequences of political demobilization on credit issues are serious for two main reasons. First, as is true for all borrowers, the remedies that can be secured from market action are likely to be limited in scope. Second, while the data presented in this chapter demonstrate that marginalized borrowers are similar to more mainstream borrowers in their propensity to blame and subsequently target market actors to deal with credit problems, I argue that it is marginalized borrowers who are most harmed by the lack of political pressure brought to bear on this issue. The lending system that emerged in response to policymakers' attempts to democratize credit produces unique harms for marginalized borrowers.

While current credit regulations may provide insufficient protection irrespective of income, banks and lenders frequently privilege wealthy borrowers by offering lower interest rates, grace periods, and many other services to which marginalized borrowers are not privy. By contrast, single women, communities of color, and less affluent borrowers are far more liable to fall subject to costlier credit, a plethora of high fees for minor mistakes, and an effective zero-tolerance policy before these fees kick in. The result is that mainstream borrowers are more insulated from the harms of the current system than are their marginalized peers, so they may have less to lose by ignoring political action. Ultimately, the demobilizing effects of credit democratization have the potential to disproportionately harm the financial security of marginalized borrowers, further widening the gap between the haves and have nots in American society.

There is, however, some cause for hope. The previous chapter described the difficulties consumer advocacy groups have experienced in trying to mobilize borrowers toward political calls for lending reform. It also explored alternative messages to improve those prospects, ultimately finding that comparing consumer financial protection to other government programs to protect economic security might be helpful. This chapter finds that, when it comes to many marginalized borrowers, a wider range of messaging strategies may be able to improve political mobilization. Because less affluent borrowers and borrowers of color are predisposed to place greater blame on government actors than their mainstream counterparts do, and they appear less likely to buy into the personal responsibility narrative, it may be easier to effectively prime governmental responsibility for consumer financial protection. As with mainstream borrowers, however, the limitation of such appeals is clear:

they are less effective in turning borrowers toward action within the federal bureaucracy.

The struggle to persuade borrowers to engage with federal regulators is especially troublesome both because federal agencies play an outsized role in implementing consumer financial protections and because they figure prominently in the growth of subprime lending that contributed to the most recent financial crisis (FCIC 2011; Jacobs and King 2016). The following chapter explores why public engagement on consumer banking and lending is particularly challenging within the administrative state, and why those challenges have considerable consequences for the protection of Americans' finances.

# 6 Race to the Bottom: Administrative Rulemaking in the Political Economy of Credit

Miranda[1] was a single mother living on the North Shore in Massachusetts when the financial crisis hit in 2008. It took a toll on her finances. Doubling Miranda's economic distress, her child's father had recently passed away, leaving no financial support to help the family. She, like many Americans, began to rely more heavily on her credit cards to make ends meet. As her balance grew, so did the interest rate on her credit card, jumping from an APR of 7 percent to 28 percent almost overnight. Iris from Oregon had a different, but no less destructive, experience with her credit card. She made her payment one day late, and her interest rate immediately ballooned from about 3 percent to 31 percent, quadrupling her outstanding balance in the process. Iris and Miranda's experiences are familiar to millions of Americans. Their responses, however, are unusual. Both Iris and Miranda took political action; they were among the 300 borrowers mobilized by AFFIL and its partner organizations to submit comments to the Federal Reserve Board in 2008 about the need to regulate credit cards—outliers, however limited, in the organization's political efforts (AFFIL 2008e).

While groups like AFFIL have struggled to generate mass political mobilization, most acknowledge that their expertise provides them with a certain amount of influence when it comes to dealing with policymakers

(1119141 November 2014). As the board members from Americans for Financial Reform (AFR) corroborated (see chapter 4), their congressional lobbying efforts helped to preserve important elements of financial reform during the legislative debate over Dodd-Frank. If expertise is indeed the primary currency with which public interest groups barter, we might expect their sway to be particularly obvious in the regulatory arena, the policymaking venue where technocracy and expertise arguably carry the most influence. Yet with respect to consumer financial protection, public interest groups have likened their battle to playing an exhausting game of Whack-a-mole (Mierzwinski 2013). For every minor concession they wring from regulators, enough loopholes remain that the financial industry has already found a way to circumvent the policy. The problem for public interest groups is further complicated because people have been reluctant to voice their concerns about consumer financial protection to federal regulatory agencies. Despite occasional exceptions like Iris and Miranda, the previous three chapters demonstrate how challenging it is to encourage borrowers to engage with federal agencies, even on behalf of policies they like and need.

Why have advocacy groups struggled to lobby regulators for more stringent consumer credit protections, and why have borrowers not been more willing to express their frustrations to the regulators tasked with protecting them? Such a result plausibly could be the product of a lax regulatory environment. The United States, however, has a far more rigorous regulatory framework than its European counterparts; yet, European bureaucrats generally take consumer financial protections more seriously than their American colleagues (Hilton 2007; Trumbull 2014). Despite the fact that Congress has granted powerful regulatory agencies the authority to make and enforce consumer financial protection rules, borrowers' interests have largely fallen between the cracks, even when advocates try to shine light on them (Levitin 2009).

Perhaps public interest lobbying and mobilization efforts are hampered by regulatory capture—the tendency for industry groups to "take over" the agencies designed to check them. While the financial industry undoubtedly wields power in this arena (see, for example, Jacobs and King 2016), plenty of recent evidence suggests that when public interest groups and citizens participate in the rulemaking process, their views influence policy outcomes (Yackee 2006; McKay and Yackee 2007). Furthermore, public interest groups have experienced success in other arenas of consumer protection—for example, food and drug lobbying—despite facing equally powerful industries (Nadel 1971; Pertschuck 1982). Scholars have also demonstrated that interest groups and citizens both believe their participation in rulemaking is influential (Furlong 1997; Kerwin and Furlong 2005; Yackee 2014)—suggesting they see value in regulatory politics.

So why do public interest groups have such a hard time both persuading regulators to take their concerns seriously and mobilizing affected borrowers to engage in the regulatory arena? I propose that untangling this puzzle requires a careful examination of the legacy of consumer financial policymaking in the United States. Chapter 2 described how policymakers since the New Deal have enacted laws that created and continue to support a consumption economy fueled by widespread access to consumer financing. At the heart of this system is the idea that lawmakers are primarily working to promote a stable national economy and not to protect individual consumers. The previous three chapters explored how the design and implementation of the resulting consumer financial regulations produce feedback effects that both shape individual preferences regarding political action and limit the ability of advocacy groups to mobilize borrowers politically. In this chapter, I argue that the political economy of credit also has implications for the politics of federal rulemaking: it led policymakers to adopt an administrative arrangement for consumer financial protection that fragmented regulatory authority for these policies across agencies designed to promote the interests of banks over borrowers, with significant consequences for public interest lobbying and political engagement in the regulatory process.

Policymakers in the late 1960s had to decide who would have rulemaking and enforcement authority for new federal consumer financial protection laws. As figure 6.1 illustrates, Congress had two important choices to make: 1) would they centralize authority in a single agency or fragment it across multiple agencies, and 2) what would be the primary mission for the agency(s) empowered to implement financial protections? Throughout this chapter, I draw on archival and legislative

| ECONOMIC SYSTEM | PURCHASING POWER | SOURCE OF SUPPORT | FORM OF REGULATION | ADMINISTRATIVE ARRANGEMENT | ADMINISTRATIVE MISSION |
|---|---|---|---|---|---|
| Production<br>vs.<br>**Consumption** | Redistribution/Wages<br>vs.<br>**Financing** | Public<br>vs.<br>**Private** | Safety<br>vs.<br>**Information** | Centralized<br>vs.<br>**Fragmented** | Protective<br>vs.<br>**Competitive** |

**FIGURE 6.1** Policy Tradeoffs in the U.S. Political Economy of Credit

analyses to explain why Congress initially chose to break up rulemaking and enforcement authority across seven different federal agencies, most of which were created to promote the stability and profitability of financial institutions and not that of individual borrowers. The chapter then relies on interviews with consumer advocates and evidence of consumer credit complaints to show how this so-called balkanization, or fragmentation, of regulatory authority for consumer financial protections presents obstacles for both public interest lobbying and borrower engagement. Ultimately, it explores how the creation of the CFPB might reshape these dynamics by centralizing much of the regulatory authority for consumer financial protection in a single agency designed explicitly to work on behalf of consumers.

While the politics of the regulatory arena often fly under the scholarly radar, they represent one of the most important sites of policymaking in the United States. By some estimates, bureaucratic rulemaking now produces 90 percent of all federal laws enacted each year. As Cornelius Kerwin and Scott Furlong sum up, "Rulemaking has become the most common and instrumental form of lawmaking" in the United States (1992: 114). Since the 1970s, protective regulations comprise an increasingly large portion of that rulemaking activity. In light of this, the ability—or inability, as the case may be—of public interest groups and citizens to meaningfully influence the rulemaking process bears significant weight on the ultimate protection of American borrowers' financial interests.

### *Public Interest Participation in the Regulatory Process*

Interest groups and citizens have a long history of sanctioned involvement in regulatory politics. When the Administrative Procedure Act (APA) became law in 1946 (P.L. 79–404), it formalized the rulemaking process for administrative agencies. According to the APA, an agency must issue a public notice when it considers a new rule. The proposed rule is then made available for public comment for a specified period. Finally, the agency must publish the final rule along with its rationale. While there are exceptions to this sequence of events, the majority of administrative regulations come to fruition through this process (Potter 2019).

The notice and comment period assures that interest groups and members of the wider public can voice their opinions about a proposed rule, but there are many other openings for these actors to engage with regulatory agencies. Interest groups can be instrumental in getting bureaucrats to investigate new regulatory issues, and they are often consulted informally when new rules are being drafted. Agencies also hold public field hearings that formally elicit participation from both interest group representatives and members of the public. And many agencies have procedures in place to collect feedback, often in the form of complaints, from people who have been affected by a regulated industry. If opportunities for consumer advocates and borrowers to participate in the rulemaking process exist, when do they choose to participate, and under what circumstances are their voices effective?

### Deciding to Participate

Scholars have proposed several theories to address the first question: when do different sets of political actors capitalize on these openings in the regulatory system? Most prominent among them are theories that attribute participation to the characteristics of the policy under consideration. Theodore Lowi (1972) and James Q. Wilson (1980) argue that the distribution of costs and benefits for a policy area determines the type of politics that emerges in response to that issue. According to their analyses, protective regulatory policies like consumer financial protections distribute benefits widely to a diffuse group of borrowers while concentrating the costs among a smaller group of financial institutions. This can have the effect of diminishing political engagement among policy beneficiaries while increasing attention from industry groups whose practices are under consideration.

Focusing on the nuances that emerge across different types of regulations, William Gormley (1986) proposes that the varied participation of public interest groups and ordinary citizens can be explained by the salience and complexity of the issue at hand. He elaborates that citizens are most likely to engage for highly salient, relatively simple regulatory issues. By contrast, for high-complexity issues, citizens are expected to be absent from the regulatory arena, while experts take over. Gormley's theory has received widespread consideration by scholars; however, it poses a conundrum for consumer financial regulation. He posits that consumer protection issues are exactly the low-complexity, high-salience topics that should generate public engagement. On the other hand, Gormley expects financial regulation to be more complex, restricting the playing field to experts (1986: 600). What does this mean for consumer financial protection, which presumably falls at the intersection of these conflicting predictions?

Given the importance of consumer credit to the everyday lives of most Americans, combined with the media coverage associated with the

2008 financial crisis, it seems reasonable to conclude that the regulation of consumer lending is a high-salience issue. But even advocates themselves differ in assessing its complexity—and thus the extent to which we might expect experts to rule the regulatory process for this issue. As one advocate I spoke with noted, "Some of [the regulations] are complicated. There's probably thousands of pages of rules . . . a lot more law than there was before, and it's complicated" (1120141 November 2014). While it is hard to argue that the specific details of consumer financial protections—as with most forms of regulation—require expertise, another consumer advocate disagreed with the idea that the issue could not be presented in relatively simple terms for the broader public:

> This was something that everyone used to get very hung up on. Like, "this is a very complicated legal issue, how do we communicate this to the public?" I think they really overstated that, because there are ways that it's really very tangible. And everybody has a credit card, right? (1120142 November 2014)

If the characteristics of the issue under consideration are not sufficient to explain borrower inaction within the regulatory sphere, perhaps we can turn to accounts that revolve around participants themselves. Mancur Olson (1965) provides an elegant articulation of the problems public interest groups encounter when trying to mobilize diffuse populations with incentives to free ride. So perhaps we shouldn't be surprised that citizens fail to engage in rulemaking. The problem, of course, is that we have already noted that borrowers are willing to take market action either on their own or at the behest of interest group appeals; it is political action specifically that borrowers are reluctant to pursue.

Maybe there is something about borrowers' beliefs about rulemaking that inhibits their willingness to take part in this crucial realm of policymaking. Focusing specifically on the regulatory context, scholars posit that participation should be predicated on feelings of political efficacy. If interest groups and citizens do not expect their participation to be meaningful, they should be less likely to engage. Initial efforts to capture people's sentiment about the value of such participation found that public interest groups do perceive that several methods of participation in regulatory policies, including informal agency contact and written comment submission, produce influence (Furlong 1997; Kerwin and Furlong 2005). Given the frequency with which these groups—like AFFIL and AFR—are active in regulatory lobbying, this is unsurprising. What might be more remarkable is Susan Webb Yackee's finding (2014) that citizens feel similarly positive about the efficacy of their participation in rulemaking. Once again, these studies offer hope that it should be possible to generate public interest participation on behalf of consumer financial protection, particularly among borrowers. But we still don't have a clear explanation for the absence of borrowers from the rulemaking process for such a key economic policy issue.

### The Efficacy of Public Interest Participation

Predicting whether public interest groups and citizens will participate in consumer financial rulemaking is only one half of the puzzle. We also need to understand when their participation will be effective. One of the earliest accounts of the efficacy of public interest participation in regulatory politics argues that industry groups hold an advantage when it comes to policy influence. Public choice theorists, for example, argue that regulation is likely to benefit the regulated industry through a process of capture (Huntington 1952; Bernstein 1955; Stigler 1971; Peltzman 1976). But this belief is not pervasive. Proponents of pluralist and associational approaches to bureaucratic politics have countered that a much wider range of interests can influence regulatory policy outcomes (Moe 1987; Lieberman 2009). Scholars have identified several policy areas for which public interest groups have achieved success lobbying on behalf of consumers (e.g., Gormley 1983; Berry 1984). New work by scholars of public administration finds increasing support for the idea that public interest groups and citizens who participate in meaningful and unified ways during the public comment period can influence regulatory policy outcomes (Cuellar 2005; Yackee 2006; McKay and Yackee 2007; Layzer 2012). The problem, these scholars note, is the frequency with which that impactful participation takes place when compared to industry lobbying.

While each of these approaches to regulatory politics offers useful insights into the patterns and results of public interest participation in support of protective regulation, none provides an adequate explanation for the case of consumer financial protection. Industry giants would surely point to recent credit card regulations and the creation of the CFPB as credible evidence that they have not captured regulators on consumer credit protections. On the other hand, public interest groups can identify a string of issues for which regulators have either failed to act at all, or enacted protections that allow lenders to subvert them with ease, as evidence that their opinions are rarely given equal weight. Despite losing battles, public interest groups continue to devote considerable resources to regulatory lobbying, while borrowers have historically avoided participating in rulemaking despite their acknowledgment (backed by research) that they might be able to influence regulators.

Rather than focusing on the attributes of the issue area or potential participants, I offer an institutional explanation[2] for the propensity of public interest actors to engage in regulatory politics, and the prospects for their success. I argue that the administrative arrangement of regulatory rulemaking and enforcement authority for an issue produces regulatory feedback effects that shape the political behavior of bureaucrats, public interest groups, and citizens.

### *Regulatory Feedback Effects and Consumer Financial Protection Rulemaking*

I propose that policies central to the political economy of credit have created obstacles for engagement in the rulemaking process for both public interest groups and citizens. While the previous three chapters focused primarily on regulatory feedback effects generated by the design and implementation of federal consumer financial protections, this chapter argues that the administration of those policies also shapes credit politics in meaningful ways. I contend that the logic of a political economy of credit, which privileges national economic stability over the protection of individual consumers, influenced policymakers' decisions to assign regulatory oversight for consumer financial regulations in important ways.

By the time the first significant regulation of consumer credit, the Truth in Lending Act (TILA), was signed into law in 1968, a number of regulatory agencies already existed to oversee different types of financial institutions. After consulting with leaders from those agencies, who expressed reservations about their ability to effectively carry out these new borrower protections, policymakers still chose to assign authority for the new credit law (and the ones that followed) to whichever of the seven preexisting agencies was responsible for overseeing the financial institution that provided the regulated type of credit. As the main goal was to support national economic stability—a familiar mission for the existing regulatory agencies, I argue that Congress felt little need to centralize these regulations under a new agency designed with consumer protection in mind.

Unfortunately for consumers, the existing regulatory infrastructure was primarily created to ensure the profit and stability of financial institutions[3]—a "safety and soundness" mission—and not the protection of consumers. Thus, regulators often lacked the expertise and resources to

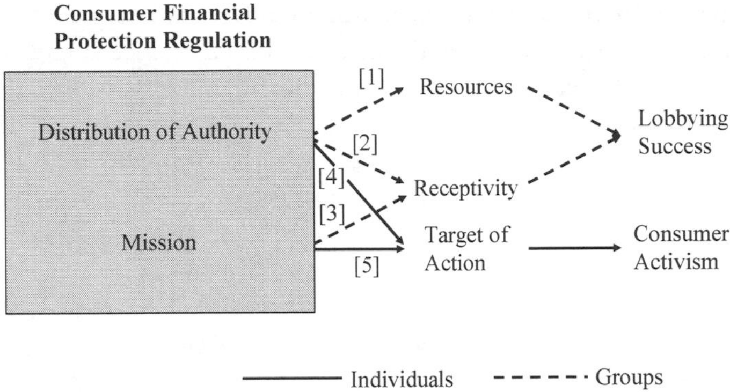


FIGURE 6.2 Consumer Financial Protection Administration Regulatory Feedback Effects

manage new borrower protection mandates. The result is that consumer financial protections were administered through a fragmented regulatory arrangement in which safeguarding borrowers took a back seat to protecting financial industry profits.

I argue that fragmenting regulatory authority for financial protections across agencies designed to defend lenders instead of borrowers produced regulatory feedback effects that shape the efficacy of public interest lobbying and the political participation of ordinary Americans. For public interest groups, this administrative arrangement makes it difficult to engage regulators on issues of consumer financial protection, while simultaneously increasing the lobbying power of industry. When regulators do turn their attention to protecting borrowers, advocates' lobbying attempts are frequently constrained by regulatory arbitrage—a so-called race to the bottom—produced by fragmented rulemaking and enforcement authority. For consumers, the inability to identify a central government agency responsible for consumer credit protection makes it hard to follow and participate in the regulatory process. Figure 6.2 illustrates the specific pathways (identified in chapter 1) along which the administrative arrangement has produced regulatory feedback effects, thereby shaping the regulatory lobbying capacity of public interest groups and the participation of consumers.

### The Efficacy of Public Interest Lobbying

As depicted, the administrative arrangement for a policy—in this case consumer financial protection—has the ability to shape the lobbying success of public interest groups relative to industry through three primary pathways. First, the degree to which rulemaking and enforcement authority for a policy is centralized in a single agency may affect both the application of interest group resources and regulators' receptivity to advocates' policy proposals. With respect to resources [1], fragmented, or decentralized, regulatory authority increases the potential cost of lobbying because it must take place across multiple venues at once. Rather than investing resources into developing relationships with regulators in a single agency, interest groups must establish and maintain connections across as many agencies as have responsibility for either making or enforcing rules for a given policy. When a new issue comes to the fore, the degree of regulatory fragmentation determines how many agencies must be lobbied simultaneously. The costs associated with lobbying in a fragmented versus a centralized regulatory environment may thus be harder to bear for public interest groups, even those that are relatively well endowed, than for highly resourced industries, ultimately limiting public interest influence.

Regulatory fragmentation may also shape the likelihood that regulators will be receptive to pro-borrower reforms [2]. The balkanization of regulatory power can incite what legal scholars refer to as "regulatory arbitrage," whereby regulated institutions—in this case financial entities—are able to play different agencies against one another in pursuit of the lowest level of regulation (see Levitin 2013; Carpenter 2014). In a fragmented system, arbitrage can take place for two related reasons. First, if multiple agencies are responsible for administering or enforcing the same rule to their respective clients, the agencies likely need to coalesce on the appropriate rule or enforcement strategy. This often leads to the lowest common denominator being adopted.

The incentive to engage in a so-called race to the bottom is further exacerbated in the case of consumer financial protection because of a loophole in the regulatory structure. Financial institutions have some flexibility to reclassify themselves (e.g., from a bank charter to a thrift charter) in order to come under the jurisdiction of their preferred regulator (Carpenter 2014). As a result of the competition generated by regulatory fragmentation, agencies have incentives to protect their turf by adopting more favorable polices (Kirsch and Mayer 2013). For public interest groups, this means that arbitrage may limit how receptive bureaucrats are to requests for more stringent consumer protection standards, instead favoring industry preferences.

The primary mission of the administrative agency tasked with implementing a protective regulation may also shape the degree to which bureaucrats are receptive to advocacy demands [3]. Some agencies are designed to engage in competitive, or safety and soundness, regulation, meaning they are tasked with ensuring the stability and profitability of a particular industry or market. Other agencies are designed primarily to protect consumers, making them responsible for the interests of individuals, even when those interests conflict with industry profitability. While the two tasks are not inherently at odds with one another, they can come into conflict (Schooner 2006). If one task is given to an agency designed to prioritize the other goal, when a conflict does arise the agency will likely decide in favor of carrying out their primary mission. So, for example, if an agency focused on competitive regulation is given authority over protective rulemaking, bureaucrats may have incentives to defer to the profitability of the financial institutions over the safety of consumers when deciding on the stringency of a particular rule. From the perspective of a public interest group, this phenomenon may once again limit how receptive bureaucrats are to the consumer-oriented concerns of advocates.

### The Propensity for Borrower Participation

Public interest groups are not the only actors whose politics might be shaped by the administrative environment for a particular policy. Ordinary citizens are affected as well. I contend that both the fragmentation of regulatory authority and the mission of the agencies responsible for administering a policy may also influence citizen participation in the rulemaking process. First, as figure 6.2 illustrates, the degree of regulatory fragmentation in the administration of a policy may further illuminate or obfuscate government's role in that issue [4]. If a single administrative agency is granted oversight for a policy area, people may come to associate that agency with its respective policy jurisdiction. By contrast, when the regulatory oversight for a particular policy area is dispersed across multiple agencies, it may be far more complicated for citizens to identify the appropriate government body responsible for addressing their particular concern. This has the potential to shape public participation because, as scholars have demonstrated, the ability to identify a clear target for action is a necessary condition of political engagement (Arnold 1990). Even if citizens choose to turn to government to voice their complaints, a fragmented system can make it far more difficult for consumers to navigate the decentralized complaint or comment process.

An agency's mission may also influence citizen political engagement in regulatory politics [5]. Agencies dedicated primarily to consumer protection may be more inclined to actively seek consumer feedback on an issue than an agency whose primary focus is competitive regulation. Studies have long demonstrated the effect of active mobilization on political engagement (see Rosenstone and Hansen 1993). Aggressively reaching out to consumers to contribute their stories and voice their policy preferences—for example, by promoting notice and comment periods through social media or hosting frequent field hearings—may generate more consumer participation in the rulemaking process.

I argue that, taken together, these feedback effects shape the politics of consumer financial protection—and indeed any protective regulatory issue—within the federal bureaucracy. This occurs by simultaneously raising or lowering both the costs of participation and the likely return on investment from that participation for both public interest groups and citizens. One key takeaway from this theory of regulatory feedback effects is that decisions about whom to assign authority to for the implementation of a particular policy, or set of policies, can shape the likelihood that regulatory capture will occur. Put simply, how much power industry lobbyists have relative to public interest groups likely stems from the institutional arrangement policymakers create when they first establish regulatory oversight for new policies. So what specific arrangement emerged for the administration of consumer financial protection in the United States?

### *Administering Consumer Financial Protection in a Political Economy of Credit*

The United States is distinctive in the degree to which it relies on regulatory agencies as active sites of policymaking (Hilton 2007). Regulatory agencies began to emerge at both the state and federal levels during the Progressive Era, increasingly replacing the courts as the primary arbiters for issues from industrial competition to health and safety (Glaeser and Shleifer 2001). The proliferation of regulatory agencies accelerated even more following the Great Depression as policymakers looked to experts to help remake the American economy (Prasad 2012). Agencies dedicated to overseeing the country's financial institutions represent some of the oldest and most significant regulatory commissions in the United States.[4]

The Office of the Comptroller of the Currency, created in 1863 as part of the Treasury Department, was one of the earliest regulatory commissions established to govern financial institutions. It is responsible for supervising federally chartered banks. The Federal Reserve System, consisting of twelve regional banks and a Board of Governors, was established by the Federal Reserve Act in 1913 (P.L. 63–43) during the Progressive Era. The Fed oversees several types of financial institutions, including U.S. branches of foreign banks and state-chartered banks that are members of the reserve system. New Deal policies ushered in the next wave of financial regulators. To better support mortgage financing, the Federal Home Loan Bank Board originated in 1932 to oversee building and loan institutions (P.L. 72–304). It was replaced with two separate regulatory agencies in 1989 in the wake of the savings and loan crisis: the Office of Thrift Supervision,[5] which was designed to supervise a variety of federally chartered savings associations, and the Federal Housing Finance Board, which maintained oversight for the Federal Home Loan Bank system (P.L. 101–73). The Federal Deposit Insurance Corporation (FDIC) was another New Deal creation designed to stabilize the banking industry. Established as part of the Banking Act of 1933 (P.L. 73–66), the FDIC insures bank deposits and manages the assets of failed banks. Finally, the National Credit Union Administration, which was initially part of the Farm Credit Administration, became an independent agency in 1970 with responsibility for both state and federal credit unions (P.L. 91–206).[6]

While each of these regulatory agencies was established with the explicit competitive mission of promoting the safety and soundness of financial institutions and markets, the list of commissions created to protect consumer finances is much shorter.[7] In fact, until the birth of the Consumer Financial Protection Bureau (CFPB) in 2010, it was a list of one—the Federal Trade Commission (FTC); and even that agency had a much broader mission than simply protecting consumers' credit transactions. The FTC was created in 1914 (P.L. 63–203) with the dual mission of protecting consumers and promoting competition. It was established with enthusiastic support from progressive reformers and President Woodrow Wilson, who saw the FTC as a critical tool for trust busting (Hovenkamp 1999). Governed by a five-person board[8] with broad authority to identify and regulate unfair and deceptive practices, the FTC comprises both a Bureau of Consumer Protection and a Bureau of Competition. As part of its activities, the FTC collects consumer complaints on a wide swath of products and practices, of which consumer financing represents a small part. Notably, the FTC does not publicly release its raw data on consumer complaints.

While the FTC was the first, and for a long time the only, agency officially empowered to protect consumers from unfair and deceptive financial practices, other forms of consumer representation in the federal government grew after President Roosevelt's administration turned its attention toward promoting consumption in the wake of the Great Depression. Most major New Deal policies—for example, the short-lived National Industrial Recovery Act—included provisions for consumer representation. Unfortunately for the average American, this token representation rarely amounted to real power over policy outcomes (Cohen 2003).

The presence of these largely symbolic consumer advisory boards across several federal agencies eventually produced a perverse consequence for those who sought genuine consumer protection in the regulatory arena. It allowed opponents to assert that the creation of new bodies empowered to protect consumer interests beyond the capacity of the FTC was unnecessary. As Esther Peterson, President Johnson's special assistant for consumer affairs, lamented in her remarks to the 1967 Consumer Assembly:

> To listen to some, the government already does far too much for the consumer. These critics are fond of citing a 1961 House Committee Report that listed 33 Federal agencies as working in the consumer interest with a total appropriation of nearly $1 billion. These critics fail to realize that the consumer interest is often incidental to the producer interest which is the principal concern of many of these agencies. (Peterson 1967)

This attitude eventually doomed the battle to create a cabinet-level consumer protection agency during the 1970s—a failure often pointed to as the watershed moment in the development of a powerful business lobby in Washington (Pertschuk 1982). But for advocates of consumer financial regulation in the 1960s and beyond, the lack of support for broader consumer protection combined with the treatment of consumer interests as ancillary to maintaining a stable political economy of credit had more immediate consequences.

When TILA was enacted in 1968, oversight for the first-of-their-kind regulations had to be assigned to an agency. The FTC was the only existing commission dedicated, at least in part, to consumer protection. But in a further sign that policymakers viewed the consumer protection aspect of TILA as only a byproduct of the more important goal of maintaining stable financial markets, the FTC did not receive primary oversight for the new law. Nor was a new regulatory commission created to administer what was sure to be a growing body of policy. In a nod to policymakers' true motivations, rulemaking and enforcement authority for the new disclosure provisions were proposed to go to the Federal Reserve—an agency designed solely to oversee bank stability and profits. The emphasis on prioritizing financial markets was clear.

In hearings for the bill, James L. Robertson, vice chairman of the

Fed, expressed his concern with the proposed administrative arrangement, despite the agency's overall support for the Act. Robertson explained that the Fed was not well suited to promulgating rules for the new law, though he acquiesced that they would be willing to take up the job for what he hoped would be a short period:

> The Board's familiarity with the trade practices that would be subject to regulation under this legislation is very limited indeed. . . . Administration of a law such as [this] is a function essentially different from the functions that Congress heretofore has considered appropriate for the Federal Reserve System. Formulating regulations under this bill would involve the Board in time-consuming consideration of trade practices about which we have very little knowledge. . . . If the Congress decides to designate the Board as the agency to prescribe regulations to implement this bill, we will do our best to carry out the assignment, but we hope that in time . . . administration of Federal disclosure requirements will be reassigned to an agency better suited to perform the function. (U.S. Senate 1967: 666–667)

Perhaps recognizing that Congress was unwilling to house the rulemaking responsibility for the bill elsewhere, Robertson eventually acquiesced that his agency would be willing to take this on. His softening stance is captured in an exchange with Senator Proxmire:

> PROXMIRE: Am I correct in assuming that the Board is reluctantly willing to assume the administration of the bill?
>
> ROBERTSON: We think that the legislation is so important that, if you don't have a better agency to do it, we will undertake to prescribe regulations to implement the law. (U.S. Senate 1967: 669)

But Robertson was explicit in his objection to assigning enforcement authority for the new provisions to the Fed:

> The task of implementing this proposed law will be complicated not only by our lack of knowledge in this field, but also by the fact that the Board has no trained investigative staff. . . . Consequently, we would hope that our only function under this legislation would be to prescribe regulations. . . . We also hope that Congress will express its desire that all Federal agencies

> endeavor to secure compliance with the law by lenders and sellers subject to their jurisdiction. (U.S. Senate 1967: 667)

Robertson went on to suggest that, in addition to assigning enforcement responsibility to the agencies who held oversight for different financial institutions, the bill should task the Justice Department with carrying out any legal actions against financial institutions who violated the provisions. The bill eventually adopted Robertson's imperfect solution. The authority to propose rules to implement the new law was given to the Fed, despite their professed lack of expertise in the area.[9] The authority to enforce compliance with the law was fragmented amongst existing agencies responsible for overseeing different types of financial institutions, with power to pursue legal action placed with the Attorney General. But these other financial regulators were similarly ill suited to the task. Like the Fed, their primary missions were to protect financial institutions and not borrowers. They had neither the expertise nor the incentive to put consumer protection at the fore of their activities. The House didn't seem to care, noting that this arrangement was ideal because it "takes care not to disturb the existing lines of responsibility presently drawn within the Federal Establishment" (U.S. House 1967: 18). In essence, the complex system was adopted without regard to how consumers themselves might navigate it.

### *The Challenging Administrative Environment*

Agencies' concerns over their ability to carry out these new consumer financial protections did not prevent Congress from relying on the same administrative strategy in subsequent legislative efforts. The consumer credit policy dataset systematically captures the administrative arrangement for the evolving constellation of protective credit regulations in the United States. First, I gauge the degree of regulatory fragmentation for consumer financial protections by exploring the assignation of rulemaking and enforcement authority for each. I operationalize this relationship with dummy variables that code whether rulemaking and enforcement authority respectively for a particular policy are assigned to a single agency (yes equals one). They are detailed in table 6.1. I then look to the stated missions of each regulator to determine whether the agency responsible for rulemaking and enforcement for a particular policy has a primary mission for consumer protection. This is also coded as a dummy variable for each, where the presence of a consumer protection mission equals one. In combination, these measures provide

**Table 6.1 Consumer Financial Protection Policy Administrative Attributes, 1934–2010**

| Year | Policy | Rulemaking Authority | Enforcement Authority |
|---|---|---|---|
| 1934 | National Housing Act (Title I) | FHA | FHA |
| 1968 | Consumer Credit Protection Act | FRB | Multiple Agencies |
| 1968 | Truth in Lending Act | FRB | Multiple Agencies |
| 1970 | Fair Credit Reporting Act | Multiple Agencies | FTC |
| 1970 | Provisions Relating to Credit Cards (Title V) | FTC | FTC |
| 1974 | Equal Credit Opportunity Act | FRB | Multiple Agencies |
| 1974 | Fair Credit Billing Act | FRB | Multiple Agencies |
| 1976 | Truth in Leasing Act | FRB | Multiple Agencies |
| 1977 | Fair Debt Collection Practices Act | FTC | FTC |
| 1978 | Electronic Funds Transfers | FRB | Multiple Agencies |
| 1980 | Truth in Lending Simplification and Reform Act | FRB | Multiple Agencies |
| 1988 | Fair Credit and Charge Cards Disclosure Act | FRB | Multiple Agencies |
| 1988 | Home Equity Loan Consumer Protection Act | FRB | Multiple Agencies |
| 1991 | Truth in Savings Act | FRB | Multiple Agencies |
| 1996 | Omnibus Consolidated Appropriations Act | FRB | Multiple Agencies |
| 1996 | Consumer Credit Reporting Reform Act | Multiple Agencies | FTC |
| 1996 | Credit Repair Organizations Act | FTC | FTC |
| 2003 | Fair and Accurate Credit Transactions Act | FTC/FRB | FTC |
| 2006 | Military Lending Act | DOD | Multiple Agencies |
| 2009 | Credit Card Accountability Responsibility and Disclosure Act | FRB | Multiple Agencies |
| 2010 | Consumer Financial Protection Act of 2010 | CFPB | Multiple Agencies |
| 2010 | Improving Access to Mainstream Financial Institutions Act | DOT | n/a |

CFPB - Consumer Financial Protection Bureau, DOD - Department of Defense, DOT - Department of Treasury, FHA - Federal Housing Administration, FRB - Federal Reserve Board, FTC - Federal Trade Commission

a comprehensive picture of the regulatory environment for consumer financial protections.

### Fragmenting Regulatory Authority

Rulemaking and enforcement authority are, indeed, fragmented to a significant degree. As table 6.1 illustrates, only four policies assign both rulemaking and enforcement authority to the same agency: Title I of

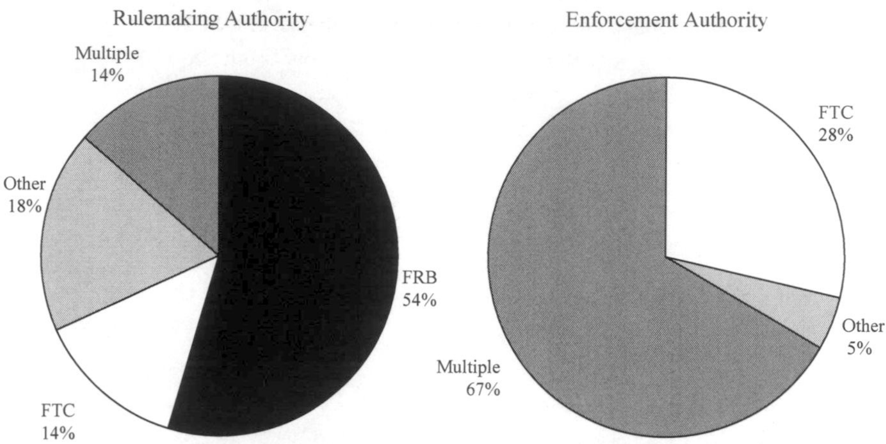


**FIGURE 6.3** Administrative Authority for Consumer Financial Protections, 1934–2010

the National Housing Act, Title V of the Fair Credit Reporting Act, The Fair Debt Collection Practices Act, and the Credit Repair Organizations Act. By contrast, sixteen policies divide rulemaking and enforcement authority across more than two agencies. Not only is the administration of consumer financial protection fragmented within individual policies, it is also fragmented across policies.

As figure 6.3 shows, the ability to promulgate rules for consumer financial protection is distributed across multiple agencies, although a small majority of laws (54 percent) designate the task of drafting new rules primarily to the Fed—the same agency that tried to escape the job when it was first assigned in 1968. Enforcement authority is even more fragmented. More than two out of every three policies divide enforcement authority among multiple regulatory agencies. In most of these cases, up to seven agencies are implicated in managing compliance for the specified rule—each responsible for enforcing regulations for credit originated by the financial institution they oversee. The FTC is given enforcement authority for just under a third of all policies. But even the FTC—the one agency whose mission is partly dedicated to consumer protection—was unsure how to carry out their task in the beginning. In a letter to Kansas State Professor of Family Economics William Fasse, Sheldon Feldman, the assistant director for consumer credit and special programs in the FTC's Bureau of Consumer Protection, wrote to request assistance:

> The Division of Consumer Credit and Special Programs . . . [is] responsible for enforcing the Truth In Lending, Fair Credit Re-

> porting and Fair Packaging and Labeling Acts. . . . My personal view is that we need much more input from those who are in a position to identify the most pressing areas of unchartered regulatory effort. (Feldman 1969)

Widespread regulatory fragmentation—both across and within policies—presented a number of problems for bureaucrats. During June 2007 hearings held before the House Financial Services Committee to discuss the state of the economy, Sheila Bair, the Republican-appointed chairperson of the FDIC, explained to lawmakers, "The greatest weakness in today's financial marketplace is the absence of clear consumer protection standards applied uniformly to all participants in the market" (U.S. House 2007: 16). She specifically referenced the problems created by dividing rulemaking and enforcement authority across different agencies with respect to unfair or deceptive acts or practices (UDAP) regulations:

> Well, we [the FDIC] enforce UDAP, but we don't have the ability to write rules. And so because there are no rules, we are finding out we have to use case-by-case determinations and consult a great deal with the Fed and the FTC about what is unfair or deceptive because we don't have the ability to define these terms. (U.S. House 2007: 27)

Beyond the ability to enact rules, regulatory fragmentation threw up another obstacle as well: it made the consumer complaint process incredibly complex. A presumably unintended consequence of regulatory fragmentation was the lack of a unified complaint system for consumers to turn to when they sought redress. Complaint-handling institutions in the realm of consumer finance have been found by consumers to be either inadequate or obscured (Best 1981). Representative Dennis Moore (D-KS) noted this problem during congressional hearings in 2007, reporting, "I looked at some of the websites, and it is very, very confusing and takes several clicks sometimes to get to a complaint form or a toll-free number" (U.S. House 2007: 25). Agency representatives acknowledged his assessment, responding that it was a difficult challenge to overcome in the existing regulatory environment.

### Protecting Consumers or Protecting Banks

The balkanization of rulemaking and enforcement authority for consumer credit policies is only half of the story. As figure 6.4 shows, very

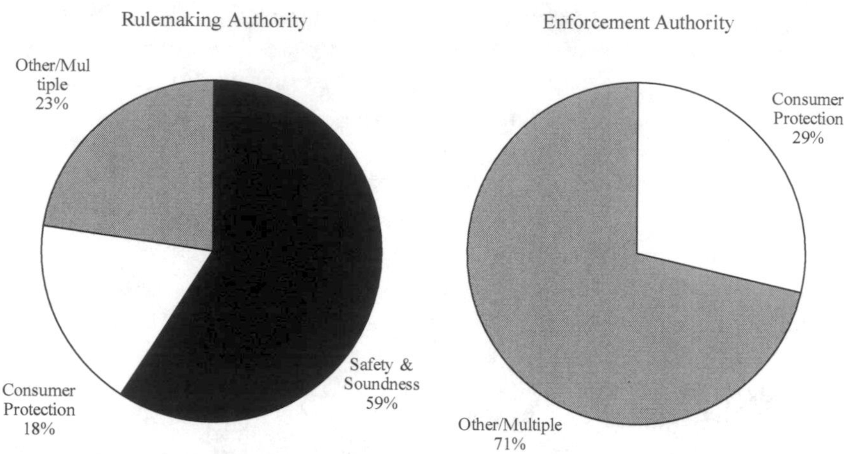


**FIGURE 6.4** Agency Mission for Consumer Financial Regulators, 1934–2010

few consumer credit policies are administered by agencies created with the primary mission of protecting consumers. Fewer than one in five policies assign rulemaking authority to an agency with a primary mission of consumer protection, and only 29 percent authorize enforcement by an agency dedicated to consumer protection. By contrast, 59 percent of consumer financial protection laws are implemented by agencies designed to promote the safety and soundness of banks with an eye toward maintaining economic stability.

For example, the Federal Reserve Board reports a major part of its mission as "maintaining the stability of the financial system and containing systemic risk that may arise in financial markets." And as Representative Frank wryly noted upon reviewing subprime mortgage rules proposed by the Fed at the outset of the 2008 crisis, "We now have confirmation of two facts we have known for some time: one, the Federal Reserve System is not a strong advocate for consumers, and two, there is no Santa Claus. People who are surprised by the one are presumably surprised by the other" (*Wall Street Journal* 2007).

Legal scholar Adam Levitin explains that the regulatory arrangement for consumer finance "made consumer protection an orphan mission that tended to 'fall between the cracks' because no agency had an exclusive role of consumer protection in financial services" (2013: 40). FDIC Chairperson Bair provides further evidence of this problem. When asked about her opinion on a number of potentially predatory lending products during congressional hearings in 2007, Bair responded, "I think those practices are highly troubling, but even assuming we thought they were unfair or deceptive, we would not have the ability to write a rule making that determination, whereas we can write rules on safety and soundness" (U.S. House 2007: 28).

Fragmenting regulatory authority for credit policies across agencies whose primary missions are promoting the safety and soundness of banks contributed to another phenomenon that decreased the protection of consumers: regulatory arbitrage. As explained earlier, because lenders have some flexibility to change their charters to come under the authority of the friendliest regulator, agencies have incentives to protect their turf by weakening regulation. Even those bureaucrats who are inclined toward greater consumer protection are constrained by this competition. The following exchange between Chairperson Bair and Representative Frank illustrates the problem of regulatory arbitrage in stark terms:

> BAIR: Since we only have 15 percent of the credit card market, even if we could find authority under safety and soundness to write a rule, we would be imposing that rule only on FDIC-supervised credit card issuers . . .
>
> FRANK: And you would pretty soon have 1.5 percent of the market and not 15 percent if you had a rule and [the other agencies] did not. (U.S. House 2007: 28)

Comptroller John Dugan, from the Office of the Comptroller of the Currency, echoed this line of thinking:

> I would just add that I agree with that. For many years it was not clear that banking agencies could even take enforcement action. . . . We do think it would be helpful to have rule-writing authority. . . . Our concern is that if one agency adopts a rule, people could use other charters to do the same activity. (U.S. House 2007: 27–28)

The result of this scheme for administering consumer financial protections is that agencies whose primary focus is on bank profitability passed relatively weak consumer protection rules that were then enforced by other agencies with incentives not to unduly anger their constituent banks. Instead of strong rules with active enforcement, consumer protection issues, when dealt with at all, were addressed "informally and confidentially" during other investigatory processes (Carpenter 2014).

It ultimately took fifty years after the enactment of TILA and a massive financial crisis before Vice Chairman Robertson's plea to relocate authority for consumer financial protection rulemaking to an agency designed specifically for that purpose was realized. The Financial Crisis Inquiry Report concluded that "widespread failures in financial regulation and supervision proved devastating to the stability of the nation's financial markets," and they singled out the Fed as the worst offender (FCIC 2011: xviii). In a 2010 *Wall Street Journal* editorial analyzing the crisis, Elizabeth Warren accused federal regulators of "play[ing] the role of lookout at a bank robbery." Even with this analysis, support for the creation of a new agency vested with protecting consumers' finances was reliant in part on the ability of supporters to explicitly tie consumer protection to national economic stability. For example, Senator Richard Shelby (R-AL), an avowed opponent of the CFPB, underlined conventional wisdom about their separation to the *New York Times* in 2010, commenting "I fully support enhancing both consumer protection and safety and soundness regulation [but] I will not support a bill that enhances one at the expense of the other" (Chan 2010).

In hindsight, of course, it seems obvious that the proliferation of risky loan products and the subsequent inability of consumers to repay their debts would have tremendous consequences for the continued profitability of lenders and the wider stability of the financial system. But prior to the recession, regulators were more concerned with the relationship between profitability and stability (Carpenter 2014)—and as noted in chapter 5, predatory loans, while risky, were certainly profitable for many institutions. Regulators like Sheila Bair eventually made the connection between the two missions explicit, noting, "Activities that are harmful to consumers also can raise safety and soundness concerns" (Bair 2007). After a difficult legislative fight, detailed in chapter 2, the CFPB was ultimately created in 2010 in an attempt to combine much of the rulemaking and enforcement authority for credit regulations under a single agency dedicated to protecting consumers.

Creating a new, independent watchdog to centralize consumer financial protection oversight was a major political challenge. Financial institutions, who had long taken advantage of regulatory arbitrage, predictably weren't excited about the proposed agency. Nor, it turned out, were some of the federal regulators who had come to benefit from their relationships with finance—most notably, and ironically given their initial reticence to take on consumer financial protections—the Fed (Kirsch and Mayer 2013; Jacobs and King 2016). The prospective agency's supporters and opponents clashed along several fronts related to the CFPB's design and authority. Would the agency be independent or would it fall under the direct supervision of an existing regulator? Who would lead it? Exactly what would the CFPB have oversight for? Most existing types of financial institutions were already regulated by other federal agencies. Would they now come under the purview of the CFPB? What about lenders like auto dealers and payday and title loan stores that were typically subject to state, not federal, regulation?

The end result was a compromise across these different issues. In order to stave off defeat of the agency, and possibly the entire 2010 financial reform package, Senator Christopher Dodd acquiesced to a compromise in which the CFPB would be housed within the Fed, albeit with a largely independent budget and policymaking power. While consumer advocates and many Democratic lawmakers detested the decision, noting how unwise it was to effectively give more power for protecting consumers to the one agency most responsible for failing to prevent the financial crisis, Dodd successfully argued that this strategy was necessary to secure support from moderate Senate Democrats and Republicans on the banking committee. Michael Barr, the Treasury Department assistant secretary for financial institutions and an architect of the original CFPB proposal, later argued that, "as long as there would be an independent budget, and independent director, independent policy making, and independent enforcement, you could put the agency on the moon and it wouldn't really matter" (Kirsch and Mayer 2013: 90).[10]

The CFPB would be managed by a director appointed to a five-year term, rather than a board, who would run the agency largely independent of Fed supervision. This decision, which divided members of the consumer advocacy community, has become the subject of controversy in the ensuing years, creating a feast or famine scenario for the agency's supporters and opponents. Because a single director has relative autonomy, pro-consumer directors theoretically are able to lead a more activist, pro-regulatory body, while anti-consumer directors will have the ability to effectively cripple the agency (SoRelle 2018). In return for this measure of autonomy for the CFPB, precarious though it might be, and much to the chagrin of many consumer advocates, Representative Barney Frank agreed to compromise during the committee markup on the issue of oversight. Auto dealers were exempt from CFPB jurisdiction, while most existing federal consumer financial protections were handed over to the new agency, though the CFPB would continue to share some administrative and enforcement authority with other financial regulators.

The creation of the CFPB did not completely eliminate the problem of regulatory arbitrage—indeed, many of the original financial regulators are still active in rulemaking and enforcement. Dodd-Frank did, however, require the centralization of regulatory authority in the CFPB for the most significant consumer financial protections. In practical terms, this meant that the rulemaking and enforcement power for consumer financial protections that had been granted to the Federal Reserve, the Office of the Comptroller of the Currency, the Office of Thrift Supervision, the Federal Deposit Insurance Corporation, the National Credit Union Administration, and select programs overseen by the Department of Housing and Urban Development were redirected to the CFPB beginning in 2011. Thus, the CFPB is a potentially powerful new player in the regulatory arena, one whose mission is entirely dedicated to protecting Americans' finances.

### *How Administrative Arrangements Shape Public Interest Lobbying*

Compounding the policymaking incentive it creates for bureaucrats, I propose that the nature of the administrative environment for consumer financial protection policies can limit the ability of public interest groups to lobby regulators for more stringent protections. Specifically, I argue that the fragmentation of rulemaking and enforcement authority places resource constraints on consumer advocates, restricting their lobbying capacity. Furthermore, regulatory arbitrage—the result of fragmenting authority across agencies tasked with safety and soundness missions—limits bureaucrats' receptivity to consumer advocates' proposed reforms. Policymakers themselves have alluded to several of these issues, but how do public interest groups perceive the dynamics of regulatory politics for consumer financial protection?

I rely on interviews with consumer advocates from four of the most active consumer credit lobbying groups to explore these two phenomena.[11] Advocates spoke about their experiences with the rulemaking process both before and after the creation of the CFPB in 2010. Because the CFPB altered the administrative environment for consumer financial protection, centralizing much of the rulemaking and enforcement power in an agency dedicated to safeguarding borrowers, I can begin to untangle how the specific features of the regulatory structure shape public interest lobbying on credit issues before and after the change.

#### Resources for Lobbying

Did the fragmentation of rulemaking and enforcement authority—which required building and maintaining relationships across multiple fronts—inhibit public interest lobbying in support of consumer financial protection by raising its costs? The evidence from advocates is mixed. As one acknowledged, "For the most part, these groups had limited resources, so it's not like they're going to three or four agencies" (0312151 March 2015). A senior staff member from a different organization agreed with this assessment, explaining, "The biggest limit for us is resources and how much we can do" (1119141 November 2014). But that person ultimately noted, "Open doors are not really a problem for us." Another advocate heavily involved in regulatory lobbying suggested that resources were not a severe problem because, for many credit issues, they could concentrate their efforts at the Fed during the rulemaking stage (0313151 March 2015). While fragmentation may not have seriously constrained consumer interest groups' abilities to get access to the people they needed to, every single advocate I spoke with agreed about one thing—access was only half the battle.

**Receptivity to Proposals**

The real struggle came with getting regulators to take their proposals seriously. As one advocate summed up, "What matters is their willingness to do something about the issues that you're calling attention to" (0312151 March 2015). Another advocate agreed, explaining what public interest groups faced once they got in the door:

> Once it's out there, it really just depends on who the partner is in the policymaking position. . . . Sometimes it falls on receptive ears and it's up to us to push it, or push it further. But sometimes we need to knock on doors and make sure people are hearing it. . . . Whether the issues are something people want to take on, that's a whole other question. (1119141 November 2014)

Advocates also agreed that prior to the CFPB, receptivity was a serious obstacle to effective lobbying. And they attributed the problem explicitly to the interaction of two structural factors of the administrative environment: fragmentation and the investiture of rulemaking authority in agencies without a consumer protection mission. One advocate explained how the lack of focus on consumer protection affected agency behavior from the outset, inhibiting the identification of products and services that needed to be addressed through rulemaking:

> [The structure] meant that it was often hard to identify problems because there was nobody whose job it was, whose primary function it was, it was on them, to look at business practices in consumer welfare. It was a secondary issue behind safety

> and soundness for virtually all of the banking lenders. (0312151 March 2015)

Even after a problem had been identified, the agencies' safety and soundness missions limited their ability to enact necessary consumer protections. As another advocate explained:

> For the most part, what the other agencies had was a secondary focus on the issues we're concerned with. Their primary focus was not consumer protection, and their primary focus was the health of the industry that they're regulating, and that often can be articulated in a way that there are contrary interests. If you eliminate this bad product, of course it has an effect on financial welfare of the industry. That's a structural difference that's really important. (1119141 November 2014)

Representatives of consumer interest groups agreed that the problem of mission mismatch combined with regulatory fragmentation to produce arbitrage, which made it incredibly challenging to get regulators to support proposals for more stringent reform. One advocate described how arbitrage shaped the process of lobbying for stronger consumer financial protections:

> The structure here, in main part, tended to make it harder for the agencies to mobilize on that problem even when they wanted to address it. . . . It took years for all the regulatory agencies [to] align behind an approach, and then the least common denominator situation meant that when they did mobilize behind it, it was pretty weak. (0312151 March 2015)

Another expanded on the problem of arbitrage:

> The agencies would compete for members, whether you're a bank, you're a state bank or a federal bank. You can switch, so it was very difficult to get uniform. First, they weren't inclined to be aggressive, and second, they couldn't be consistent. And even if they wanted to act together, it's like getting five agencies together—that's very difficult to do. (1119141 November 2014)

The experiences of consumer advocates mimic some of the problems identified by regulators themselves. They also provide strong evidence to support the argument that the administrative environment for consumer financial protection policies produced feedback effects that inhibited public interest lobbying efforts. That argument is made even stronger when contrasting these accounts with advocates' descriptions of their regulatory lobbying after the creation of the CFPB, which centralized a significant amount of the rulemaking and enforcement authority for consumer financial protection in the capable hands of an organization dedicated to putting borrowers first. One advocate, who was completing comments in response to several hundred pages of new regulations prior to our meeting, confirmed that working with the new agency was a whole different ballgame (0313151 March 2015).

Getting rid of the incentive for regulatory arbitrage was a key factor in opening the doors to more receptive regulators:

> For us, the most important was the [CFPB's] broad rulemaking authority, and its broad enforcement authority, and its independence and independent financing. All that was the key. . . . That's very different than what the other agencies had. . . . It is true that having this blanket ability to deal with the issues in their area is unique, because before, one agency could act but the other agencies wouldn't, and you'd have inconsistent rules. Now, it's all in one. (1119141 November 2014)

Another agreed, summing up the difference succinctly: "Primary focus and market-wide coverage. So no gaps. No potential for regulatory arbitrage" (0312151 March 2015). Not only did the new administrative arrangement eliminate many of the incentives to engage in arbitrage, but the CFPB also expanded oversight beyond the scope of the lenders covered by existing financial regulators. One advocate described the expansion of regulatory reach as "totally new, totally fresh, and rather eye-popping" (1119141 November 2014). This advocate went on to underscore the ultimate result for public interest lobbyists: "In terms of the history of the [organization], I think this is the most influential we've ever been, since the 70s. I think it's halcyon days for our staff in that regard. They feel they're really accomplishing things."

### *How Administrative Arrangements Shape Citizen Engagement*

The deleterious effect of the original administrative arrangement for consumer financial protection on public interest lobbying is clear, as is the turnaround jumpstarted by the creation of the CFPB. But what about citizen engagement in the regulatory process? This chapter theorizes that the same features that led to regulatory arbitrage—fragmentation of authority across agencies dedicated to protecting banks instead of consumers—also limited citizen participation in the regulatory arena. First, by fragmenting regulatory authority across a number of agencies, it may be difficult for borrowers to identify which, if any, federal agency is working on their behalf. From a theoretical perspective, this has the potential to further diminish borrowers' beliefs that government is responsible for consumer financial protection. From an instrumental perspective, fragmentation might make it hard for someone to navigate the disjointed comment and complaint systems even if they do want to participate. Finally, giving responsibility for consumer protection to agencies whose focus and expertise are oriented toward protecting banks may diminish agency outreach to borrowers, taking away an important political mobilizing agent. Evidence collected from archival material and advocacy interviews is consistent with this explanation.

In 1969, the National Consumer Law Center (NCLC) administered a survey to legal aid offices around the country. Several of the questions were designed to see whether attorneys or their consumers were filing credit complaints to the FTC under the new TILA provisions. Nine of every ten responding offices (90 percent) said that they did not believe the FTC had been active with respect to consumer protection in their state, so it should be no surprise that very few said they had ever filed, or even considered filing, a complaint on behalf of one of their clients (NCLC 1969). A decade of enforcing consumer credit protections did nothing to change this pattern. As chapter 3 discussed, virtually no respondents to the Fed's 1977 Survey of Consumer Finance said they contacted a federal agency to make a complaint about consumer credit problems. An analysis of the results noted, "It is particularly interesting that not one consumer contacted an existing Federal regulatory agency. This fact may indicate . . . a lack of familiarity" (Board of Governors 1977: 29).

The Fed's own analysis is consistent with the idea that the fragmentation of regulatory authority, which resulted in a patchwork consumer complaint system, made it challenging for ordinary people to identify or to utilize that system. Even more support for this conclusion is generated by a strange anomaly in consumer responses to the 1977 survey. While 1 percent of respondents reported contacting a federal agency, analysts found that the few people who reported submitting comments sent them to agencies that did not actually exist (Board of Governors 1977). Today, of course, most financial regulators accept complaints via phone or online complaint forms, potentially easing the submission process, although as Representative Moore found, even the advent of the Internet could not smooth the navigation of the complaint process in the fragmented regulatory environment.

Consumer advocates I spoke with argued that the introduction of the CFPB consumer complaint system represented a game changer for consumers' ability and incentive to voice their credit issues to government. As one veteran of the consumer movement explained:

> One of the huge changes is the CFPB complaint database. It's so much more accessible, I think, to consumers. It's responsive, gives them an incentive because it requires a response from the [company] . . . supposedly they do respond, so that's a whole new level of power for consumers. (1120141 November 2014)

The complaint process was initiated in 2011. It began by accepting credit card complaints, and the CFPB has added new complaint categories over time.[12] As of April 2018, the CFPB had taken in almost 1.5 million consumer credit complaints (CFPB 2018). The agency accepts complaints directly from consumers online or via telephone, mail, email, or fax. Once submitted, the complaint is reviewed by staff and routed to the appropriate financial institution, which then responds to the consumer. This ability to instigate company action is one of the strong suits of the new system. As one advocate marveled:

> There was a newspaper article talking about somebody [who] complained about overdraft fees with their bank [and] sent a complaint to the CFPB. After complaining and complaining to the bank that they were being mistreated, [they] did not get any response until they filed a [CFPB] complaint, then got a call the next day from somebody at the level of the bank that they could make a change, and they made a change. I suspect that doesn't happen at every bank, but it happens at some, and that's an incredible difference. (1120141 November 2014)

Of the complaints handled in 2017, for example, 78 percent were forwarded to companies. About 16 percent of complaints fell under the jurisdiction of another agency and were forwarded to the appropriate regulator.[13] The remaining 5 percent were incomplete and returned to the consumer for more information (CFPB 2018). Companies responded to an astounding 95 percent of the complaints sent to them via the CFPB in 2017. One in four borrowers who complained about either credit cards or bank accounts received some form of monetary or non-monetary relief from the company.

The centralization of the complaint process in the hands of an agency actively promoting consumer financial protection should, according to the theory presented in this chapter, lead to the growth in consumer complaint making to the CFPB over time, especially relative to both existing governmental agencies and market organizations. I explore the trajectory of consumer complaint making to see whether the various administrative arrangements, before and after the CFPB, affect the propensity for borrowers to make complaints about credit to a federal agency. While perhaps not as pointedly political as submitting a comment during the rulemaking process, filing a complaint with a federal consumer agency is a useful measure of citizen political engagement for two reasons. First, filing a complaint is a direct action in response to a credit grievance, and as we learned in chapters 3 and 5, most consumers opt to direct that type of response toward market entities. Choosing to submit a complaint to a federal agency instead suggests that a consumer recognizes the regulatory power of that agency. Second, the complaints filed with a government agency—and the consumer narratives that the CFPB collects as well—provide direct evidence of consumer grievances that may be used in the rulemaking process (Board of Governors 1977: 29).

The following section explores the patterns in complaint data collected directly by the CFPB from 2011 to 2018 as well as data aggregated by Consumer Sentinel between 2008 and 2018.[14] First, we can see whether consumers make increased use of the CFPB complaint database over time. Figure 6.5 charts the number of complaints submitted by quarter for credit cards, bank accounts, and consumer installment loans. While the magnitude of growth varies across each type of loan, there is a clear upward trajectory in consumer complaint making over time for each product. This is consistent with the argument that borrowers are increasingly able to identify the CFPB as the appropriate federal authority to help manage their problems with consumer financing. However, this data cannot tell us how the increase in people's recognition of the CFPB might shape patterns of engagement with other federal and non-governmental actors. For that, we need to look at a wider range of organizations that receive consumer complaints.

Consumer Sentinel aggregates consumer complaints across all products and services in its jurisdiction, including those filed with federal government agencies and participating state agencies and private mar-

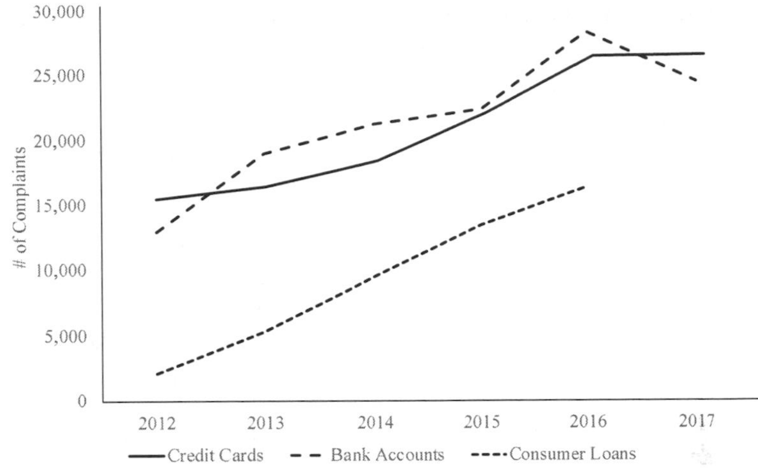


**FIGURE 6.5** Growth of Consumer Credit Complaints Filed with CFPB, 2011–2018

ket organizations. The breadth of the data they incorporate makes it a unique snapshot of complaint making across the political-market divide. Descriptive metrics have been made available to the public every year since 2006, and they began to incorporate CFPB complaints in 2011. Consumer Sentinel collects complaints in three broad categories: fraud, identity theft, and other. Consumer finance complaints are included primarily in the fraud and other categories.

The evidence presented in figure 6.6 suggests that changing the administrative arrangement has indeed reshaped complaint making for issues of consumer financial protection. It reports the percent of all fraud and other consumer complaints submitted to three major organizations—the FTC; the Better Business Bureau (BBB), a private, market-based organization; and the CFPB—since the CFPB first began submitting to the system in 2011. In fact, the CFPB has quickly become one of the three largest sources of consumer complaints in the database, which is both a remarkable achievement given the relatively narrow set of complaints it invites relative to other data partners and a clear indication that the organization is indeed gaining traction among the public.

As expected, CFPB complaints represent a growing percent of the total complaint population. In 2012, the CFPB's first full year reporting consumer complaints, the agency contributed only 4 percent of all fraud and other complaints in Consumer Sentinel's network. By 2018, that number had nearly tripled, comprising 11 percent of fraud and other complaints. At the same time, complaints filed with the FTC and the non-governmental BBB fell. In 2011, 28 percent of all fraud and other

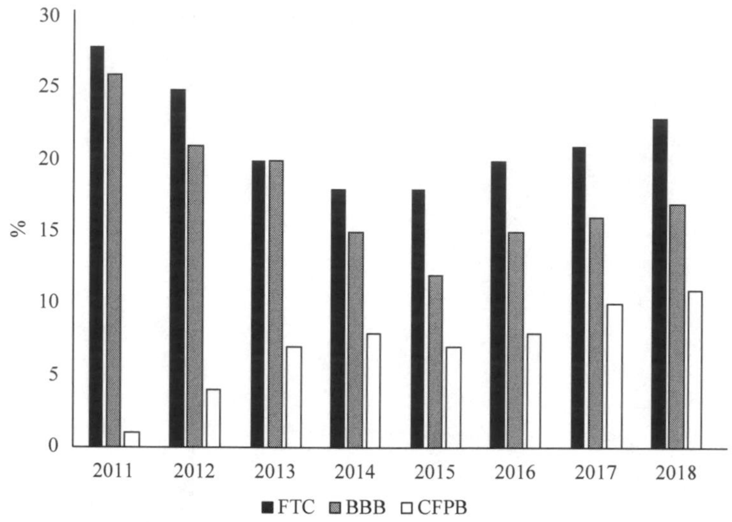


**FIGURE 6.6** Percent of Consumer Complaints by Organization, 2011–2018
Source: Calculated from Consumer Sentinel, Network Reports, 2008–2018

complaints were submitted through the FTC, while another 26 percent were submitted through the BBB. By 2015, those numbers had declined to lows of 18 percent for the FTC and 12 percent for the BBB. Interestingly, while complaints have risen some for these two organizations between 2016 and 2018, the number submitted to the market-based BBB has not recovered as much—falling ten percentage points from their mark.

These trends are particularly striking for two reasons. First, they occur in a period when the total number of complaints increased from 1.9 million in 2011 to 2.9 million in 2018, magnifying the absolute impact of the growing percent of complaints filed through the CFPB. Second, while the CFPB captures only consumer financial complaints, the measures for both of the other organizations include complaints from the entire universe of consumer goods (e.g., consumer software, health care, sweepstakes).[15] Taken together, these trends suggest that the CFPB is indeed playing an increasingly significant role in the minds of borrowers, one that may be displacing their tendency to report to market-based agencies like the BBB.

It is, however, challenging to draw clear conclusions from this data because the different organizations don't collect comparable complaints. Another way of examining the potential effect of a more visible government agency—the CFPB—compared with its less visible or market-based counterparts, is to look at how much the CFPB contributes to a specific subset of complaints relative to the larger pool over time. Since the CFPB has been collecting credit card complaints longer than other types, figure 6.7 shows the volume of all credit card complaints reported by the CFPB relative to the total collected by Consumer Sentinel partners, including both governmental and non-governmental organizations.

As the figure 6.7 illustrates, credit card complaints submitted to the CFPB have grown relative to other sources in the last eight years. By 2014, CFPB credit card complaints represented nearly 60 percent of all similar complaints filed with Consumer Sentinel's partners—a remarkably short period of time for people to begin to identify the CFPB as the appropriate landing place for their problems. This trend is particularly noteworthy because it suggests that people are increasingly likely to turn to the CFPB with their credit concerns, and they also appear increasingly likely to turn to a political actor—the CFPB—instead of a previously sought out market actor—the BBB.

There is also some evidence to suggest that the emergence of the CFPB corresponds with an overall increase in the submission of consumer lending complaints. Consumer Sentinel ranks the most frequent types of complaints each year. Figure 6.8 presents the average rank for both "credit cards" and "banks and lenders" in the periods prior to (2008–2011) and after (2012–2018) the CFPB began to collect and report complaints for each area. As the figure demonstrates, credit cards

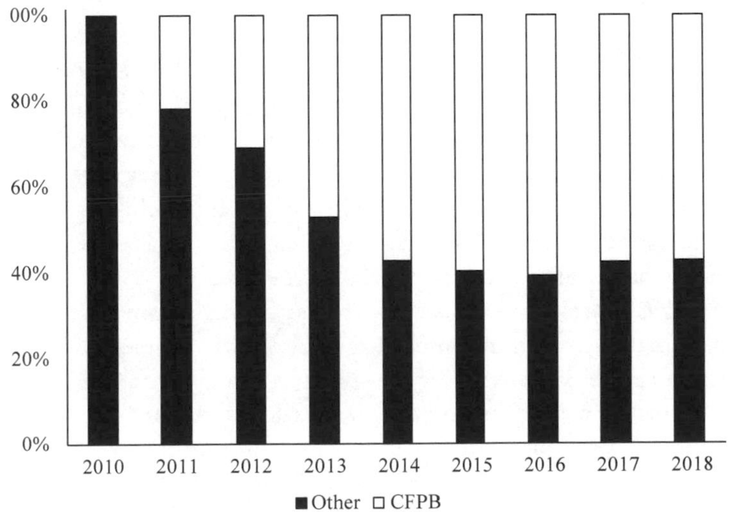


**FIGURE 6.7** Credit Card Complaints Submitted by Organization, 2011–2018
Source: Calculated from CFPB Complaint Data, 2018, and Consumer Sentinel, Network Reports, 2008–2018

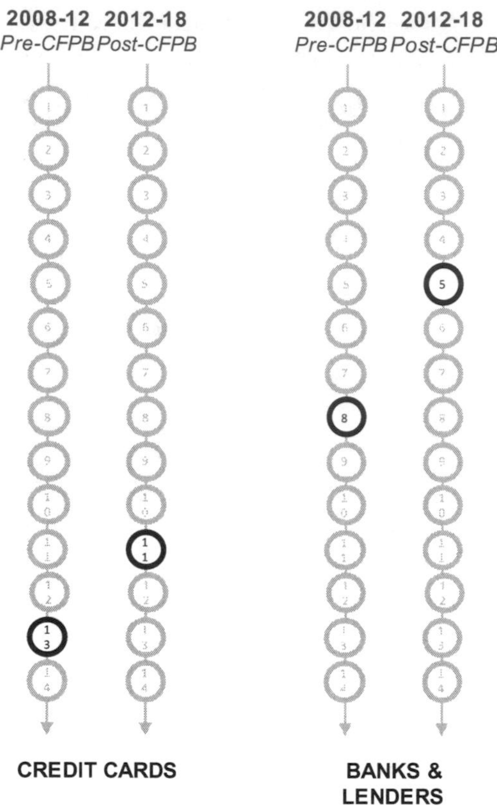


**FIGURE 6.8** Changing Rank of Credit Card and Bank and Lender Complaints
Source: Calculated from Consumer Sentinel, Network Reports, 2008–2018

moved up the list about two places and banks and lenders three after the CFPB started collecting complaints. This represents an increase in both the number and relative volume of complaints for each. It's hard to imagine this jump reflects an actual increase in the number of problems people are experiencing with credit cards and banking, particularly since the latter period is further removed from the financial crisis. Once again, the pattern is consistent with what we would expect to see if the CFPB elicits more borrowers to take political action by easing the process and making political avenues for redress more visible.

These changing patterns of consumer complaint making after the creation of the CFPB intimate that the structure of the administrative environment does produce feedback effects for ordinary Americans' participation in the regulatory arena. Moving from a fragmented scheme of administration, in which the agencies responsible for carrying out consumer financial protections had neither the expertise nor the incentive to make it a priority, to a system where regulatory authority is centralized in a consumer-oriented agency, corresponds with a boost in the number of folks who turn to government with credit grievances. While it is difficult to conclude with certainty the precise mechanisms in play, several seem plausible.

Perhaps the centralization of authority in a single consumer protection agency has made it easier for citizens to identify a relevant political actor to turn to. This scenario may have been amplified by the extensive and proactive borrower outreach the new bureau conducted—an approach that regulatory agencies mainly focused on their relationship with financial institutions would be less likely to pursue. Former CFPB Director Richard Cordray elaborated on this point in a 2014 address to the American Bar Association:

> We are the first federal agency ever created with the sole purpose of protecting consumers and seeing that they are treated fairly in the financial marketplace. . . . It means an agency that prides itself on using technology and other new tools to achieve broad outreach to communities across the country and to the individual consumers we were created to serve. (Cordray 2014)

Indeed, on May 5, 2016, the CFPB held its 34th field hearing since its inception in 2011—an average of seven field hearings every year. As of 2018, the CFPB also had more than 83 thousand Twitter followers for its main account. By way of comparison, the FTC had 58 thousand followers despite a much larger portfolio of rulemaking and enforcement activities. The public release of closed complaint data is another important feature of the CFPB's public outreach. Indeed, the simple practice of making raw complaint data available to the public—something the FTC does not do—shouldn't be overlooked as a powerful tool to engage borrowers with the agency. Industry groups and powerful Republicans, including the lobbying organization run by the Koch brothers, have fought tooth and nail to eliminate the public complaint database (Watzman 2012). Both of these activities support the idea that the CFPB has been particularly diligent in reaching out to consumers directly, even when it angers powerful industry and political groups.

### *The Importance of Public Interest Participation in Regulation*

It seems clear that the administrative environment for consumer financial protection has the potential to significantly influence the policies that regulators pursue, the success of public interest group lobbying efforts, and the frequency with which borrowers engage with the regulatory process. The original administrative arrangement was designed in a way that thwarted borrower interests at every turn. Driven primarily by national economic concerns, federal policymakers assigned regulatory and enforcement authority for the growing corpus of consumer financial regulation to existing agencies that had few resources for or incentives to look out for the average American. The result was a fragmented system of regulatory authority that consistently favored banks over borrowers. Not only did this system mean that consumer advocates had trouble finding receptive bureaucrats with whom to partner, but also the patchwork approach to protecting consumers made it difficult for people to find ways to engage in the rulemaking process.

When the Dodd-Frank Act established the CFPB in 2010, the regulatory infrastructure was fundamentally altered. Once policymakers were convinced that the stability of the financial system was, in fact, tied to protecting people from risky loan products, they created a robust agency with the authority to make and enforce rules for all sorts of financial products and services, taking those tasks out of the hands of regulators who were ill equipped to look out for borrowers. This regulatory restructuring has clearly improved the fortunes of consumer advocacy groups, and it may be increasing people's engagement with the regulatory system as well.

Each of these changes represents a significant step forward for the future of consumer financial protection. But does the CFPB have the power to alter the political landscape for advocates and average American families beyond the borders of bureaucracy? The book's conclusion considers whether this new watchdog agency will create a critical juncture in the political economy of credit, disrupting the feedback loop that has for so long depoliticized the issue of consumer financial protection. It explores the potential for the CFPB to fundamentally reshape future policy remedies and reorient borrowers toward broader political engagement on credit issues, and the major political obstacles that stand in the way.

# 7 A New Lease? The Uncertain Political Future of Consumer Financial Protection

Shortly after Barack Obama's historic victory in the 2008 presidential election, *Time* magazine ran a cover with the president-elect's face superimposed onto a famous photograph of a smiling President Franklin Roosevelt driving a convertible with a cigarette in his mouth. The headline read "The New New Deal: What Barack Obama can learn from FDR—and what the Democrats need to do." The comparison was understandable. Both men were elected in the midst of the most devastating economic crisis of their respective generations. Both were propelled into office by a wave of public hope that they could turn things around. Both were Democrats poised to reshape their party's legacy. Three years later, journalist Matt Taibbi harkened back to this comparison in a *Rolling Stone* article that eloquently assessed the administration's thwarted response to the financial crisis. Taibbi set the stage noting, "Upon entering office, FDR was in exactly the same position Obama found himself in after his inauguration in 2009" (Taibbi 2012).

With no attempt to disguise his disappointment, the reporter lamented that, despite inheriting similar circumstances, President Obama failed to live up to the policy legacy of his predecessor. According to Taibbi, "President Franklin D. Roosevelt launched an audacious rewrite of the rules governing the American economy following the

Great Crash of 1929," while the financial reform package supported by President Obama and congressional Democrats "was never such a badass law to begin with." Taibbi's frustration with the lack of meaningful financial reform is reasonable; it is, after all, an opinion that was shared by most consumer advocates, many ordinary Americans, and a number of politicians. But his claim that the Roosevelt and Obama administrations inherited similar situations, while only one (Roosevelt) managed the economic crisis successfully, overlooks a fundamental truth about the political system: policymakers today face a tremendously more challenging task than their predecessors, in part because of the very success those predecessors achieved.

Scholars of historical institutionalism have long acknowledged that, once established, political institutions—the "rules of the game" that shape political decision making—become an enduring part of the political landscape. Karen Orren and Stephen Skowronek explain, "All political change proceeds on a site, a prior political ground of practices, rules, leaders, and ideas, all of which are up and running" (2004: 20). In short, politicians are rarely able to operate from a clean slate. And over time, responding to the progressively more complex—and sometimes contradictory—institutional arrangements created in previous eras becomes increasingly challenging.

Public policies work the same way. Once enacted, policies—especially those that become enduring features of the political landscape—create rules and incentives that political actors must contend with moving forward. After a policy is created to address a particular issue, lawmakers confront that policy every time they pursue legislative activity for that issue in the future. Suzanne Mettler coined the term "policyscape" to describe a political landscape that is cluttered with existing policy programs (Mettler 2016). The policyscape for consumer financial protection, as this book has hopefully demonstrated, influences the political preferences and actions of a variety of actors, including policymakers, organized interest groups, and citizens, ultimately building a political economy of credit in the United States.

Taibbi's acknowledgment that Roosevelt undertook "an audacious rewrite of the rules governing the American economy" is true. But I argue it was exactly this rewrite that sowed the first seeds of today's predatory lending problem and the seemingly lackluster response to consumer financial protection in the aftermath of the 2008 financial crisis. It would be more accurate to say that, despite inheriting what appeared to be similar situations, Obama and his colleagues faced institutional and political challenges that Roosevelt never encountered. It was, ironically, Roosevelt's successful response to the Depression—and future policymakers' choices to perpetuate that system—that eventually inhibited the efforts of his political descendants, and indeed consumers and advocacy organizations, to do the same.

### *The Political Economy of Credit from Great Depression to Great Recession*

This book opened with a series of puzzles about the politics of consumer financial protection in the United States: Why have policymakers consistently embraced disclosure requirements as the main form of consumer financial protection, even when evidence (and many experts) suggest they are insufficient? Why are American borrowers, who face increasingly dire consequences from their reliance on costly and risky financing, not motivated to take political action to demand a fairer financial deal? Why have consumer advocacy groups been stymied in their efforts to elicit a political response from distressed borrowers, when mobilization usually increases participation? And why has the regulatory environment not been more welcoming of borrowers and public interest groups, even when bureaucrats are tasked with consumer financial protection?

I argue that these puzzling aspects of the politics of U.S. consumer financial protection originate with the policy decisions made by New Deal lawmakers. When confronted with the economic ravages of the Great Depression, President Roosevelt's Brain Trust turned to the idea of a consumption-driven economy as the best way forward. They pursued a number of programs to realize that vision, but chief among them was a little-heralded provision of the National Housing Act—the Title I Home Modernization Loan Program. Policymakers might have chosen to pursue a more European-style welfare system to provide the purchasing power necessary to reignite the engine of a consumption economy. But the United States had already moved away from that model (Skocpol 1992). While notable Keynesian public programs like Social Security were created, it's unlikely that the political will existed to establish a sufficiently large federal welfare system to boost consumption on the scale needed. Lawmakers might also have considered new wage laws to generate consumer purchasing power. Indeed, the 1938 Fair Labor Standards Act set a national minimum wage of 25 cents per hour for a subset of industries. However, with an unemployment rate surpassing 20 percent in the early years of the Depression, a tendency for policymakers to ignore professions that disproportionately employed marginalized groups, and an unfriendly Supreme Court, it is again difficult to conceive that wage laws would have been a viable scheme for mass economic recovery. Instead, the Roosevelt administration turned to credit as the solution to the problem of underconsumption.

With the stroke of a pen, the President signed into law the first building block in the U.S. political economy of credit on June 28, 1934. Chapter 2 described the political rationale behind the home loan modernization program and the spark it provided for the proliferation of consumer lending in the United States. Along with chapter 5, it demonstrates how the policy foundation for a political economy of credit subsequently forced federal lawmakers to maintain and later expand widespread access to financing to promote national economic growth and stability. Once enacted, these policies introduced constraints that would reshape the future politics of consumer financial protection, setting into motion a political economy of credit.

### The Primacy of Disclosure

The political economy of credit influenced the trajectory of future policymaking in two ways that ultimately restricted the potential for more efficacious consumer financial protections. It constrained the types of remedies that Congress could enact, and it created an administrative scheme that inherently diminished the prospects for more borrower-friendly regulation. For members of Congress, the political economy of credit meant that any future policymaking had to be attentive to the issue of access to financing. The system depends on increasingly broad access to consumer credit, but it also requires borrowers to be confident in their ability to use financial products and services. When Congress was confronted with the need to regulate the growing consumer lending market in the 1960s, lawmakers had to identify a policy remedy that could accomplish the second goal without threatening the first.

Congress landed on information disclosure as an ideal solution. By forcing lenders to provide people with more information about their financial products, the problem of adverse selection was corrected to a degree. Consumers, the logic went, would feel empowered to make smart choices when shopping for financial products. And unlike the implementation of prohibitions on specific risky lending practices, information disclosures didn't restrict the supply of credit. As a result of the political economy of credit, policymakers found themselves locked into a path-dependent process wherein information disclosure was perceived to be the only appropriate way to protect consumer finances in most cases.

The demands of maintaining such a system spilled over into the administrative arrangement for consumer financial regulations as well. Lawmakers chose information disclosure in response to the need to prioritize credit access over consumer protection. Likewise, the need to promote the financial security of institutions influenced who was assigned rulemaking and enforcement authority for the new financial protections. With their focus firmly on questions of systemic stability and profitability, members of Congress gave authority for each new consumer financial protection policy to whichever of the preexisting financial regulators was charged with overseeing the institution that provided the regulated type of credit. The result, as I detailed in chapter 6, was that rulemaking and enforcement authority for these policies was fragmented across a number of different federal agencies, only one of which—the Federal Trade Commission—had a mission partially geared toward consumer protection.

In this system, regulators faced their own constraints when carrying out their responsibilities for the new financial protection laws. First, as the testimony from bureaucrats like Sheila Bair detailed, the fragmentation of rulemaking and enforcement authority made it difficult for a single agency to carry out their mandate without consulting other agencies. Regulators were further hampered by the fact that they had incentives to appease the financial institutions under their oversight to avoid losing jurisdiction for them. In the worst-case scenario, which was unfortunately a common one, these problems combined to incite regulatory arbitrage, or a race to the bottom. The least onerous policy, from the perspective of the financial institutions, was frequently adopted as the only politically viable solution. Between their mission and the institutional arrangement of rulemaking authority, regulators had neither the expertise nor the incentive to take a more active stance in favor of stronger borrower protections.

The demands of maintaining a political economy of credit clearly limited federal policymakers' ability to enact more substantive consumer financial protections. This, alone, had the potential to produce significant political and economic consequences. But, as the book argues, the regulatory feedback effects generated by consumer financial protection policies extend well beyond the purview of policymakers. They also shape the politics of individual citizens and consumer interest groups in important ways.

### The Market for Mobilization

The federal consumer financial protections enacted between 1968 and 2010 had several distinctive features with respect to their design, implementation, and administration, as detailed in chapters 3, 5, and 6. First, the adoption of information disclosure as the primary policy remedy served to personalize borrowing. Disclosures are premised on the idea that providing information allows consumers to make rational decisions in the marketplace. This policy design teaches consumers that they simply have to be responsible credit shoppers to protect themselves from bad deals. By this logic, when problems with consumer financing occur, it is either the fault of the lender for being deceptive or the fault of the borrower for making poor choices. Government is nowhere to be found in the equation—an issue further exacerbated by the implementation and administration of these remedies.

Consumer financial protections are implemented and administered in ways that obscure government's involvement in financial markets, thus privatizing the borrowing experience. When New Deal policymakers decided to create consumer financing where the free market had not, they chose not to engage in direct government lending. Instead, they would seduce private financial institutions to lend to a growing swath of Americans with the promise of government insurance to cushion losses—thus guaranteeing profit. When policymakers in the 1960s and '70s were faced with the need to regulate the consumer financial market that emerged, they too created policies that were implemented through existing market transactions. Information disclosures appeared in contracts for banking and credit as though companies had conjured the idea on their own, with no indication that government policy was responsible. And because financial products and services didn't have to pass inspection or safety protocols, consumer-financing contracts lacked visible indicators that a government agency had approved them for use. Furthermore, the initially fragmented administration for consumer financial protection made it difficult for people to identify a single government agency that they could associate with protecting their interests as borrowers.

The result of these dynamics, I argue, is that borrowers came to view their banking and lending transactions as existing solely within the realm of the market. Government's role in both the creation and the continued oversight of the consumer financial industry was completely obscured from borrowers. And policy remedies further the notion that using financial products and services entails a relationship solely between lender and borrower. So, when something goes wrong, I argue, borrowers lack the incentive to turn to political actors for redress. Instead, they attempt to get resolution for both their specific credit problems and their more general dissatisfaction with lenders by engaging directly with market actors. When people shy away from voicing their concerns with financial products and services directly to legislators and regulators, it further reduces policymakers' motivations to consider more fundamental reforms, reinforcing the existing political economy of credit.

### Obstacles to Consumer Advocacy

The constraints placed on policymakers and the diminished incentives for ordinary borrowers to make claims on political actors put significant obstacles in the path of consumer advocacy organizations as well. As chapter 6 details, the administrative arrangement for consumer financial regulation—especially prior to the formation of the Consumer Financial Protection Bureau (CFPB)—reduced bureaucrats' receptivity to public interest group lobbying. Not only was it sometimes challenging for advocates to coordinate their resources across the multiple agencies overseeing a particular regulatory issue, but their proposals had trouble gaining traction with agencies designed to support banks and not borrowers.

The efficacy of lobbying—both in the legislative and administrative arenas—was further complicated because these groups had trouble mobilizing borrowers to support campaigns for reform. As chapter 4 illuminated, public interest groups faced a particularly difficult task creating an appeal for political action that resonated with borrowers, who tended to place the blame for consumer credit problems solely on the shoulders of market actors—both their own and their lenders'. Groups like AFFIL and AFR, while engaging in heroic insider lobbying, never fully overcame the disconnect between people's attitudes and the need for political action, removing a crucial component from their campaign for reform.

: : :

From the perspective of borrowers, supportive policymakers, and consumer advocates, the previous pages paint a bleak picture for the prospects of consumer financial protection. The political economy of credit appears to have induced a self-reinforcing cycle that forecloses on more borrower-friendly financial practices. Lawmakers are motivated to rely on the status quo—information disclosures. This policy regime produces regulatory feedback effects that teach people that consumer financial protection lies entirely in the realm of the market, removing their incentives for political action. Without receptive lawmakers or demanding citizens, public interest groups face a nearly impossible task convincing government officials to consider new methods of consumer financial protection regulation. And the cycle begins again.

Is the story of the American borrower doomed to a bad ending? Perhaps not. There are, as the previous chapters uncover, some possibilities to disrupt the political economy of credit and rewrite the narrative of consumer financial protection in the United States.

## *The CFPB: A New Lease?*

The creation of the CFPB may have the potential to interrupt this cycle. Chapter 6 already demonstrated some of the ways in which the new agency has changed the regulatory landscape, making bureaucrats more receptive to consumer advocates and increasing borrower political action via complaint making. Does the creation of the CFPB represent what scholars call a critical juncture?[1] That is to say, can the creation of the CFPB serve as a catalyst for reshaping the politics of consumer financing in the United States? The following sections consider the agency's potential to rewrite the rules on consumer financial protection and the major hazards that stand in the way.

### Embracing New Approaches

Both legislators and bureaucrats have bolstered the maintenance of the existing consumer financial protection regime. Does the creation of a new agency, one designed with the explicit purpose of protecting consumers across the gamut of financial products, have the potential to shift this dynamic? Chapter 6 provides initial evidence to suggest that the CFPB has been more receptive to the lobbying efforts of public interest groups. The agency has also demonstrated its willingness to go after new targets in the fight against predatory lending. For example, in 2015, it launched a major rulemaking initiative to crackdown on payday lenders heretofore ignored by federal regulators (Puzzanghera 2015).

While the CFPB holds tremendous potential to move toward a more expansive model of consumer financial protection, welcoming the input of public interest groups along the way, there are a number of obstacles to realizing this vision. First, the agency's approach to consumer protection is still, at heart, oriented toward educating consumers. Their own mission statement reads, "Our mission is to make markets for consumer financial products and services work for Americans. . . . Above all, this means ensuring that consumers *get the information they need to make the financial decisions they believe are best* for themselves and their families."[2] The agency also reinforces this market-based logic in defining their role for the public:

> In a market that works, the prices, risks, and terms of the deal are clear upfront so that consumers can understand their options and comparison shop. . . . To achieve this vision, the CFPB works to: Empower. We create tools, answer common questions, and provide tips that help consumers navigate their financial choices and shop for the deal that works best for them. . . .[3] Educate. We encourage financial education and capability from childhood through retirement, publish research, and educate financial companies about their responsibilities. (CFPB 2018)

### Enabling Consumer Political Engagement

Even in the absence of transformative policymaking, the mere presence of an identifiable, centralized government agency dedicated to safeguarding consumers in their financial transactions could reshape another facet of the politics of borrower protection: the political engagement of borrowers themselves. I have argued that one of the major obstacles preventing greater consumer political action in response to credit problems is the obscurity of government in the realm of financial transactions. The CFPB may not ultimately lead to less personalizing consumer financial protections, but the organization does have the capacity to serve as a beacon, signaling the presence of government in consumer financial protection. Like the Food and Drug Administration (FDA), its well-entrenched colleague, the CFPB's active consumer outreach combined with its unique mission may raise its profile sufficiently so that the ordinary borrower recognizes the CFPB as a viable option to consider when something goes wrong. Additionally, the CFPB has begun to require that their own educational materials be provided to borrowers with certain types of credit contracts; while this has primarily applied to mortgage financing to date (e.g., 12 CFR 1024.6), it could be expanded to improve the visibility of the federal agency in other types of borrowing as well. Over time, such measures could facilitate broader public recognition that government is actively engaged in consumer financial protection, thus increasing the odds of borrower political engagement.

The shift in complaint making toward the CFPB, even in its first few years of existence, is a positive indicator of this potential. But the agency's name recognition still has a long way to go before catching

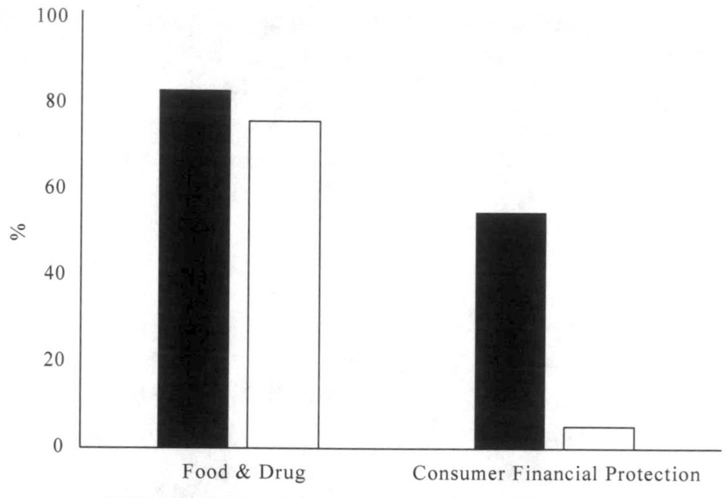


**FIGURE 7.1** Knowledge of Federal Government Agencies

up with its better-known peers. For example, in a series of annual polls commissioned by AFR each year since the CFPB's inception, respondents were asked to report their opinion of the agency. The average favorability ratings from 2013 through 2017 (between 36 and 51 percent support) are considerably higher than the unfavorables (between 10 and 12 percent). But the largest category of respondents reports no opinion or no knowledge of the agency (between 37 and 53 percent) (Lake Research Partners 2017).

The 2017 Survey of Consumer Credit takes a more direct approach in gauging people's familiarity with the CFPB. Respondents were asked whether they thought an agency existed to protect consumers against unsafe and deceptive financial products and services. Those who said yes were then asked if they could name that agency off the top of their heads. For comparison, respondents were asked the same sequence of questions about food and drug protection, a much more common set of regulatory agencies. Figure 7.1 reports the results of those two questions.

Just over half of respondents thought there was a federal agency for protecting consumer finances, while over 80 percent said such an agency existed for food and drug regulation. More important, even amongst those who thought an agency existed, only 5 percent could name the CFPB, a further 18 percent could name another financial regulator like the Securities and Exchange Commission, FTC, or FDIC. By contrast, over 75 percent of respondents could name either the FDA or the USDA (and frequently, both) as the agency responsible for regulating food and drugs. This level of recognition is presumably helped by the relative age of these two agencies, but the fact that the average American is confronted directly with a notice of either USDA or FDA approval every time she shops for meat or vitamins must surely contribute to the agencies' respective high profiles. The results for consumer financial protection demonstrate reasons both for optimism and caution when considering whether the CFPB can serve as a clear target for future political engagement.

**Attacks by Unfriendly Policymakers**

The most substantial obstacle to the success of the CFPB and its subsequent potential to disrupt the political economy of credit comes from unfriendly lawmakers. First, the agency must survive attempts by external policymakers—members of Congress and the President—to either weaken its power or overrule its decisions. Practically before the ink was dry on President Obama's signature on the Dodd-Frank Act, congressional Republicans—with backing from Wall Street—were engaged in legislative attempts to dismantle or defang the CFPB. Senator Richard Durbin (D-IL) quipped that Wall Street hates the CFPB "like the devil hates holy water" (Shelbourne 2017). Representative Jeb Hensarling (R-TX) summed up Republican complaints with the CFPB by calling it a "rogue agency" (NPR 2017).

Abolishing the CFPB was a prominent piece of the 2016 Republican Party Platform, and Republicans have proposed, though not yet successfully enacted, bills to weaken the agency by challenging its independence, funding, leadership structure, oversight, and complaint database. Congress can also curtail the agency's power by overturning the consumer financial protections it issues. After regaining unified control of the federal government in 2016, for example, Republicans used the Congressional Review Act[4] to overturn the CFPB's rule banning mandatory arbitration (a practice discussed in chapter 4). Opponents have also challenged the constitutionality of the CFPB's one-person director in the courts, potentially threatening the agency's ability to continue operating.

The second major threat to the CFPB's ability to serve as a critical juncture emanates from within the agency itself. While it is staffed by civil servants, the agency is managed by a single director who is appointed by the president. The fight over whether the CFPB should be run by a single director or a multi-member board was a huge point of contention during the legislative debate on its creation. As one advocate explained:

> We had a big discussion as the legislation was moving through about what the right structure was. And the truth is, there are pros and cons to both. Neither is perfect, and people like me—I initially favored a board before because I worried about a single individual being able to . . . turn on a dime. But, Barney Frank in particular insisted on a single director, and it has been important as they have geared up, having that unify lines of support. (0312151 March 2015)

Advocates recognized early on, however, that what would be a strength under a pro-consumer director could quickly turn into a weakness under more bank-friendly leadership. A senior staffer at one of the public interest groups acknowledged, "Absolutely. This is a one-person show, and so a new appointment could radically change things" (1119141 November 2014). Another advocate envisioned that potential scenario and its effect on the CFPB's direction:

> The truth is that consumer financial agencies have their good years and their bad years with a single director. . . . If we get a Republican president . . . Richard Cordray decides to leave office and run for governor of Ohio, which is a reasonably good possibility, and he's replaced by a Republican who works with the American Bankers Association, you'll see a very sharp shift. Live by the sword, die by the sword. It's one of the disadvantages to the single realm. (0312151 March 2015)

This, it turns out, was a prophetic assessment. Richard Cordray was the agency's first director. Appointed by Barack Obama, Cordray was a strong proponent of consumer financial protection. The agency fully embraced its role as an advocate for borrowers under his watch. In 2017, with whispers that he might be fired leaking from the Trump White House and a long-held interest in running for higher office, Cordray stepped down from his position to run for governor of Ohio. The process of replacing him played out more like an episode from *Game of Thrones* than a typical bureaucratic transition. Cordray's deputy, Leandra English, attempted to take the reins of the organization, but President Trump appointed the head of the Office of Management and Budget, Mick Mulvaney, as interim director instead. Mulvaney's appointment stood up in court, leaving an avowed opponent of the CFPB in charge of running it.

Before ascending to the directorship, Mulvaney had called the agency a "sick, sad" joke and said its executive position was like "a one-person dictator" (CNN 2017). Despite his criticism of the agency's structure, Mulvaney was quick to capitalize on the power of his new position. In his first two months at the helm, he began to weaken the agency's regulatory stance. Mulvaney decided the CFPB would reconsider landmark payday lending regulations drafted under Cordray (Lane 2018). He also scaled back several of the agency's ongoing investigations—including one into a massive Equifax data breach that threatened millions of Americans' financial information. Mulvaney subsequently attempted to remove the public's access to the consumer complaint database, joking to an audience of the American Bankers Association that the CFPB doesn't need to run a "Yelp for financial services, sponsored by the federal government" (McKenna 2018).

Even more significant than these actions on individual rules and enforcements, Mulvaney made several strategic changes to the agency's overall strength and direction. He made headlines early in his tenure for refusing to request funding for the CFPB, saying it could function on its emergency reserve fund instead (Grunwald 2018). This is notable because the agency's funding, which is not dependent on the Congressional appropriations process, has long been a selling point among consumer advocacy groups. As one I spoke with admired, "The CFPB is, if you compare it to comparable regulatory agencies, in terms of its jurisdiction, authority, and funding, particularly funding, which was a special interest of mine, was very strong" (0312151 March 2015).

Mulvaney also officially changed the name of the agency to the "Bureau of Consumer Financial Protection." He argued that this was in line with the name listed in the original legislation creating the agency, but observers noted that it seemed more like an attempt to undermine the CFPB's public standing. As consumer advocate Karl Frisch explained to the *Washington Examiner*, "Only an idiot would walk away from such a successful investment in this brand. An idiot or someone who wants to make the CFPB look, feel, and sound more bureaucratic and less like an accessible champion for consumers" (Lawler 2018). While Mulvaney's permanent replacement, Trump-appointee Kathy Kraninger, softened the blow by keeping the name change for official and legal purposes while using CFPB for everyday purposes, the possibility for confusion still remains. And that confusion could undermine public identification of the fledgling agency, potentially inhibiting its ability to serve as a target for mass politics.

The most significant potential change, however, came from Mulvaney's decision to alter the CFPB's mission statement. Mulvaney described his vision as a CFPB that works on behalf of banks and lenders in addition to ordinary Americans (Mulvaney 2018). All press releases began to feature a new mission statement that emphasized the CFPB's role in "regularly identifying and addressing outdated, unnecessary, or unduly burdensome regulations." That is a dramatic reversal from what Democrats envisioned when they designed the consumer watchdog.

As chapter 6 explained, the CFPB was novel precisely because it was the first federal agency explicitly designed to focus on the needs of borrowers and not the needs of banks, making it unique among financial regulatory agencies. Undermining this mission—in essence, making the CFPB more like all of the existing prudential regulators—would seriously limit the agency's potential both to improve the lobbying prospects of public interest groups and to cultivate a reputation among borrowers that might boost political engagement. It may also make the agency more susceptible to regulatory capture. One advocate suggested with resignation, "At some point [the CFPB] may, like most agencies, be more or less captive or under the influence of the people they're regulating, but that isn't true now. And hopefully won't be true for a decade or two. But it'll probably happen" (1119141 November 2014).

Of course, appointees who are fundamentally opposed to the agency's work will not always be in charge of the CFPB, but the recent changes highlight its tenuous position. If the CFPB can survive these current attempts to undermine its authority, it has the potential to reshape many aspects of the politics of consumer financial protection in the United States. As the previous sections caution, however, it must endure potentially dramatic swings in leadership, avoid regulatory capture, and potentially undergo a slow process of public recognition to realize that potential. The prospects for the CFPB to rewrite the story of consumer financial protection politics are enticing precisely because they offer a long-term solution. But are there other possibilities to change the politics of consumer financial protection?

### *Economic Security: A Broader Appeal?*

For those who desire reform, one of the most concerning policy legacies of consumer financial regulation is that it powerfully limits political action by convincing borrowers that government isn't the appropriate place to take up the issue. In the absence of a wholesale shift in how policymakers design consumer financial protection—an unlikely scenario given the path-dependent logic of the political economy of credit—is there a way to overcome the demobilizing effects of policies like this? Can American borrowers be marshaled to take political action on behalf of issues that they have come to think of as matters of market, rather than government, responsibility? The book offers another, albeit shorter-term, opportunity to reinject borrowers' concerns into political discourse on banking and lending: changing the way we frame consumer financial protection.

Chapters 4 and 5 explore how drawing parallels between consumer financial regulation and more traditional, and visible, policy programs that protect the financial security of Americans might make people more willing to acknowledge government's role in financial protection. This, in turn, produces a more powerful mobilizing effect on participants than the appeals that groups have historically employed—messages that portray borrowers as helpless victims of corporate abuse who can be saved only by the government. The goal of this approach is to convince borrowers that consumer finance is simply another form of economic—not regulatory—policy, thus financial protections have the same goal of bolstering our economic security that policies like Social Security or popular tax programs do. It is a particularly promising strategy because it appears most efficacious for the marginalized borrowers who stand to reap the greatest benefit from political engagement on behalf of more robust consumer financial protection.

Ironically, this approach mirrors the logic of the political economy of credit. It treats consumer financing exactly how policymakers since the New Deal have treated it—as fuel for consumption akin to welfare, wages, or other sources of support that government frequently provides. It offers a template that advocacy groups might use to subvert the demobilizing pressure of existing financial protections. It is, of course, an imperfect solution. Frames rarely lead to lasting change in people's perceptions about issues. And they do nothing to minimize the larger pressures policymakers face to maintain the political economy of credit. Even success at the margins of consumer financial protection, however, would be meaningful for the millions of American borrowers who rely on credit to finance their daily lives.

*The Politics of the American Borrower*

Borrowing has become the American way of life. From credit and debit cards to bank accounts and loans, most of us rely on financing to pay for everything from a cup of coffee to a college education. For many, borrowing is the only way to afford daily necessities in the absence of better wages or more robust welfare benefits. But borrowing to live is a double-edged sword. For every person who survives, or even thrives, with the aid of consumer credit, the danger of financial ruin from high interest rates, fees, and mounting debt lurks close behind. One need only recall the 2008 financial crisis to see how the boom in consumer borrowing under increasingly costly, and sometimes predatory, lending terms threatens the financial security of American families and the national economy.

For a nation whose political economy and culture are fundamentally tied to the promise, and sometimes the peril, of mass consumption—a so-called consumer's republic—it is imperative that we know more about the main fuel for that system. This book has taken up that mission, contributing both to scholars' understanding of the politics of consumer finance—and regulatory policy more broadly—and to the practical politics associated with each. Hopefully the book has convinced you, beyond the specifics of its argument, that the politics of consumer financing and financial protection deserve more of our attention.

The centrality of consumer banking and lending to the expansion and substantiation of a robust national economy has made consumer financial regulation an attractive subject for economic analysis for several generations. Researchers have explored the economic efficiency of a variety of consumer credit products and policies, focusing particularly on the growth of consumer borrowing. As chapter 1 described, however, it has only been in the last two decades that scholars have turned their attention to political topics related to consumer finance. Social scientists have crafted compelling narratives to describe how policy, politics, and culture reshaped American consumption and consumer finance. More recently, scholars have articulated a vision of the U.S. political economy as one that embraces consumer credit as an American-style welfare state.

Each of these works is masterful in its own way, but they collectively overlook two important dimensions of the politics of consumer financing. First, while we have several accounts for the expansion of consumer credit in the United States, few scholars have explored the politics of consumer financial protection for the growing ranks of American borrowers. One consequence is that we have paid insufficient attention to the role of individual versus macroeconomic welfare in understanding both the political motivations and political consequences of a credit-fueled economy. I suggest that individual welfare concerns have rarely superseded policymakers' investment in protecting the national economy and the credit marketplace that undergirds it. This orientation toward national economic performance is crucial for understanding the specific policies that federal lawmakers adopted over time with respect to consumer financial protection.

If individual welfare was foremost in the minds of policymakers, it is hard to imagine they would have produced a system of consumer financial protection that so thoroughly ignored restrictions that could better ensure borrowers' well-being. An anecdote from one of the advocates I spoke with provides a good counterfactual for what consumer financial protections might have looked like if individual welfare was the primary legislative goal. He described the growing use of prepaid cards to distribute unemployment and other forms of public assistance—quite literally using credit for welfare. He then went on to explain what happened when policymakers found out that some of these cards had predatory terms:

> We did a report on prepaid cards used for public benefits. . . . We put that out with a grade for every single state, and within weeks, states were so embarrassed that reforms were taking place. . . . I think they were just mortified that they had walked into these horrible relationships. (1119141 November 2014)

Mortified reactions and immediate attempts to fix the problems of predatory credit have not, however, been the modal response from policymakers who find out that credit cards or bank accounts have exorbitant interest rates and fees—at least not when those cards are used for something other than the direct disbursement of government benefits. Instead, when policymakers respond at all, they have simply increased the information disclosed to consumers, arguing that people can use that information to protect themselves. This reaction makes sense only when considering the real goals and constraints of federal policymakers. They have opted into a self-perpetuating system that requires them to choose credit regulations that preserve widespread access to financing, something they believe would be impossible by restricting risky lending terms. And these policy details are important, as I argue, because they produce distinctive political consequences.

The second blind spot with the existing work on consumer finance stems directly from this last point. While scholars have explored some of the political causes that contributed to the growth of consumer credit in the United States, they have paid far less attention to the political consequences of that outcome. Political consequences are central to this book. I have emphasized how the creation of a political economy of credit in the United States influences the political behavior of federal policymakers (both legislative and bureaucratic), public interest groups, and ordinary citizens in meaningful ways—ways that have significant implications for future policy reform efforts.

This project ultimately expands what we know about consumer financing specifically and how public policies shape politics more broadly. With respect to the first, the book raises new questions about how consumer credit works in the U.S. political economy, it explores why and how specific policy details were adopted, and it demonstrates that those policy details produce an interconnected political response from elected officials, bureaucrats, interest groups, and citizens. With respect to the second, it makes three key innovations in the study of policy feedback effects. First, the theory presented and applied in this book offers a necessary expansion of the logic of policy feedback into a centrally important yet underexplored realm of policymaking: protective regulation. The framework articulated in the previous chapters has the potential to shed light on political dynamics for a range of essential policy issues, from environmental protection to food and drug regulation. Second, and relatedly, this study expands the scope of policy feedback theory to explain how elements of a policy's administrative arrangement constrain bureaucratic rulemaking and influence the participation of interest groups and ordinary citizens in the rulemaking process—a key site for the vast majority of federal laws made each year. Finally, it broadens the scope of inquiry for examining how the privatization of welfare provision influences political behavior in the United States to include consumer credit, an increasingly important stand-in for a more robust welfare state.

The discussion of regulatory feedback effects on collective borrower action also lays the groundwork for future scholarship to more fully address how policies condition broader social movements. To date, the relationship between policy feedback and collective action hasn't been fully conceptualized.[5] But the theory of the political economy of credit presented in this book begins to demonstrate how the two may be linked. Scholars of contentious politics typically coalesce around three necessary factors for large-scale mobilization: expansion of political opportunities for previously excluded groups to influence the political process, mobilization of structures that provide necessary resources for organizing, and collective action frames to instigate mass engagement (see Tarrow 1998). The political economy of credit demonstrates how policies create feedback effects that might shape each of these dimensions—the opportunity for policy reform; the creation, motivation, and capacity of organizations; and finally, the receptivity of the public to collective action frames.

Not only is it important to understand these phenomena from a scholarly perspective, but the process of policy development detailed in this study, and the political consequences it produces, are also relevant to real-world politics. The book explains how the feedback effects generated by consumer financial protections diminish the political pressure that citizens and public interest groups bring to bear on government actors. I have already identified one specific takeaway for consumer advocates: they must find a way to reframe government's responsibility for protecting consumer finances in order to have a chance to spark borrower political mobilization. But there are other lessons to be learned as well.

Perhaps supportive policymakers and consumer advocates would have better luck introducing more substantive policy reform if they could directly tie those measures to national economic stability. Proponents of reform might also be better served to think creatively about non-disclosure policy alternatives that do not restrict the credit supply. Or perhaps they should focus their efforts on existing proposals, for example, debt collection reforms, that are less clearly tied to the supply of consumer financing. They would also be well served to consider lobbying for more government visibility in the implementation of consumer financial protections. Better understanding the motivations behind and resulting dynamics of consumer financial protection policymaking in the United States can allow advocates to improve their strategic decision making on these issues.

It is easy to imagine several additional questions we might want to ask about the politics of consumer credit. For example, despite its centrality to economic citizenship in the United States, we have very little knowledge of, or data with which to study, how access to banking and credit and its associated debt might affect people's politics more broadly. We know that socioeconomic resources shape people's engagement with the political system (e.g., Wolfinger and Rosenstone 1980; Brady et al. 1995), but does consumer debt factor into this equation? If so, how? Might the growth of consumer debt, exacerbated by the 2008 financial crisis, have contributed to the mounting dissatisfaction with mainstream political candidates and institutions?

We also know that the poorest Americans, who lack access to mainstream credit and banking, rely on an alternative set of financial markets (Bolton and Rosenthal 2005; Baradaran 2015). Does access to mainstream credit, or the lack thereof, affect people's politics? Has the dramatic rise in payday lending and check cashing since the 1990s (Casey 2005), which has quite visibly taken over Main Street in many towns across the country, reshaped people's engagement with their own communities? Can the presence of community credit and banking programs improve trust and civic engagement? There are plenty of questions that need to be asked and answered.

Expanding both our scholarly and practical knowledge of consumer lending politics is necessary to produce policy reform and avoid a continuation of the consequences that stem from the current arrangement. Not only did the existing policy regime fail to protect the financial stability of the national economy, but also it failed to protect the economic security of the average American. The current scheme of consumer financial protection regulation is especially impotent when it comes to safeguarding the most vulnerable borrowers from high-cost, risky lending practices, which only serves to exacerbate existing socioeconomic inequality in the United States. Reversing the gap that has grown between the top 20 percent of Americans and the bottom 80 percent is unlikely to be achieved without considerable reform to U.S. consumer financial protection regulation.

: : :

Matt Taibbi's rather dismal assessment of the response to the financial crisis was echoed by a number of prominent journalists and scholars in the aftermath of the 2008 recession. Taibbi and his colleagues accused policymakers from the Obama administration of failing to meet the same standards that their predecessors in the Roosevelt administration achieved. But I argue that it is the very regime enacted by New Deal policymakers—one that has been lauded by liberals for decades—that set in motion some of the specific constraints that future generations had to wrangle with in order to regulate the system of consumer banking and credit created in 1934.

Whether intentionally embracing the logic of regulatory feedback effects or not, however, Taibbi gets it right at the end when he concludes, "The system has become too complex for flesh-and-blood people, who make the mistake of thinking that passing a new law means the end of the discussion, when it's really just the beginning of a war." As the war over consumer financial protection continues to unfold, it is worth remembering that our current battlefield is indelibly marked by the decisions of previous generations of lawmakers, and the outcome of today's battles will make a lasting impression not only on the economic fortunes of future generations of American borrowers but on their politics as well.

## Acknowledgments

Debt takes many forms, not all of which are predatory or burdensome. I have had the great privilege to accumulate many debts of gratitude while writing this book, and they began, as does this story, right before the 2008 financial crisis. When I joined the National Consumer Law Center in 2006, I had no idea that I was about to watch a global financial crisis unfold from a front row seat. My colleagues were tireless advocates for the most vulnerable Americans, and I witnessed firsthand the heroic battles they waged to warn policymakers about an impending financial collapse and to stave off its worst effects. This project would not have been possible without the opportunity to learn from and work alongside the brilliant, dedicated, and infinitely kind staff there; I offer them—and all of the other consumer advocates who work to build a fairer financial system—my foremost thanks.

If my experience at NCLC provided the initial intellectual deposit for this book, many colleagues and friends have since shared their wisdom to help it flourish. I am tremendously grateful to Suzanne Mettler for helping me to build the theoretical toolkit to bring this book to fruition. Suzanne has been a champion for me and for this project, and working with her has been one of the true pleasures of my career. Elizabeth Sanders and Richard Bensel provided invaluable comments on the process of historical development outlined in the book. Jamila Michener and Adam Seth Levine, in addition to their extensive substantive comments, were both extraordinarily helpful to me in navigating the publication process. Many other colleagues have provided feedback in various forms that moved the book forward at different stages in its development, including Michael Jones-Correa, Peter Enns, Chloe Thurston, Ken Roberts, Louis Hyman, Patricia Posey, Helena Silverstein, Seo-Hyun Park, Il Hyun Cho, Andrew Clarke, and Angelika von Wahl. Thank you also to the anonymous reviewers whose incisive feedback has undoubtedly strengthened this manuscript.

Of course, this book would not exist without funding, research, and editorial support. Thank you to the Consumer Movement Archives at Kansas State University, the Center for the Study of Inequality at Cornell University, and the Academic Research Council at Lafayette College for providing financial support (with no hidden fees). I am particularly grateful for the help of archivists Jane Schillie and Anthony Crawford at the CMA, Virginia Lewick and Kirsten Carter at the FDR Presidential Archives, and Brian McNerney at the LBJ Presidential Archives. I also extend my thanks to the consumer advocates who agreed to be interviewed; their honest (and astonishingly prophetic) insights provide invaluable data for this book. Tina Slater, Laurie Dorsey, Rebecca Stoker, and Alicia Sparrow have offered essential administrative support throughout, and Mary Corrado's editorial work on the final manuscript was indispensable. I am extremely appreciative of Chuck Myers, my editor at the University of Chicago Press, for enthusiastically supporting the project and shepherding it to its conclusion. Larry Jacobs was also instrumental in the final stages of the book, helping me navigate the feedback I received and encouraging me to trust my instincts in carrying it out. I couldn't have asked for a better pair of editorial guides.

I am fortunate to have a wonderful group of friends and family members who have also left their marks on this book. I am especially indebted to my Downstairs Reading Group partners, Delphia Shanks and Sarah Maxey; through five years of weekly writing workshops and (mis)adventures, these two formidable friends and scholars offered unyielding encouragement and constructive criticism that strengthened the book immeasurably. Tamar Malloy has also been an irreplaceable sounding board at critical moments in this project's development. Her analysis and encouragement have been steadfast throughout. And I am grateful to my brother, Elliott SoRelle, with whom I have enjoyed trading stories about our ongoing research projects—mine in political science, his in biophysics.

My wife, Carrie Baldwin-SoRelle, deserves an especially profound thank you. Carrie's contribution extends well beyond the love, support, and enduring patience required to see a project like this to its conclusion; she has also been an invaluable research and editorial associate. Putting her social science librarian superpowers to full use, Carrie transcribed the advocacy interviews, helped to compile references, advised on copyright, and provided detailed feedback for every chapter. I am truly grateful for all of her support.

Finally, I want to extend my deepest gratitude to my parents, Jim and Cindy SoRelle, to whom this book is dedicated. This book would not have been possible without their endless love and encouragement and the type of editorial support that comes from having two professors as parents. Most importantly, however, both of my parents have taught me how to be a compassionate scholar, one who is determined to investigate problems that matter in the world. That is a debt that can never be repaid.

Mallory E. SoRelle
Easton, Pennsylvania
June 2019

# Data Appendix

**Table A.1 Comparative Descriptive Statistics of Survey Sample**

| | 2017 Survey of Consumer Credit | American National Election Study 2012 |
|---|---|---|
| Gender | | |
| % Female | 50 | 52 |
| % Male | 50 | 48 |
| Race | | |
| % White | 69 | 59 |
| % Non-white | 31 | 41 |
| Age | | |
| Range | 18–73 | 17–75+ |
| Mean | 42 | 48 |
| Education | | |
| % <High School Degree | 2 | 10 |
| % High School Credential | 19 | 25 |
| % Some College | 39 | 33 |
| % Bachelor's Degree | 27 | 19 |
| % Graduate Degree | 12 | 12 |
| Median Category | Some College | Some College |
| Income | | |
| % <$25,000 | 22 | 31 |
| % $25,000–49,999 | 26 | 24 |
| % $50,000–74,999 | 18 | 17 |
| % $75,000–99,999 | 14 | 11 |
| % $100,000–124,999 | 10 | 7 |
| % $125,000–149,999 | 4 | 3 |
| % $150,000+ | 6 | 7 |
| Median Category | $50,000–74,999 | $25,000–49,999 |
| Party ID | | |
| % Democrat | 39 | 40 |
| % Republican | 27 | 24 |
| % Independent | 35 | 36 |

**Table A.2 Effect of Credit Usage on Blame Gap**

| | (1) | (2) | (3) | (4) |
|---|---|---|---|---|
| Use Bank Account (1=yes) | . . . | 0.140* | . . . | . . . |
| | | (0.059) | | |
| Use Credit Card (1=yes) | . . . | . . . | 0.140* | . . . |
| | | | (0.055) | |
| Use Other Loan (1=yes) | . . . | . . . | . . . | 0.153* |
| | | | | (0.056) |
| Race (1=non-white) | −0.205* | −0.194* | −0.212* | −0.210* |
| | (0.054) | (0.054) | (0.054) | (0.054) |
| Gender (1=female) | 0.020 | 0.010 | 0.011 | 0.008 |
| | (0.046) | (0.047) | (0.047) | (0.047) |
| Education | 0.039* | 0.038* | 0.037* | 0.041* |
| | (0.015) | (0.015) | (0.015) | (0.015) |
| Income | 0.013 | 0.010 | 0.003 | 0.007 |
| | (0.015) | (0.015) | (0.015) | (0.015) |
| Age | 0.002 | 0.002 | 0.002 | 0.003 |
| | (0.002) | (0.002) | (0.002) | (0.002) |
| Party ID | 0.074* | 0.076* | 0.075* | 0.074* |
| | (0.011) | (0.011) | (0.011) | (0.011) |
| Constant | 0.048 | −0.053 | −0.042 | 0.018 |
| | (0.093) | (0.101) | (0.099) | (0.094) |
| N | 1495 | 1479 | 1479 | 1479 |
| $R^2$ | .06 | .07 | .07 | .07 |

Notes: Figures in columns are ordinary least squares (OLS) regression coefficients. Coefficient standard errors are in parentheses.

*p<.05

**Table A.3 Predicted Effect of Blame on Consumer Action**

| | (1) Market Action | (2) Political Action | (3) Future Market Action | (4) Future Political Action | (5) Contact Congress | (6) Contact Federal Agency |
|---|---|---|---|---|---|---|
| Market Blame | 2.163* | 0.629 | 0.209* | −0.018 | 0.039 | −0.030 |
| | (0.633) | (0.166) | (.028) | (.038) | (0.057) | (0.055) |
| Government Blame | 0.637 | 2.165* | 0.090* | 0.279* | 0.255* | 0.297* |
| | (0.178) | (0.548) | (0.024) | (0.032) | (0.047) | (0.046) |
| Race (1=non-white) | 0.649 | 1.052 | −0.067 | 0.023 | 0.106 | 0.232* |
| | (0.282) | (0.415) | (0.046) | (0.062) | (0.091) | (0.089) |
| Gender (1=female) | 1.599 | 0.925 | −0.032 | −0.213* | −0.091 | −0.165* |
| | (0.651) | (0.320) | (0.040) | (0.053) | (0.077) | (0.065) |
| Education | 1.021 | 1.074 | 0.016 | 0.002 | 0.001 | −0.009 |
| | (0.132) | (0.118) | (0.013) | (0.017) | (0.025) | (0.024) |
| Income | 0.847 | 1.205 | −0.004 | −0.013 | −0.062* | −0.051* |
| | (0.109) | (0.137) | (0.012) | (0.017) | (0.024) | (0.024) |
| Age | 1.044* | 0.974* | 0.008* | 0.004* | 0.010* | 0.001 |
| | (0.017) | (0.013) | (0.001) | (0.002) | (0.003) | (0.003) |
| Party ID | 0.943 | 1.115 | −0.023* | −0.031* | −0.044* | −0.025 |
| | (0.091) | (0.092) | (0.010) | (0.013) | (0.019) | (0.018) |
| Constant | . . . | . . . | 2.357* | 2.090* | 1.999* | 2.187* |
| | | | (0.116) | (0.157) | (0.231) | (0.227) |
| N | 355 | 355 | 1495 | 1495 | 1063 | 1063 |
| $R^2$/Pseudo $R^2$ | .12 | .08 | .11 | .08 | .06 | .07 |

Notes: Figures in columns 1 and 2 are odds ratios from logistic regression. Figures in columns 3 through 6 are ordinary least squares (OLS) regression coefficients. Coefficient standard errors are in parentheses for all four models.
*$p<.05$

**Table A.4 Predicted Effect of Open-End Attitudes on Consumer Action**

| | (1) Support Overdraft Reform | (2) Contact Congress on Reform | (3) Contact Fed. Agency on Reform | (4) Contact Bank on Reform |
|---|---|---|---|---|
| Predatory (1=yes) | 0.582* | 0.250+ | 0.262+ | −0.121 |
| | (0.123) | (0.147) | (0.245) | (0.146) |
| Consumer Protect (1=yes) | 0.625* | 0.687* | 0.091 | −0.147 |
| | (0.301) | (0.343) | (0.339) | (0.341) |
| Fairness (1=yes) | 0.541* | 0.199* | 0.068 | 0.104 |
| | (0.084) | (0.101) | (0.100) | (0.101) |
| Information (1=yes) | 0.441* | 0.005 | −0.091 | −0.001 |
| | (0.100) | (0.121) | (0.120) | (0.121) |
| Per. Responsibility (1=yes) | −0.909* | −0.573* | −0.437* | −0.418* |
| | (0.106) | (0.169) | (0.167) | (0.168) |
| Experience (1=yes) | 0.815* | 0.519* | 0.375* | 0.406* |
| | (0.093) | (0.095) | (0.094) | (0.094) |
| Race (1=non-white) | −0.106 | 0.174+ | 0.296* | 0.363* |
| | (0.159) | (0.091) | (0.091) | (0.091) |
| Gender (1=female) | 0.267* | −0.076 | −0.136+ | 0.013 |
| | (0.058) | (0.078) | (0.077) | (0.077) |
| Education | 0.030+ | −0.005 | −0.009 | −0.047+ |
| | (0.019) | (0.025) | (0.025) | (0.025) |
| Income | −0.032+ | −0.051 | −0.043+ | −0.029 |
| | (0.018) | (0.024) | (0.024) | (0.024) |
| Age | 0.014* | 0.011* | 0.003 | −0.002 |
| | (0.002) | (0.003) | (0.003) | (0.003) |
| Party ID | −0.027+ | −0.052* | −0.041* | 0.002 |
| | (0.032) | (0.019) | (0.018) | (0.019) |
| Constant | 3.213* | 2.694* | 2.859* | 3.352* |
| | (0.118) | (0.162) | (0.160) | (0.161) |
| N | 1429 | 1045 | 1045 | 1045 |
| $R^2$ | .21 | .08 | .05 | .05 |

Notes: Figures in columns are ordinary least squares (OLS) regression coefficients. Coefficient standard errors are in parentheses.

*p<.05, +p<.1

**Table A.5 Treatment Effects of Government Primes on Consumer Action**

| | Control | Government Prime | Competitive Rebuttal | Competitive Reframing |
|---|---|---|---|---|
| **Contact Congress** | | | | |
| Mean | 2.77 | 3.08 | 2.96 | 2.81 |
| *n* | 194 | 193 | 195 | 206 |
| Difference | — | .31* | .19⁺ | .03 |
| **Contact Bank** | | | | |
| Mean | 3.25 | 3.33 | 3.24 | 3.23 |
| *n* | 194 | 193 | 195 | 206 |
| Difference | — | .08 | −.01 | −.02 |

*p<.05, ⁺p<.1 for one-tailed test

**Table A.6 Effect of Government Primes on Willingness to Contact Congress**

| | (1) | (2) | (3) |
|---|---|---|---|
| Government Prime (1=yes) | 0.336*<br>(0.131) | . . . | . . . |
| Rebuttal Prime (1=yes) | . . . | 0.202<br>(0.134) | . . . |
| Reframe Prime (1=yes) | . . . | . . . | 0.043<br>(0.132) |
| Race (1=non-white) | −0.087<br>(0.159) | 0.112<br>(0.167) | 0.199<br>(0.164) |
| Gender (1=female) | −0.118<br>(0.131) | 0.031<br>(0.134) | 0.007<br>(0.134) |
| Education | −0.035<br>(0.042) | −0.021<br>(0.041) | 0.035<br>(0.042) |
| Income | −0.077⁺<br>(0.042) | −0.017<br>(0.043) | −0.082*<br>(0.041) |
| Age | 0.014*<br>(0.005) | 0.017*<br>(0.005) | 0.011*<br>(0.005) |
| Party ID | −0.116*<br>(0.031) | −0.097*<br>(0.032) | −0.066*<br>(0.031) |
| Constant | 2.651*<br>(0.260) | 2.342*<br>(0.271) | 2.497*<br>(0.269) |
| N | 384 | 387 | 399 |
| $R^2$ | .06 | .05 | .02 |

Notes: Figures in columns are ordinary least squares (OLS) regression coefficients. Coefficient standard errors are in parentheses.
*p<.05, ⁺p<.1

**Table A.7 Treatment Effects of Similarity Scenarios on Consumer Action**

| | Control | Consumer Similarity Scenario | Economic Security Similarity Scenario |
|---|---|---|---|
| Contact Congress | | | |
| Mean | 2.77 | 2.99 | 3.33 |
| *n* | 194 | 147 | 133 |
| Difference | — | .21⁺ | .56* |
| Contact Bank | | | |
| Mean | 3.25 | 3.27 | 3.46 |
| *n* | 194 | 147 | 133 |
| Difference | — | .02 | .21⁺ |

*p<.05, ⁺p<.1 for one-tailed test

**Table A.8 Effect of Similarity Scenarios on Willingness to Contact Congress**

| | (1) All Participants | (2) Support Regulation | (3) All Participants | (4) Support Regulation |
|---|---|---|---|---|
| Consumer Scenario (1=yes) | 0.117<br>(0.130) | 0.216⁺<br>(0.143) | . . . | . . . |
| Econ. Sec. Scenario (1=yes) | . . . | . . . | 0.429*<br>(0.128) | 0.560*<br>(0.144) |
| Race (1=non white) | 0.004<br>(0.159) | 0.057<br>(0.174) | −0.045<br>(0.159) | −0.160<br>(0.178) |
| Gender (1=female) | 0.157<br>(0.132) | 0.162<br>(0.143) | −0.035<br>(0.131) | −0.069<br>(0.145) |
| Education | −0.040<br>(0.042) | −0.045<br>(0.046) | −0.011<br>(0.041) | −0.025<br>(0.045) |
| Income | −0.078*<br>(0.040) | −0.056<br>(0.044) | −0.056<br>(0.042) | −0.046<br>(0.046) |
| Age | 0.011*<br>(0.004) | 0.012*<br>(0.005) | 0.013*<br>(0.005) | 0.014*<br>(0.005) |
| Party ID | −0.131*<br>(0.032) | −0.132*<br>(0.034) | −0.088*<br>(0.030) | −0.102*<br>(0.034) |
| Constant | 2.677*<br>(0.274) | 2.626*<br>(0.294) | 2.532*<br>(0.273) | 2.580*<br>(0.300) |
| N | 383 | 339 | 388 | 326 |
| $R^2$ | .07 | .07 | .05 | .08 |

Notes: Figures in columns are ordinary least squares (OLS) regression coefficients. Coefficient standard errors are in parentheses.
*p<.05, ⁺p<.1

**Table A.9 Predicted Effect of Blame Gap on Action for Marginalized Borrowers**

| | (1) Non-white | | (2) Women | | (3) Low Income | |
|---|---|---|---|---|---|---|
| | Market | Political | Market | Political | Market | Political |
| More Blame | 1.977⁺ | 0.452⁺ | 1.682 | 0.504⁺ | 1.733 | 0.612 |
| | (0.787) | (0.203) | (0.786) | (0.187) | (0.734) | (0.214) |
| Race (1=non-white) | . . . | . . . | 1.168 | 0.561 | 0.779 | 1.154 |
| | | | (0.885) | (0.394) | (0.539) | (0.672) |
| Gender (1=female) | 1.521 | 0.610 | . . . | . . . | 1.421 | 0.733 |
| | (0.938) | (0.409) | | | (0.858) | (0.370) |
| Education | 0.973 | 0.704⁺ | 0.918 | 1.319⁺ | 1.085 | 1.167 |
| | (0.182) | (0.147) | (0.213) | (0.221) | (0.229) | (0.185) |
| Income | 0.814 | 1.333 | 0.921 | 1.102 | . . . | . . . |
| | (0.146) | (0.253) | (0.243) | (0.207) | | |
| Age | 1.034 | 0.976 | 1.087* | 0.974 | 1.044⁺ | 0.975 |
| | (0.925) | (0.026) | (0.036) | (0.019) | (0.027) | (0.019) |
| Party ID | 0.943 | 1.140 | 1.432⁺ | 0.982 | 0.855 | 1.084 |
| | (0.142) | (0.179) | (0.295) | (0.134) | (0.126) | (0.135) |
| N | 109 | 109 | 161 | 161 | 175 | 109 |
| Pseudo $R^2$ | .09 | .13 | .21 | .09 | .09 | .05 |

Notes: Figures in columns are odds ratios from logistic regression. Coefficient standard errors are in parentheses.
*p<.05, ⁺p<.1

**Table A.10 Effect of Blame on Future Market Action for Marginalized Borrowers**

| | (1) Non-white | | (2) Women | | (3) Low Income | |
|---|---|---|---|---|---|---|
| | Market | Political | Market | Political | Market | Political |
| Market Blame | 0.280* | 0.064 | 0.175* | −0.038 | 0.233* | 0.029 |
| | (0.053) | (0.069) | (0.041) | (0.056) | (0.042) | (0.056) |
| Government Blame | 0.037 | 0.087 | 0.091* | 0.237* | 0.098* | 0.230* |
| | (0.046) | (0.060) | (0.034) | (0.047) | (0.035) | (0.047) |
| Race (1=non-white) | . . . | . . . | −0.014 | 0.009 | −0.082 | 0.048 |
| | | | (0.068) | (0.093) | (0.066) | (0.088) |
| Gender (1=female) | 0.056 | −0.216* | . . . | . . . | 0.016 | −0.207* |
| | (0.074) | (0.096) | | | (0.058) | (0.078) |
| Education | 0.040 | 0.016 | 0.010 | −0.028 | 0.014 | −0.002 |
| | (0.025) | (0.032) | (0.018) | (0.025) | (0.020) | (0.026) |
| Income | −0.019 | −0.015 | −0.016 | −0.005 | . . . | . . . |
| | (0.025) | (0.032) | (0.018) | (0.024) | | |
| Age | 0.009* | 0.003 | 0.008* | 0.003 | 0.006* | 0.005 |
| | (0.003) | (0.003) | (0.002) | (0.003) | (0.002) | (0.003) |
| Party ID | −0.009 | −0.017 | −0.030* | −0.037* | −0.019 | −0.028 |
| | (0.020) | (0.026) | (0.014) | (0.019) | (0.014) | (0.019) |
| Constant | 2.098* | 2.425* | 2.450* | 2.117* | 2.264* | 2.032* |
| | (0.191) | (0.247) | (0.155) | (0.213) | (0.161) | (0.216) |
| N | 463 | 463 | 744 | 744 | 718 | 718 |
| Pseudo $R^2$ | .15 | .02 | .09 | .05 | .12 | .06 |

Notes: Figures in columns are ordinary least squares (OLS) regression coefficients. Coefficient standard errors are in parentheses.

*p<.05

**Table A.11 Treatment Effects for Marginalized Groups**

| Non-White Borrowers | | | | |
|---|---|---|---|---|
| | Control | Competitive Rebuttal | Consumer Similarity | Econ. Security Similarity |
| **Contact Congress** | | | | |
| Mean | 2.64 | 3.28 | 3.38 | 3.27 |
| *n* | 42 | 50 | 39 | 33 |
| Difference | — | .64* | .74* | .63* |
| **Contact Federal Agency** | | | | |
| Mean | 2.74 | 3.22 | 3.18 | 3.27 |
| *n* | 42 | 50 | 39 | 33 |
| Difference | — | .48* | .44⁺ | .53* |

| Low-Income Borrowers | | | | |
|---|---|---|---|---|
| | Control | Competitive Rebuttal | Consumer Similarity | Econ. Security Similarity |
| **Contact Congress** | | | | |
| Mean | 2.78 | 2.93 | 3.07 | 3.39 |
| *n* | 80 | 100 | 75 | 62 |
| Difference | — | .16 | .29⁺ | .61* |
| **Contact Federal Agency** | | | | |
| Mean | 2.74 | 2.82 | 2.81 | 2.97 |
| *n* | 80 | 100 | 195 | 62 |
| Difference | — | .08 | .08 | .23 |

*p<.05, ⁺p<.1 for one-tailed test

## *A.12 Survey Experimental Protocol*

Please take a moment to read the following press release describing a new proposal about overdraft fees and answer some questions about it:

(see figure 3.18 for proposal)

1. What do you think about this proposal? Do you oppose it, support it, or neither?
   (1= Strongly oppose to 5= Strongly support)
2. Still thinking about the previous question you just answered, I'd like you to tell me what ideas came to mind as you were answering the question. Exactly what things went through your mind?
   (open-ended)
3. **For those receiving either consumer or economic similarity scenario only**

   Do you agree or disagree with the following statement: Policymakers in Congress and in federal agencies are responsible for passing laws to [protect people like you from deceptive sales practices and unsafe products when you shop for things like food, drugs, and all sorts of other goods and services/ to help people like you be financially secure by providing things like tax breaks or social security benefits].
   (1= Strongly disagree to 5= Strongly agree)
4. [Experimental Treatment] Still thinking about the proposal to change overdraft fees from the previous page, if a consumer organization asked you to take any of the following actions to <u>voice your support</u> for this proposal to change overdraft fees, how likely would you be to contact [your member of Congress/your bank/a federal agency like the Federal Trade Commission]?
   (1= Very unlikely to 5= very likely)

## Notes

CHAPTER ONE

1. Some might say that credit cards and toasters are very different from one another, so it makes sense that policymakers would treat them differently. But they share important similarities from the consumer's, and more importantly from the market's, perspectives. Both cost money to use; they must be "purchased." Consumers are expected to shop around for the best deals for both. Both are promoted with advertising campaigns designed to get people to buy them. Both are subject to information asymmetries between producers and consumers, meaning that consumers are at a knowledge disadvantage about the product's characteristics. Both have the potential to significantly harm those who use them.

2. A uniform legal definition of predatory lending does not exist in the United States, but a number of federal agencies have applied their own descriptions to the term. The Federal Deposit Insurance Corporation (FDIC), for example, explains that a predatory loan "typically involves imposing unfair and abusive loan terms on borrowers, often through aggressive sales tactics; taking advantage of borrowers' lack of understanding of complicated transactions; and outright deception" (Office of Inspector General FDIC 2006). The Federal National Mortgage Association (Fannie Mae) describes a predatory loan as one that is "characterized by excessively high interest rates or fees, and abusive or unnecessary provisions that do not benefit the borrower" (Carr and Kolluri 2001).

3. Subprime loans are those offered to borrowers who are considered to be less creditworthy or who pose a greater risk

of loan default. To compensate for the higher risk to lenders, subprime loans frequently feature higher interest rates and less favorable lending terms than prime loans.

4. Fee-harvester credit cards charge high fees on low credit limits, which results in the consumer having as little as 50 dollars of usable credit for an exorbitant cost; they were sold to millions of consumers in the years prior to the crisis (Jurgens and Wu 2007). Refund anticipation loans, which make small, short-term loans that must be repaid with income tax refunds, charge consumers an interest rate equivalent to between 390 and 520 percent APR, compared to rates ranging from zero to 20 percent for regular revolving credit accounts (Wu and Fox 2006). Overdraft charges are a flat fee levied when customers overdraw their bank accounts. On the eve of the financial crisis, about 86 percent of banks employed this program, charging an average fee of 27 dollars for a single overdraft. This amounted to nearly two billion dollars in revenue for banks—accounting for almost three-quarters of all service charges on bank accounts (FDIC 2008).

5. The beginning of the recession was identified by the Business Cycle Dating Committee of the National Bureau of Economic Research (NBER 2008).

6. For information on the missions of these two organizations, see Mayer 2012.

7. Analyses of the Dodd-Frank bill and resulting creation of the CFPB suggest that, while the new agency changes the underlying regulatory architecture of consumer financial protection, the law did not fundamentally change the substance of consumer financial protection policies (see, for example, Levitin 2009 and Carpenter 2014).

8. The book will use the terms consumer credit, consumer lending/loans, and consumer finance/financing interchangeably. While the term consumer credit is often employed loosely to refer to any type of financial product that costs money to use, this book relies on a narrower definition of consumer credit to include types of financing that 1) are not backed by real estate or other financial assets, 2) are intended to finance general consumption and not specific asset building, and 3) are regulated primarily at the federal rather than state level. The first qualification, differentiating between asset-backed and non–asset-backed credit, reflects common practice within the field (see Durkin et al. 2014) as well as the Federal Reserve Board's own definitions. The second qualification, focusing on credit for general consumption rather than specific asset building, acknowledges that policymakers employ different rationales when creating and regulating financing designed to help Americans build specific assets (like mortgages for home buying and student loans for education) versus financing to support general consumption. This decision also helps address a large gap in the scholarly literature; we have far more research on the politics of credit used to help Americans build assets (e.g., Schwartz 2009; Prasad 2012; Mettler 2014; Kwak 2015; Rose 2018; Thurston 2018; Quinn 2019) than we do on credit to finance broader consumption, despite the proliferation and importance of the latter. Finally, I restrict analysis to financing that is primarily regulated by the federal government because types of credit that are subject to different constellations of state policies (e.g., payday loans)

are regulated in a variety of different ways with different political goals and consequences.

9. Bank accounts are included in this book because they represent an important source of consumer financing for the average American. As with other forms of financing, banking costs money to use. While bank accounts themselves are not a form of credit, they often carry finance charges—like overdraft fees—that operate like short-term loans. They also increasingly have credit products tied to their use, like bank or debit cards.

CHAPTER TWO

1. It is not the goal of this chapter to provide an exhaustive history of the evolution of consumer lending in the United States. Anyone interested in that topic should consult the excellent works of Martha Olney (1991), Lendol Calder (1999), and Louis Hyman (2011), among others.

2. There are a number of scholarly explanations for why policymakers might bend to the desires of business interests, focusing on structural incentives for policymakers (Lindblom 1982), the role business elites play in policy subsystems (e.g., Sabatier 1987; Baumgartner and Jones 1993), and the distribution of policy costs and benefits for certain types of policies (Lowi 1972; Wilson 1980).

3. See, for example, Carpenter 2002.

4. As will be discussed in greater detail in this chapter, not only does the federal government follow a distinctive approach to regulating credit when compared to the states, but also the federal government has gone so far as to preempt—or overrule—state consumer protections like usury caps for many types of consumer credit. This also indicates a distinct motivation on the part of federal policymakers.

5. This strategy was consistent with the observation made by economist Ben Bernanke, who served as Chair of the Fed during the 2008 financial crisis, that the protracted recession of the 1930s was attributable in part to the inability of some borrowers to obtain credit, and that "intermediation between some classes of borrowers and lenders requires non-trivial market-making" by the state in order to correct the situation (1983).

6. For a concise description of positive path dependence see Pierson 2004; also see Arthur 1994 and David 2000.

7. For much of the world's history, according to Raymond Williams (1999), the word "consumer" was primarily used as a pejorative term to describe those who used up valuable resources in a gluttonous or unrestrained manner. By the eighteenth century, however, "consumer" became part of the lexicon of the emergent bourgeoisie political economy that separated the functions of the making (production) and using (consumption) of goods. The terms "producer" and "consumer" described each of the primary actors of the capitalist market economy.

8. The appointment of Moffett, with his corporate credentials, rankled Ickes, leading to constant—and occasionally public—battles between the two administrators. In a confidential telegram sent November 27, 1934, from White House Press Secretary Stephen Early to President Roosevelt's traveling secretary Marvin H. McIntyre, Early writes, "I sincerely hope that you will be able to keep Jimmy suppressed so far a[s] publicity goes while he is in Warm

Springs. He and Ickes to all appearances are keeping their armistice agreement and are not continuing their row. Feeling[s] run deep, however, and while they personally may not be talking and may be keeping their promise they made me not to talk, I notice almost every day stories appearing without attribution . . . describing Jimmy as victor in the clash with Ickes."

9. Interestingly, the CAC eventually decided to merge the Consumer Credit committee with the committee on Economic Welfare (CAC 1963), a further indication of the perceived relationship between the two areas.

10. For example, Prasad 2012 and Vogel 2003.

11. The United States has a dual banking system in which banks can choose to charter as either state or national banks. While state banks are bound more tightly by state regulations, historically national banks were still subject to many of the state consumer regulations where they did business.

12. The *Marquette* ruling marked a watershed moment in banking regulation, but it followed a long trend in the Supreme Court ruling in favor of national banks over state regulators. The Court's ruling was based in the National Bank Act of 1864, passed during the Civil War to promote a system of national banks in order to support a more stable national economy. Long before consumer credit existed in any modern form, the Act provided some exemptions from state banking regulation for nationally chartered banks. The *Marquette* decision is notable because it extended those exemptions in dramatic fashion to consumer credit transactions.

13. Despite the conventional wisdom that the 1970s and '80s saw a return by federal Republicans to promoting states' rights, federal preemption of state law increased dramatically beginning in 1970, with both parties preempting at equal rates. Republicans in particular were anxious to embrace ceiling preemptions—like those capping or removing protective financial regulations—in an effort to limit the amount of regulation states could enact (SoRelle and Walker 2016).

14. Double cycle billing is the process of calculating the interest charge in a given billing period by accounting for the average daily balance of both the current period and the previous period.

15. Another consequence of this outcome is that borrowers have been forced to rely on other mechanisms to manage the fallout of predatory lending. Bankruptcy is one alternative, providing an ex post facto cushion of sorts for the consequences of weak financial protection. Even this option has been weakened since reforms in 2005 raised obstacles to filing and limits to remediation. More recently, state attorney generals are leveraging generic unfair or deceptive acts or practices (UDAP) statutes—typically used for consumer goods and services—to bring claims against predatory lenders in the absence of more robust financial protections. Neither of these are adequate solutions, nor are they preventive in the same way that more stringent protective financial regulations would be.

## CHAPTER THREE

1. Gregg's story, including the following quotes, appeared in a *New York Times* article on the rise of overdraft loans (Berenson 2003).

2. A 2011 study conducted by the Federal Deposit Insurance Corporation (FDIC) found that 70 percent of large banks and more than half (54 percent) of midsize banks employed an automated overdraft system (CFPB 2013).

3. In 2009, the Fed amended Regulation E (implementing the Electronic Funds Transfer Act) to eliminate automatic opt-in programs for overdraft protection. The new regulation requires consumers to affirm their participation in the program after they are provided with information on overdraft policies (Regulation E 2009). The rule went into effect in 2010. More stringent protections have not been successfully enacted.

4. While a precise measure of bank profits derived from overdraft fees is difficult to obtain because they are often reported along with other account service charges, studies have estimated that consumer overdraft and insufficient funds charges combined account for between $12.6 (in 2011) and $32 (in 2012) billion dollars (see CFPB 2013).

5. The Consumer Sentinel Network is a federally managed database for law enforcement professionals that aggregates consumer complaints gathered from a nationwide network of around fifty data providers.

6. Scholars have continually shown that socioeconomic resources, including education, age, and income, are a key indicator of political engagement (see, for example, Wolfinger and Rosenstone 1980; Brady et al. 1995).

7. The Fed uses census tract income as a proxy for borrower income. They divide income into four categories calculated by comparing the median family income in a tract with the median income in the larger metropolitan or nonmetropolitan statistical area in which the tract is located: low income (<50 percent), moderate income (50–79 percent), middle (80–119 percent), and high (≥120 percent).

8. The survey was conducted online to reduce social desirability bias and to mitigate the effects of asking potentially sensitive questions about people's personal finances and their use of consumer credit (Kreuter et al. 2008).

9. The survey was administered June 16–23, 2017, to a nationally representative pool—targeted for age, income, education, race, partisanship, and Census region—from Survey Sampling International's online pool. The descriptive statistics for the sample are available in the appendix. The survey was offered on computer, laptop, tablet, and mobile phone. SSI, a commonly used sample for social science research, employs a multi-platform, managed recruitment panel (they recruit from more extensive sources than a traditional web intercept "river" approach). Pool participants are randomly matched to specific survey projects, undergo a quality control and identification verification screening process, and are compensated in various ways (e.g., monetary rewards, points, prize options). The survey was pretested in both 2015 and 2017 through Amazon's Mechanical Turk system, and the results presented in the following sections are consistent across all three waves. Taken together, these results are robust across multiple years, platforms, and more than 3,000 respondents.

10. Answer options included a checking account, credit or bank card, prepaid credit card, mortgage loan, payday loan, refund anticipation loan, or personal loan. The remaining analysis will focus on the use of checking

accounts, credit/bank cards, and other personal loans because these products meet the criteria outlined in chapter 1.

11. Adverse credit experiences, as typically measured by the Federal Reserve Board and replicated in the 2017 Survey of Consumer Credit, include denial of credit, denial of the full amount of credit requested, charged high rates or fees for credit, received other poor credit terms, provided insufficient information about credit terms, billing errors, other mistakes with credit accounts, problems with debt collection or harassment, property repossession to clear debt, or respondent-identified problems not included in the above list.

12. This measure was created by subtracting the mean blame for political actors from the mean blame for market actors for each respondent.

13. The results of the full OLS regression models are in the appendix.

14. Respondents in both surveys were allowed to select multiple actions, so they could affirm all types of action taken in response to an adverse credit experience.

15. Complaining to a creditor might seem an obvious first step, perhaps one designed to address a different type of problem than a borrower might seek political remedies for. It is worth including here, however, for three important reasons. First, complaining to a creditor does have a direct political analogue: filing a complaint with a federal agency. Second, the Fed included the option on their 1977 survey designed to capture what I am asking; including it maintains consistency with their measurement and reasoning. Finally, variation exists among people who contact, or say they would contact, a creditor based on their level of market blame, suggesting that this action fits the broader pattern of blame and action discussed in the following sections and thus makes sense to include in the analysis.

16. The ability of governmental agencies to resolve financial disputes will be addressed more fully in chapter 6.

17. The individual items included in the market and political action variables are divided as in table 3.2.

18. People are often guilty of overreporting their willingness to take a particular type of action, but there is no theoretical reason to expect that respondents in this survey should be more likely to overreport preferences for one type of action over another.

19. Income is measured on a seven-point scale where each one-point increase corresponds to 25,000 additional dollars of annual household income. A person's highest level of education is measured on an eight-point scale from some high school to graduate degree. Age is a continuous variable. Gender and race are both dummy variables where one equals female and non-white, respectively. Party identification is measured on a seven-point scale from strong Democrat to strong Republican. All demographic variables are centered on the median response for the following analyses to enable more meaningful interpretation of coefficients.

20. Could a general lack of trust in government or a sense that government is ineffective be driving people's turn to market actors? If people's feelings of government distrust or political inefficacy were influencing their attribution

of blame to the market, and ultimately their lack of political mobilization, we wouldn't expect these trends to be restricted to the issue of consumer financial protection. We would also expect to see people participate less in traditional forms of political engagement like voting or contacting a member of Congress. However, increasing market blame does not negatively correlate with these other political acts (in fact, the opposite is true). This suggests that the relationship between market blame and market action is specific to consumer financing.

21. The Federal Trade Commission was selected as the example for this question because pre-tests demonstrate it is currently the most familiar federal regulator of consumer credit—data that will be discussed in greater detail in chapter 6.

22. A prime example of the growing discourse surrounding the politics of consumption is presented in the special edition of the *Annals of the American Academy of Political and Social Science*: The Politics of Consumption/The Consumption of Politics, May 2007. See also, for example, Cohen 2003, Breen 2004, Jacobs 2005, and Hilton 2009.

23. See, for example, Micheletti 2003 and Stolle, Hooghe, and Micheletti 2006.

CHAPTER FOUR

1. Emphasis in original text.

2. Given labor's prominent role in early consumer credit lobbying, is it possible that the decline of organized labor led to the weakening of public interest group efforts to stimulate political action? There are a few reasons to be dubious. First, unions have a complex relationship with consumer financial protections (see Trumbull 2014). While union power may have declined over time, unions have become more supportive of financial protection, suggesting they should be more likely to mobilize in later decades. Second, while private sector unionization was in decline during the early quest to enact consumer financial protections, public sector unions grew, complicating the story of declining union power (Walker 2014). Finally, if the diminution of organized labor is responsible for failed mobilization efforts, we would expect to see that play out across multiple venues, yet consumer groups—including labor partners—were able to mobilize large cohorts to protest market actors in the aftermath of the financial crisis.

3. Consumers' Research was founded in 1929 primarily as a product testing organization. After an internal labor dispute, a group splintered from Consumers' Research to form Consumers Union.

4. Initially, much of this educational activity had to be carried out in secrecy. As consumer advocate and economist Richard Morse explained, "Consumer Research was launched in a sea fearful of reprisal. Copies were confidential and members signed statements pledging to keep the copies out of circulation even among their friends . . . a far cry from today's practice of selling Consumers Union Reports" (1963: 3). The clandestine provision of information for consumers was understandable given that organizations like Consumers Union were eventually added to the House Un-American Activi-

ties Committee list of subversive organizations, a position they would not be removed from until the mid-1950s (Morse 1963).

5. Annual reports for years before 1975 were not available at the Consumer Movement Archives.

6. Each of the variables discussed in the following section on email content analysis were coded as dummies, where the presence of the variable (e.g., calling for political action) equals one and the absence equals zero.

7. Emails were also coded for whether they requested an organizational action, for example, making a donation to AFFIL. Thirty percent of the emails requested organizational actions either in addition to or in lieu of a market or political action.

8. The dummy variables for market action and political action account for the presence and not the number of respective actions requested in the email. So, for example, if an email asked the recipient both to call a member of Congress and to submit a comment to the Fed, that email is still coded one for political action.

9. Terms included educat*, smart decision*, smart shop*, responsibil* (when discussing consumers).

10. Terms included right* (when referring to consumers), justice, discriminat*.

11. Terms included fair*, unfair*, decept*.

12. Terms included protect*, saf*, unsafe, victim*.

13. Terms included predator*, abus*, greed*, trick*, trap*, fraud*, scam*.

14. Interestingly, the majority of appeals combining a request for market action with frames highlighting personal responsibility were tips for safe holiday shopping released around Christmas.

15. I calculated the effective page views by source by multiplying the number of visits from each source by the average pages per visit from each source using AFFIL's Google analytics data from April 20, 2007 through June 5, 2008, which was preserved in the archives (AFFIL 2008c).

16. Responses were not restricted to the presence of only one of these variables, although in practice the personal responsibility narrative rarely overlapped with either the predatory or consumer protection.

17. Only 8 percent of respondents left the open-end probe blank or wrote something unintelligible.

18. The mean willingness to contact Congress to support the reform was 3.13 (with .095 standard error) for participants who did not receive the additional predatory lending frame and 3.10 (with .094 standard error) for those who did.

19. Specifically, I included separate dummy variables for whether a respondent mentioned predatory lending, consumer protection, fairness, information, personal responsibility, or a personal experience with overdraft fees.

20. These variables are described in greater detail in the previous chapter.

21. The following experiment employs a between-subjects design that attempts to balance internal and external validity. The text of the overdraft reform reflects real advocacy appeals in language and length. Furthermore, the substance and length of the frames are in line with other political science

experiments asking participants to read news clips, policy proposals, political scenarios, etc., to gauge policy support. The experiment was also pretested in 2015 and through two waves in 2017 for purposes of internal validity. The results remain consistent throughout, as do the open-end responses to the prompt. I also conducted informal cognitive interviews to gauge people's comprehension of the treatments before pretests were administered in 2017.

22. The size of each experimental group is presented along with the full table of results in the appendix.

23. All experimental analysis in this chapter includes only those respondents who acknowledged using a bank account in the last year (about 80 percent of survey respondents). It makes sense to restrict the results to the category of people who would be most directly affected by the proposed reform, especially since we have demonstrated that people who use a particular financial product hold different preconceptions about who is to blame for problems with that product.

24. Full statistical results for the effect of each treatment with controls are available in the appendix.

25. This is consistent with an approach used by Jerit (2009).

CHAPTER FIVE

1. By 1969, the NWRO had 540 local chapters across the United States with 25,000 active members, primarily women of color (Reese and Newcombe 2003).

2. Former Fed Governor Lawrence Lindsey is credited with first using the term "democratization of credit" in 1997. Democratization of credit is now commonly employed to describe the expansion and deepening of access to a variety of types of consumer financing to middle- and lower-income households and other borrowers, like racial minorities, who previously lacked access to many mainstream credit products.

3. Preemption, as discussed in chapter 2, refers to the practice of federal policymakers limiting state and local authority for a given issue.

4. See also Hyman 2011, Krippner 2011, and Baradaran 2015.

5. Other measures were proposed to increase economic development in the inner city, for example, directing federal funds to local businesses to promote job growth or promoting local entrepreneurship, but they were overshadowed by the consumption-driven approach to political economy.

6. Proxmire and others attributed blame for this credit gap in consumer, mortgage, and business finance not to the lack of creditworthy inner-city borrowers but instead to the absence of sufficient private financial investment (U.S. Senate 1968; Congressional Record 1969).

7. When the House Banking Committee marked up the original antidiscrimination bill, it didn't specify sex or marital status. Representative Marie "Lindy" Boggs (D-LA), upon noticing the omission, added the provisions without consulting her colleagues on the Committee. When she distributed copies that she had made herself, she addressed her colleagues saying, "Knowing the members composing this committee as well as I do, I'm sure it was just an oversight that we didn't have 'sex' or 'marital status' included. . . . I've taken

care of that, and I trust it meets with the committee's approval" (Good 2013). They did not argue.

8. One side effect of this law is that lenders began to rely on geographic, rather than demographic, information to help determine a borrower's credit risk. This resulted in de facto racial discrimination, as many communities had been "redlined" by financial institutions. Redlining, which involved the systematic denial of credit to entire communities based, historically, on race meant that residents in these areas did not have the opportunity to build a credit history—a common, and legal, prerequisite for creditworthiness. Congress enacted the Community Reinvestment Act of 1977 with the goal of reducing the effects of redlining and further expanding access to financing to low-income, predominantly minority communities.

9. Revolving credit, described briefly in chapter 1, means a borrower does not pay off the full amount of the outstanding debt balance before it incurs interest and rolls over to the next payment period (typically each month). When credit is revolved it accrues more interest, generating larger profit margins for lenders.

10. Recall that the scores reflect the mean blame assigned to each actor, where one equals no blame and five equals all of the blame.

11. Recall that the blame gap was calculated by subtracting the mean blame score for political actors from the mean blame score for market actors ([banks and lenders + consumers]/2) – ([Congress + president + federal agencies]/3) for a score ranging from –5 to 5.

12. Recall these question and answer categories mirror those included in the 1977 Survey of Consumer Finances conducted by the Federal Reserve.

13. Marginalized and mainstream borrowers reported similar numbers of problems; the median respondent from each category reported two different types of credit problems.

14. Respondents were allowed to select multiple actions, so they could affirm all types of action taken in response to an adverse credit experience.

15. The individual items included in the market and political action variables are divided as in table 5.1.

16. Measures of market and government blame are identical to those used in chapter 3. The same controls for demographic and political characteristics are used in these models as well.

17. One reason non-white and low-income borrowers may place greater emphasis on government's role in consumer finance (even though it does not surpass their blame for market actors) is that these groups typically report more willingness to look to government as a solution to a number of policy issues—a fairly consistent finding in survey instruments like the American National Election Study. Furthermore, scholars note that the state—particularly as a punitive force—has historically been far more visible in the lives of race-class subjugated communities in the United States than it has for affluent white Americans (e.g., Thurston 2018). As such, even as marginalized borrowers' experiences with consumer credit might privatize the issue, these borrowers may be more likely to "see" the state in other realms of daily life and, thus, respond to primes of state visibility.

18. Sample sizes for each of the experiments are included along with the full results in the Appendix. The sample sizes range from a low of 33 to a high of 195. While the survey contains more specific ethnoracial information about borrowers, the sample is not broken down further to distinguish among participants because of the relatively small sample sizes when restricting to non-white borrowers.

CHAPTER SIX

1. Names changed to preserve anonymity.

2. To the extent that other scholars have considered institutional explanations for regulatory behavior, they have focused primarily on the effect of resource allocations, political independence, and relationship with Congress on the policy choices agencies adopt (e.g., Moe 1987; Teske 1991, 2004).

3. This was no accident. Scholars have documented how lobbying by financial interests shaped the mission and institutional structure of many of these bodies from the outset in order to ensure not only that agencies were tasked with prudential regulation, but also that the agencies' very power was often tied to the profitability (and policy preferences) of the industry it sought to regulate. For a thorough account of this process in the Federal Reserve, see Jacobs and King 2016.

4. Mark Jickling and Edward Murphy (2010) provide an excellent overview of the U.S. system of financial regulation in "Who Regulates Whom? An Overview of U.S. Financial Supervision."

5. The Dodd-Frank Act abolished the Office of Thrift Supervision in 2011.

6. There are, of course, other important financial regulatory agencies that, while not responsible for the safety and soundness of financial institutions, nevertheless are responsible for maintaining competition in the financial sector. These include the Securities and Exchange Commission (established in 1934) and the Commodity Futures Trading Commission (established in 1974).

7. Beyond the area of finance, only three other regulatory agencies exist whose sole focus is on consumer protection: the Food and Drug Administration (established in 1906), the National Highway Traffic Safety Administration (established in 1970), and the Consumer Product Safety Commission (established in 1972).

8. Board members are appointed by the president and confirmed by the Senate to seven-year terms. No more than three members can be from the same political party.

9. In fact, the report on the bill authored by the House Banking and Currency Committee completely disregards the Fed's own testimony, stating that "No one can deny [the Fed's] experience and expertise in these matters" (U.S. House 1967: 18).

10. For an exceptionally detailed account of this battle, see Kirsch and Mayer 2013.

11. In theory, looking at lobbying expenditures would provide a more quantifiable method to address the question of resources, but many consumer advocates are not actually forced to register as lobbyists, so it is impossible to get an accurate picture of activity from lobbying disclosures.

12. The CFPB began collecting complaints on mortgages in December 2011; bank accounts and services, private student loans, and other consumer loans in March 2012; credit reporting in October 2012; money transfers in April 2013; debt collection in July 2013; payday loans in November 2013; prepaid cards, credit repair, debt settlement, pawn and title loans in July 2014; virtual currency in August 2014; federal student loan servicing in February 2016; and marketplace lending in March 2016.

13. The fact that a considerable number of complaints were erroneously submitted to the CFPB could mean that the remaining regulatory fragmentation is still confusing to consumers; however, it may also be a sign that ordinary Americans are already coming to identify the CFPB as a government actor looking out for their interests.

14. Consumer Sentinel, established in 1997 for the benefit of law enforcement officials, is a database of consumer complaints that is managed by the FTC.

15. The Consumer Sentinel data available to the public offer limited opportunities to disaggregate complaint type by agency, so it is impossible to see how many FTC complaints, for example, were for credit issues.

CHAPTER SEVEN

1. A critical juncture is typically defined as a significant choice, or shift, in political life that has the potential to set a new path forward while foreclosing other options (Lipset and Rokkan 1967; Collier and Collier 1991).

2. Emphasis added by author.

3. The third plank of their agenda focuses on enforcement.

4. The Congressional Review Act allows Congress to review major rules enacted by executive agencies. Congress can overturn the rule with majority votes in the House and Senate and the signature of the President. While the CRA has historically been seldom used, Republicans employed it frequently after retaking control of government in 2016.

5. Suzanne Mettler (2005b) offers one of the few—if not the only—chapters addressing this link, but her analysis is largely restricted to applying the traditional individual feedback mechanisms of resource and interpretive effects to an aggregate, or collective, context.

## References

0312151, [Senior Director] March 12, 2015, Personal Interview.

0313151, [Managing Director] March 13, 2015, Personal Interview.

1119141, [Executive Director] November 19, 2014, Personal Interview.

1120141, [Deputy Director] November 20, 2014, Personal Interview.

1120142, [Campaign Manager] November 20, 2014, Personal Interview.

Ackerman, James M. 1981. "Interest Rates and the Law: A History of Usury." *Arizona State Law Journal* 1: 61–110.

Administrative Procedure Act, P.L. 79–404, 60 Stat. 237, 5 U.S. Code § 500.

American National Election Studies. 2012. "The ANES 2012 Time Series Study." Stanford University and the University of Michigan.

Americans for Fairness in Lending. 2004. "Transcript from Cleveland Conference," AFFIL Box 1, Folder 19, Consumer Movement Archives, Manhattan, KS.

Americans for Fairness in Lending. 2006. "Perspective—2006," AFFIL Box 2, Folder 25, Consumer Movement Archives, Manhattan, KS.

Americans for Fairness in Lending. 2007a. "Strategic Plan," AFFIL Box 1, Folder 3, Consumer Movement Archives, Manhattan, KS.

Americans for Fairness in Lending. 2007b. "Youth Outreach Campaign Review," AFFIL Box 1, Folder 16, Consumer Movement Archives, Manhattan, KS.

Americans for Fairness in Lending. 2007c. "AFFIL Talking Points 2007," AFFIL Box 1, Folder 3, Consumer Movement Archives, Manhattan, KS.

Americans for Fairness in Lending. 2008a. "Credit Card Campaign 2008 Activities," AFFIL Box 2, Folder 19, Consumer Movement Archives, Manhattan, KS.

Americans for Fairness in Lending. 2008b. "Board and Staff Retreat Notes," AFFIL Box 1, Folder 15, Consumer Movement Archives, Manhattan, KS.

Americans for Fairness in Lending. 2008c. "Annotated Google Analytics," AFFIL Box 2, Folder 21, Consumer Movement Archives, Manhattan, KS.

Americans for Fairness in Lending. 2008d. "Audio Press Conference Overview," AFFIL Box 3, Folder 19, Consumer Movement Archives, Manhattan, KS.

Americans for Fairness in Lending. 2008e. "Federal Reserve Board Comments," AFFIL Box 2, Folder 19, Consumer Movement Archives, Manhattan, KS.

Americans for Fairness in Lending. 2010. "Membership," AFFIL Box 2, Folder 19, Consumer Movement Archives, Manhattan, KS.

Americans for Fairness in Lending. 2018. "About." Retrieved from https://americansforfairnessinlending. wordpress.com/about-2/.

Americans for Financial Reform. 2009. "AFR Joins National Mobilization for Financial Reform," Press Release, retrieved from http://ourfinancialsecurity.org/2009/10/afr-joins-national-mobilization-for-financial-reform-events-across-country/.

Americans for Financial Reform. 2010. "Steering Committee Minutes," AFFIL Box 3, Folder 5, Consumer Movement Archives, Manhattan, KS.

Arkansas State Constitution, Article 19, Section 13 [repealed].

Arnold, R. Douglas. 1990. *The Logic of Congressional Action.* New Haven: Yale University Press.

Arrighi, Giovanni. 1994. *The Long Twentieth Century: Money, Power, and the Origins of Our Times.* London: Verso.

Arthur, W. Brian. 1994. *Increasing Returns and Path Dependence in the Economy.* Ann Arbor: Michigan University Press.

Bair, Sheila C. June 13, 2007. "Statement of Sheila C. Bair, Chairman, Federal Deposit Insurance Corporation on Improving Federal Consumer Protection in Financial Services." U.S. House of Representatives.

Banking Act of 1933, P.L. 73–66, 48 Stat. 162, enacted June 16, 1933.

Baradaran, Mehrsa. 2015. *How the Other Half Banks: Exclusion, Exploitation, and the Threat to Democracy.* Boston: Harvard University Press.

Baumgartner, Frank, and Bryan D. Jones. 1993. *Agendas and Instability in American Politics.* Chicago: University of Chicago Press.

Beales, Howard, Richard Craswell, and Steven C. Salop. 1981. "The Efficient Regulation of Consumer Information." *Journal of Law and Economics* 24(3): 491–539.

Beldon Russonello and Stewart Strategies. 2006. "Communicating on Fairness in Lending." AFFIL Box 3, Folder 21, Consumer Movement Archives, Manhattan, KS.

Benford, Robert D., and David A. Snow. 2000. "Framing Processes and Social

Movements: An Overview and Assessment." *Annual Review of Sociology* 26: 611–639.

Berenson, Alex. January 22, 2003. "Banks Encourage Overdrafts, Reaping Profit." *New York Times.*

Bernanke, Ben S. 1983. "Nonmonetary Effects of the Financial Crisis in the Propagation of the Great Depression." *American Economic Review* 73(3): 257–276.

Bernstein, Marver H. 1955. *Regulating Business by Independent Commission.* Princeton: Princeton University Press.

Berry, Jeff. 1984. *Feeding Hungry People: Rulemaking in the Food Stamp Program.* New Brunswick, NJ: Rutgers University Press.

Best, Arthur. 1981. *When Consumers Complain.* New York: Columbia University Press.

Board of Governors of the Federal Reserve System. 1977. "1977 Consumer Credit Survey." Richard Morse Papers Box 138, Folder 9, Consumer Movement Archives, Manhattan, KS.

Board of Governors of the Federal Reserve System. 2007. "Report to the Congress on Credit Scoring and Its Effects on the Availability and Affordability of Credit."

Board of Governors of the Federal Reserve System. 2016. "Survey of Consumer Finances 1970–2016." [Dataset, codebook, and chart book].

Board of Governors of the Federal Reserve System. 2017a. "Changes in U.S. Family Finances from 2013 to 2016: Evidence from the Survey of Consumer Finances." *Federal Reserve Bulletin* 103(3).

Board of Governors of the Federal Reserve System. 2017b. "Report on the Economic Wellbeing of U.S. Households in 2016."

Board of Governors of the Federal Reserve System. Accessed 2018. "Consumer Credit-G.19."

Bolton, Patrick, and Howard Rosenthal. 2005. *Credit Markets for the Poor.* New York: Russell Sage.

Brady, Henry E., Sidney Verba, and Kay Lehman Schlozman. 1995. "Beyond SES: A Resource Model of Political Participation." *American Political Science Review* 89(2): 271–294.

Branscombe, Martha. 1969. "Foreword." *Official Proceedings of the Annual Meeting.* National Conference on Social Welfare, ix–xii.

Breen, Timothy Hall. 2004. *The Marketplace of Revolution: How Consumer Politics Shaped American Independence.* New York: Oxford University Press.

Brooks, Rick, and Ruth Simon. 2007. "Subprime Debacle Traps Even Very Credit-Worthy; As Housing Boomed, Industry Pushed Loans to a Broader Market." *Wall Street Journal*, December 3.

Byrnes, Sarah. April 20, 2008. "Is the Consumer Movement a Horseless Headman?" Caveat Emptor (blog). Retrieved from http://caveatemptorblog.com/578/is-the-consumer-movement-a-horseless-headman/.

Calder, Lendol Glen. 1999. *Financing the American Dream: A Cultural History of Consumer Credit.* Princeton: Princeton University Press.

Campbell, Andrea Louise. 2002. "Self-Interest, Social Security, and the Distinctive Participation Patterns of Senior Citizens." *American Political Science Review* 96(3): 565–574.

Campen, Jim. 2008. "Self Assessment," AFFIL Box 2, Folder 29, Consumer Movement Archives, Manhattan, KS.

Canaday, Ward. August 23, 1934. "Letter to Stephen Early." Official Files 1091 Box 1, Folder "Jan–Aug 1934," Franklin Delano Roosevelt Presidential Archives, Hyde Park, NY.

Caplovitz, David. 1963. *The Poor Pay More: Consumer Practices of Low-Income Families*. New York: Free Press.

Carpenter, Daniel P. 2002. "Groups, the Media, Agency Waiting Costs, and FDA Drug Approval," *American Journal of Political Science* 46(3): 490–505.

Carpenter, David H. 2014. "The Consumer Financial Protection Bureau: A Legal Analysis." Congressional Research Service.

Carr, James H., and Lopa Kolluri. 2001. "Predatory Lending: An Overview." Fannie Mae Foundation. Retrieved from http://www.knowledgeplex.org/kp/text_document_summary/article/relfiles/hot_topics/Carr-Kolluri.pdf.

Carruthers, Bruce G., and Laura Ariovich. 2010. *Money and Credit: A Sociological Approach*. Cambridge: Polity Press.

Casey, John P. 2005. "Fringe Banking and the Rise of Payday Lending." In *Credit Markets for the Poor*, edited by Patrick Bolton and Howard Rosenthal, 17–45. New York: Russell Sage.

Chan, Sewell. 2010. "Talks with G.O.P. on Financial Bill at 'Impasse,' Dodd Says." *New York Times*, February 5.

Chong, Dennis, and James N. Druckman. 2007. "Framing Theory." *Annual Review of Political Science* 10: 103–126.

CNN. 2017. "Mick Mulvaney Takes Helm of Consumer Financial Protection Bureau." *New Day*, November 27.

Cohen, Lizabeth. 2003. *A Consumers' Republic: The Politics of Mass Consumption in Postwar America*. New York: Knopf.

Cohen, Lizabeth. 2010. "Colston E. Warne Lecture: Is It Time for Another Round of Consumer Protection? The Lessons of Twentieth Century U.S. History." *Journal of Consumer Affairs* 44(1): 234–246.

Collier, Ruth Berins, and David Collier. 1991. *Shaping the Political Arena: Critical Junctures, the Labor Movement, and Regime Dynamics in Latin America*. Princeton: Princeton University Press.

Congressional Record, 1934a. CR-1934–0613.

Congressional Record, 1934b. CR-1934–0616.

Congressional Record, 1967. CR-1967–0711.

Congressional Record, 1968. CR-1968–0201.

Congressional Record, 1969. CR-1969–0513.

Congressional Record, 1974a. CR-1974–0205.

Congressional Record, 1974b. CR-1974–0613.

Consumer Advisory Council. 1963. "Preliminary Report." Caroline Ware Papers Box 15, Folder "Economic Committee #6," Franklin Delano Roosevelt Presidential Archives, Hyde Park, NY.

Consumer Credit Protection Act, P.L. 90–321, 82 Stat. 146, enacted May 29, 1968.

Consumer Federation of America. 1975–2014. "Annual Reports." Consumer Federation of America, unprocessed, Consumer Movement Archives, Manhattan, KS.

Consumer Financial Protection Bureau. 2013. "CFPB Study of Overdraft Programs." Retrieved from http://files.consumerfinance.gov/f/201306_cfpb_whitepaper_overdraft-practices.pdf.

Consumer Financial Protection Bureau. 2018. "Consumer Response Annual Report: January 1–December 31, 2017." Retrieved from https://files.consumerfinance.gov/f/documents/ cfpb_consumer-response-annual-report_2017.pdf.

Consumer Financial Protection Bureau. Accessed 2018. "The Bureau." Retrieved from https://www.consumerfinance.gov/about-us/the-bureau/.

Consumer Sentinel. 2008–2018. "Network Reports." Federal Trade Commission.

Cordray, Richard. April 3, 2014. "Prepared Remarks of CFPB Director Richard Cordray." American Bar Association.

CQ Almanac. 1947. "Consumer Credit Controls." Washington, DC: Congressional Quarterly, 09–510–09–513, 1948.

CQ Almanac. 1967. "Truth-In-Lending Bill Passed by Senate." Washington, DC: Congressional Quarterly, 11–717–11–726, 1968.

CQ Almanac. 1968a. "Congress Enacts Strong Truth-In-Lending Law." Washington, DC: Congressional Quarterly, 12–205–12–211, 1969.

Credit Card Accountability Responsibility and Disclosure Act, P.L. 111–24, 123 Stat. 1734, enacted May 22, 2009.

Creighton, Lucy Black. 1976. *Pretenders to the Throne: The Consumer Movement in the United States*. Lexington, MA: Lexington Books.

Cuellar, Mariano-Florentio. 2005. "Rethinking Regulatory Democracy." *Administrative Law Review* 75: 412–499.

David, Paul. 2000. "Path-Dependence, Its Critics, and the Quest for Historical Economics." In *Evolution and Path Dependence in Economic Ideas: Past and Present*, edited by P. Garrouste and S. Ioannides, 15–40. Cheltenham, UK: Edward Elgar.

Department of Defense. 2006. "Report on Predatory Lending Practices Directed at Members of the Armed Forces and Their Dependents." Retrieved from https://archive.defense.gov/ pubs/pdfs/Report_to_Congress_final.pdf.

Depository Institutions Deregulation and Monetary Control Act of 1980. P.L. 96–221, 94 Stat. 132, enacted March 31, 1980.

Derthick, Martha, and Paul Quirk. 1985. *The Politics of Deregulation*. Washington, DC: Brookings Institution.

Dettling, Lisa J., Joanne W. Hsu, Lindsay Jacobs, Kevin B. Moore, and Jeffrey P. Thompson. 2017. "Recent Trends in Wealth-Holding by Race and Ethnicity: Evidence from the Survey of Consumer Finances." *FEDS Notes*, September 27.

Dodd-Frank Wall Street Reform and Consumer Protection Act of 2010, P.L. 111–203, 124 Stat. 1376, enacted July 21, 2010.

Druckman, James N. 2004. "Political Preference Formation." *American Political Science Review* 98(4): 671–86.

Durkin, Thomas A., Gregory E. Elliehausen, Michael E. Staten, and Todd J. Zywicki. 2014. *Consumer Credit and the American Economy*. New York: Oxford University Press.

Durkin, Thomas A., and Michael E. Staten. 2002. *The Impact of Public Policy on Consumer Credit*. Boston: Kluwer.

Dynan, Karen E., and Donald L. Kohn. 2007. "The Rise in U.S. Household Indebtedness: Causes and Consequences." Federal Reserve Board, Washington, DC.

Early, Stephen. November 27, 1934. "Telegram to Marvin McIntyre." Official Files 1091 Box 2, Folder "Nov-Dec 1934," Franklin Delano Roosevelt Presidential Archives, Hyde Park, NY.

Eccles, Marriner S., and Sydney Hyman, eds. 1951. *Beckoning Frontiers: Public and Personal Recollections*. New York: Alfred A. Knopf.

Electronic Funds Transfer Act, P.L. 95–630, 92 Stat. 3641, enacted November 10, 1978.

Elliott, Stuart. 2007. "Critics of Lending Practices Adopt a Harder Edge." *New York Times*, March 6.

Engel, Stephen M. 2016. "Seeing Sexuality: State Development and the Fragmented Status of LGBTQ Citizenship." In *The Oxford Handbook on American Political Development*, edited by Richard M. Valelly, Suzanne Mettler, and Robert C Lieberman, 682–703. Oxford: Oxford University Press.

Entman, Robert M. 1993. "Framing: Toward Clarification of a Fractured Paradigm." *Journal of Communication* 43(4): 51–58.

Equal Credit Opportunity Act of 1974, P.L. 93–495, 88 Stat. 1500, enacted October 28, 1974.

Equal Credit Opportunity Act Amendments, P.L. 94–239, 90 Stat. 251, enacted March 23, 1976.

Fair and Accurate Credit Transactions Act of 2003, P.L. 108–159, 117 Stat. 1952, enacted December 4, 2003.

Fair Credit and Charge Card Disclosure Act of 1988, P.L. 100–583, 102 Stat. 2960, enacted November 3, 1988.

Fair Credit Billing Act of 1974, P.L. 93–495, 88 Stat. 1500, enacted October 28, 1974.

Fair Credit Reporting Act of 1970, P.L. 91–508, 84 Stat. 1114, enacted October 26, 1970.

Fair Debt Collection Practices Act of 1977, P.L. 95–109, 91 Stat. 874, enacted September 20, 1977.

Federal Credit Union Act of 1970, P.L. 91–206, 73 Stat. 628, enacted March 10, 1970.

Federal Deposit Insurance Act of 1970 (Title V), P.L. 91–508, 84 Stat. 1114, enacted October 26, 1970.

Federal Deposit Insurance Corporation. 2008. "FDIC Study of Bank Overdraft

Programs." Retrieved from http://www.fdic.gov/bank/analytical/overdraft/FDIC138_Report_Final_v508.pdf.
Federal Home Loan Bank Act of 1932. P.L. 72–304, 47 Stat. 251, 12 U.S. Code §1421.
Federal Housing Administration. 1934a. "Community Campaign." Official Files 1091 Box 2, Folder "Jan.–Aug. 1934," Franklin Delano Roosevelt Presidential Archives, Hyde Park, NY.
Federal Housing Administration. 1934b. "Modernization Is Important Part of the New Deal." Official Files 1091 Box 2, Folder "Jan.–Aug. 1934," Franklin Delano Roosevelt Presidential Archives, Hyde Park, NY.
Federal Housing Administration. 1935. "Total Volume of Federal Housing Administration Business." Official Files 1091 Box 2, Folder "December 1935," Franklin Delano Roosevelt Presidential Archives, Hyde Park, NY.
Federal Reserve Act of 1913. P.L. 63–43, 38 Stat. 251, enacted December 23, 1913.
Federal Trade Commission. 1968. *Economic Report on Installment Credit and Retail Sales Practices of District of Columbia Retailers*. Washington, DC: Government Printing Office.
Federal Trade Commission. Accessed 2016. "What We Do." Retrieved from https://www.ftc.gov/ about-ftc/what-we-do.
Federal Trade Commission Act of 1914. P.L. 63–203, 38 Stat. 717, 15 U.S. Code §41.
Feldman, Sheldon. 1969. "Letter to Professor William Fasse." Richard Morse Papers Box 4, Folder 9, Consumer Movement Archives, Manhattan, KS.
Financial Crisis Inquiry Commission. 2011. *Financial Crisis Inquiry Report*. Washington, DC: Government Printing Office.
Financial Institutions Reform, Recovery, and Enforcement Act of 1989, P.L. 101–73, 103 Stat. 183, enacted August 9, 1989.
Fleming, Anne. 2012. "The Borrower's Tale: A History of Poor Debtors in Lochner Era New York City." *Law and History Review* 30(4): 1053–1098.
Folger, Robert. 1986. "A Referent Cognition Theory of Relative Deprivation." In *Relative Deprivation and Social Comparison: Ontario Symposium on Personality and Social Psychology*, edited by James M. Olson, C. Peter Herman, and Mark P. Zanna, 33–56. New York: Lawrence Erlbaum Associates.
Furlong, Scott R. 1997. "Interest Group Influence on Rulemaking." *Administration and Society* 29: 325–347.
Furness, Betty. 1967. "Remarks of Betty Furness." Consumer Federation of America, unprocessed, Consumer Movement Archives, Manhattan, KS.
Gallup. 2016. "Congress and the Public." Retrieved from http://www.gallup.com/poll/1600/congress-public.aspx.
Gamson, William A. 1992. "The Social Psychology of Collective Action." In *Frontiers in Social Movement Theory*, edited by Aldon Morris and Carol McClurg Mueller, 53–76. New Haven: Yale University Press.
Gamson, William A., and Katherine E. Lasch. 1983. "The Political Culture of Social Welfare Policy." In *Evaluating the Welfare State*, edited by S. E. Spiro and E. Yuchtman-Yaar, 397–415. New York: Academic Press.

Gamson, William A., and Andre Modigliani. 1989. "Media Discourse and Public Opinion on Nuclear Power: A Constructionist Approach." *American Journal of Sociology* 95(1): 1–37.
Gelpi, Rosa-Maria, and François Julien-Labruyère. 2000. *The History of Consumer Credit: Doctrines and Practice*. New York: St. Martin's Press.
Glaeser, Edward L., and Andrei Shleifer. 2001. *The Rise of the Regulatory State*. Cambridge, MA: National Bureau of Economic Research.
Glickman, Lawrence B. 2012. "Consumer Activism, Consumer Regimes, and the Consumer Movement: Rethinking the History of Consumer Politics in the United States." In *The Oxford Handbook of the History of Consumption*, edited by Frank Trentmann, 399–417. Oxford: Oxford University Press.
Good, Chris. 2013. "Former Congresswoman and Ambassador Lindy Boggs Dies at 97." *ABC News*, July 27.
Gormley, William T., Jr. 1983. *The Politics of Public Utility Regulation*. Pittsburgh, PA: University of Pittsburgh Press.
Gormley, William T., Jr. 1986. "Regulatory Issue Networks in a Federal System." *Polity* 18(4): 595–620.
Gould, Elise. 2015. "2014 Continues a 35-Year Trend of Broad-Based Wage Stagnation." *Economic Policy Institute*, Issue Brief 393.
Gramm-Leach-Bliley Financial Modernization Act of 1999. P.L. 106–102, 113 Stat. 1338, enacted November 12, 1999.
Grodzins, Morton. 1966. *The American System: A New View of Government in the United States*. Chicago: Rand McNally.
Grunwald, Michael. 2018. "Mulvaney Requests No Funding for CFPB." *Politico*, January 18.
Hacker, Jacob. 2006. *The Great Risk Shift: The New Economic Security and the Decline of the American Dream*. Oxford: Oxford University Press.
Hacker, Jacob, and Paul Pierson. 2010. *Winner-Take-All Politics: How Washington Made the Rich Richer—and Turned Its Back on the Middle Class*. New York: Simon and Schuster.
Hadfield, Gillian K., Robert Howse, and Michael J. Trebilcock. 1998. "Information-Based Principles for Rethinking Consumer Protection Policy." *Journal of Consumer Policy* 21(2): 131.
Harris, Richard. 2012. *Building a Market: The Rise of the Home Improvement Industry, 1914–1960*. Chicago: University of Chicago Press.
Harris Interactive. 2012. "Oil, Pharmaceutical, Health Insurance, Tobacco, Banking and Utilities Top the List of Industries That People Would Like to See More Regulated." December 18.
Heider, Fritz. 1958. *The Psychology of Interpersonal Relations*. New York: Wiley.
Higgs, Robert. 1987. *Crisis and Leviathan: Critical Episodes in the Growth of American Government*. New York: Oxford University Press.
Hilton, Matthew. 2007. "Consumers and the State since the Second World War." *Annals of the American Academy of Political and Social Science*: The Politics of Consumption/The Consumption of Politics 611(1): 66–81.
Hilton, Matthew. 2009. *Prosperity for All: Consumer Activism in an Era of Globalization*. Ithaca, NY: Cornell University Press.

Hochschild, Jennifer L. 1981. *What's Fair? American Beliefs about Distributive Justice*. Cambridge, MA: Harvard University Press.
Home Equity Loan Consumer Protection Act of 1988, P.L. 100–709, 102 Stat. 4725, enacted November 23, 1988.
Howard, Christopher. 1997. *The Hidden Welfare State: Tax Expenditures and Social Policy in the United States*. Princeton: Princeton University Press.
H.R. 11601, July 20, 1967. 90th Congress, 1st Session.
Hovenkamp, Herbert. 1999. *Federal Antitrust Policy: The Law of Competition and Its Practice*. 2nd ed. St. Paul, MN: West Group.
Huntington, Samuel P. 1952. "The Marasmus of the ICC: The Commission, the Railroads, and the Public Interest." *Yale Law Journal* 61: 467–509.
Hyman, Louis. 2011. *Debtor Nation: The History of America in Red Ink*. Princeton: Princeton University Press.
Iyengar, Shanto. 1990. "Framing Responsibility for Political Issues: The Case of Poverty." *Political Behavior* 12: 19–40.
Jacobs, Lawrence, and Desmond King. 2016. *Fed Power: How Finance Wins*. Oxford: Oxford University Press.
Jacobs, Meg. 2005. *Pocketbook Politics: Economic Citizenship in Twentieth-Century America*. Princeton: Princeton University Press.
Jacobs, Meg. 2011. "The Politics of Consumption." *Reviews in American History* 39(3): 561–573.
Jappelli, Tullio, and Marco Pagano. 1993. "Information Sharing in Credit Markets." *Journal of Finance* 43(5): 1693–1718.
Jappelli, Tullio, and Marco Pagano. 2002. "Information Sharing, Lending and Defaults: Cross-Country Evidence." *Journal of Banking and Finance* 26: 2017–2045.
Jerit, Jennifer, 2009. "How Predictive Appeals Shape Policy Opinions." *American Journal of Political Science* 53(2): 411–426.
Jickling, Mark, and Edward V. Murphy. 2010. "Who Regulates Whom? An Overview of U.S. Financial Supervision." Congressional Research Service.
Johnson, Lyndon. 1964. "Message to Congress: President's on Consumer Interests." In *CQ Almanac 1964*, 20th ed., 889–891. Washington, DC: Congressional Quarterly.
Johnson, Lyndon. 1967. "Remarks of President Lyndon Johnson." Consumer Federation of America, unprocessed, Consumer Movement Archives, Manhattan, KS.
Johnson, Simon, and James Kwak. 2010. *13 Bankers: The Wall Street Takeover and the Next Financial Meltdown*. New York: Pantheon Books.
Jurgens, Rick, and Chi Chi Wu. 2007. "Fee-Harvesters: Low-Credit, High-Cost Cards Bleed Consumers." National Consumer Law Center.
Kelly, Margo. 2009. "Assessment Report," AFFIL Box 2, Folder 8, Consumer Movement Archives, Manhattan, KS.
Kennedy, John F. March 15, 1962. "Special Message to the Congress on Protecting the Consumer Interest." Public Papers of the Presidents of the United States: John F. Kennedy.
Kerner Commission. 1968. "Report of the National Advisory Commission on Civil Disorders." Washington, DC: Government Printing Office.

Kerwin, Cornelius M., and Scott R. Furlong. 1992. "Time and Rulemaking: An Empirical Test of Theory." *Journal of Public Administration Research and Theory* 2: 113–138.

Kerwin, Cornelius M., and Scott R. Furlong. 2005. "Interest Group Participation in Rulemaking: A Decade of Change." *Journal of Public Administration Research and Theory* 15: 353–370.

Kidneigh, John C. 1969. "The New York Conference Story." In *Official Proceedings of the Annual Meeting*, 178–184. National Conference on Social Welfare.

Kingdon, John. 1984. *Agendas, Alternatives, and Public Policies*. Boston: Little, Brown.

Kirsch, Larry, and Robert N. Mayer. 2013. *Financial Justice: The People's Campaign to Stop Lender Abuse*. Santa Barbara, CA: Praeger.

Klandermans, Bert. 1997. *The Social Psychology of Protest*. Oxford: Blackwell Publishers.

Klein, Ezra. 2010. "Elizabeth Warren on Elizabeth Warren." *Washington Post*, September 17.

Kornbluh, Felicia. 1997. "To Fulfill Their 'Rightly Needs': Consumerism and the National Welfare Rights Movement." *Radical History Review* 69: 76–113.

Kornbluh, Felicia. 2007. *The Battle for Welfare Rights: Politics and Poverty in Modern America*. Philadelphia, PA: University of Pennsylvania Press.

Kreuter, Frauke, Stanley Presser, and Roger Tourangeau. 2008. "Social Desirability Bias in CATI, IVR, and Web Surveys: The Effects of Mode and Question Sensitivity." *Public Opinion Quarterly* 72(5): 847–865.

Krippner, Greta R. 2005. "The Financialization of the American Economy." *Socio-Economic Review* 3(2): 173–208.

Krippner, Greta R. 2011. *Capitalizing on Crisis: The Political Origins of the Rise of Finance*. Cambridge, MA: Harvard University Press.

Krippner, Greta R. 2017. "Democracy of Credit: Ownership and the Politics of Credit Access in Late Twentieth-Century America." *American Journal of Sociology* 123(1): 1–47.

Kwak, Nancy H. 2015. *A World of Homeowners: American Power and the Politics of Housing Aid*. Chicago: University of Chicago Press.

Lake Research Partners. 2017. "Toplines: AFR/CRL Poll June 24–29, 2017." Retrieved from https://ourfinancialsecurity.org/wp-content/uploads/2017/07/topline.AFRCRL.timeseries.f.2017.07.24.pdf.

Lane, Sylvan. 2018. "New CFPB Director Puts Target on Payday Loan Rules." *The Hill*, January 17.

Lawler, Joseph. 2018. "Mick Mulvaney Quietly Changes the CFPB's Name." *Washington Examiner*, April 23.

Layzer, J. A. 2012. *The Environmental Case: Translating Values into Policy*. Washington, DC: CQ Press.

Leighley, Jan E., and Jonathan Nagler. 2013. *Who Votes Now? Demographics, Issues, Inequality, and Turnout in the United States*. Princeton: Princeton University Press.

Levine, Adam S. 2015. *American Insecurity: Why Our Economic Fears Lead to Political Inaction.* Princeton: Princeton University Press.

Levitin, Adam J. 2009. "The Consumer Financial Protection Agency." Briefing Paper #3. PEW Financial Reform Project.

Levitin, Adam J. 2013. "The Consumer Financial Protection Bureau: An Introduction." *Review of Banking and Financial Law* 32(2): 321–369.

Lieberman, Robert. 2009. "Civil Rights and the Democratization Trap: The Public Private Nexus and the Building of American Democracy." In *Democratization in America: A Comparative-Historical Analysis*, edited by Desmond King, Robert Lieberman, Gretchen Ritter, and Laurence Whitehead, 211–230. Baltimore, MD: Johns Hopkins University Press.

Lindblom, Charles. 1982. "The Market as Prison." *Journal of Politics* 44(2): 324–336.

Lipset, Seymour M., and Stein Rokkan. 1967. *Party Systems and Voter Alignments: Cross-National Perspectives.* Free Press.

Loftus, Joseph A. April 7, 1963. "Consumer Units Cool to Kennedy." *New York Times.* Caroline Ware Papers Box 15, Folder 2, Franklin Delano Roosevelt Presidential Archives, Hyde Park, NY.

Logemann, Jan. 2012. "From Cradle to Bankruptcy: Credit Access and the American Welfare State." In *The Development of Consumer Credit in Global Perspective: Business, Regulation, and Culture*, edited by Jan Logemann, 201–219. New York: Palgrave.

Lowi, Theodore. 1972. "Four Systems of Policy, Politics, and Choice." *Public Administration Review* 32(4): 298–310.

Maney, Ardith, and Loree Gerdes Bykerk. 1994. *Consumer Politics: Protecting Public Interests on Capitol Hill.* Westport, CT: Greenwood Press.

Mann, Bruce H. 2002. *Republic of Debtors: Bankruptcy in the Age of American Independence.* Cambridge, MA: Harvard University Press.

Manning, Robert D. 2000. *Credit Card Nation: The Consequences of America's Addiction to Credit.* New York: Basic Books.

*Marquette Nat. Bank of Minneapolis v. First of Omaha Service Corp.* 1978, 439 U.S. 299.

Mayer, Robert N. 2012. "The US Consumer Movement: A New Era amid Old Challenges." *Journal of Consumer Affairs* 46(2): 171–189.

McAdam, Doug. 1982. *Political Process and the Development of Black Insurgency, 1930–1970.* Chicago: University of Chicago Press.

McAdam, Doug, John D. McCarthy, and Mayer N. Zald. 1996. *Comparative Perspectives on Social Movements: Political Opportunities, Mobilizing Structures, and Cultural Framings.* Cambridge, UK: Cambridge University Press.

McCarthy, John D., and Mayer N. Zald. 1973. *The Trend of Social Movements in America: Professionalization and Resource Mobilization.* Morristown, NJ: General Learning Press.

McCarty, Nolan, Keith T. Poole, and Howard Rosenthal. 2008. *Polarized America: The Dance of Inequality and Unequal Riches.* Cambridge, MA: MIT Press.

McCarty, Nolan, Keith T. Poole, and Howard Rosenthal. 2013. *Political Bubbles: Financial Crises and the Failure of American Democracy.* Princeton: Princeton University Press.

McCorkell, Peter L. 2002. "The Impact of Credit Scoring and Automated Underwriting on Credit Availability." In *The Impact of Public Policy on Consumer Credit*, edited by Thomas A. Durkin and Michael E. Staten, 209–220. Boston: Kluwer.

McGhee, Heather. 2015. "Dodd Frank and the Future of Wall Street Reform." *Demos*, July 21.

McKay, Amy, and Susan Webb Yackee. 2007. "Interest Group Competition on Federal Agency Rules." *American Politics Research* 35(3): 336–357.

McKenna, Francine. 2018. "Mulvaney: CFPB Doesn't Have to Run a Yelp for Bank Customers." *Market Watch*, April 25.

Mettler, Suzanne. 1998. *Dividing Citizens: Gender and Federalism in New Deal Public Policy.* Ithaca, NY: Cornell University Press.

Mettler, Suzanne. 2005a. *Soldiers to Citizens: The G.I. Bill and the Making of the Greatest Generation.* New York: Oxford University Press.

Mettler, Suzanne. 2005b. "Policy Feedback Effects for Collective Action: Lessons from Veterans' Programs." In *Routing the Opposition: Social Movements, Public Policy, and Democracy*, edited by David S. Meyer, Valerie Jenness, and Helen M. Ingram, 211–235. Minneapolis: University of Minnesota Press.

Mettler, Suzanne. 2011. *The Submerged State: How Invisible Government Policies Undermine American Democracy.* Chicago: University of Chicago Press.

Mettler, Suzanne. 2014. *Degrees of Inequality: How the Politics of Higher Education Sabotaged the American Dream.* New York: Basic Books.

Mettler, Suzanne. 2016. "The Policyscape and the Challenges of Contemporary Politics to Policy Maintenance." *Perspectives on Politics* 14(2): 1–22.

Mettler, Suzanne, and Mallory SoRelle. 2017. "Policy Feedback Theory." In *Theories of the Policy Process*, 4th ed., edited by Christopher Weible and Paul A. Sabatier, 103–134. Boulder, CO: Westview Press.

Mettler, Suzanne, and Joe Soss. 2004. "The Consequences of Public Policy for Democratic Citizenship: Bridging Policy Studies and Mass Politics." *Perspectives on Politics* 2(1): 55–73.

Michener, Jamila. 2018. *Fragmented Democracy: Medicaid, Federalism, and Unequal Politics.* Cambridge: Cambridge University Press.

Micheletti, Michele. 2003. *Political Virtue and Shopping: Individuals, Consumerism, and Collective Action.* New York: Palgrave.

Mierzwinski, Ed. 2013. "Playing Whack-a-Mole with Predatory Lenders." *U.S. News and World Report*, August 13.

Military Lending Act of 2007. P.L. 109–364, 32 Stat. 232, enacted October 17, 2006.

Mincer, Jilian. 2011. "Credit Union Business Grows as Consumers Sour on Banks." *Reuters*, November 4.

Moe, Terry M. 1987. "Interests, Institutions, and Positive Theory: The Politics of the NLRB." *Studies in American Political Development* 2: 236–299.

Moley, Raymond. 1966. *The First New Deal*. New York: Harcourt, Brace, and World.

Morse, Richard. 1963. "The Consumer Reconsidered." Richard Morse Papers Box 101, Folder 1, Consumer Movement Archives, Manhattan, KS.

Mulvaney, Mick. 2018. "The CFPB Has Pushed Its Last Envelope." *Wall Street Journal*, October 2.

Nadasen, Premilla. 2005. *Welfare Warriors: The Welfare Rights Movement in the United States*. New York: Routledge.

Nadel, Mark V. 1971. *The Politics of Consumer Protection*. Indianapolis: Bobbs-Merrill.

National Bureau of Economic Research. 2008. "Determination of the December 2007 Peak in Economic Activity." Washington, DC: Government Printing Office.

National Commission on Consumer Finance. 1972. "Consumer Credit in the United States: Report of the National Commission on Consumer Finance." Washington, DC: U.S. Government Printing Office.

National Consumer Law Center. 1969. "National Consumer Law Center Questionnaire to Legal Services." NCLC Box 7, Folder 7, Consumer Movement Archives, Manhattan, KS.

National Housing Act of 1934, P.L. 73–479, 48 Stat. 847, enacted June 28, 1934.

Nelson, Thomas E., Rosalee A. Clawson, and Zoe M. Oxley. 1997. "Media Framing of a Civil Liberties Conflict and Its Effect on Tolerance." *American Political Science Review* 91(3): 567–583.

*New York Times*. 1933. "Ickes Corporation to Rebuild Slums." October 29.

*New York Times*. 1934. "$1,001,091 House Loans by National City Bank." Official Files 1091 Box 2, Folder "Federal Housing Administration Sept.–Oct. 1934," Franklin Delano Roosevelt Presidential Archives, Hyde Park, NY.

NPR. 2017. "Rep. Jeb Hensarling Calls Consumer Financial Protection Bureau a 'Rogue Agency.'" Morning Edition, February 24.

Obama, Barack. 2010. "Remarks by the President at Signing of Dodd-Frank Wall Street Reform and Consumer Protection Act." White House, July 21.

Office of the Inspector General. 2006. "Challenges and FDIC Efforts Related to Predatory Lending." Federal Deposit Insurance Corporation.

Olney, Martha L. 1991. *Buy Now, Pay Later: Advertising, Credit, and Consumer Durables in the 1920s*. Chapel Hill: University of North Carolina Press.

Olson, Mancur. 1965. *The Logic of Collective Action*. Cambridge, MA: Harvard University Press.

Omnibus Consolidated Appropriations Act of 1996, P.L. 104–208, 110 Stat. 3009, enacted September 30, 1996.

Orren, Karen, and Stephen Skowronek. 2004. *The Search for American Political Development*. Cambridge: Cambridge University Press.

Pennsylvania Title 41 §§201, 202.

Patman, Wright. 1967. "Remarks of Representative Wright Patman," Consumer Federation of America, unprocessed, Consumer Movement Archives, Manhattan, KS.

Peltzman, Sam. 1976. "Toward a More General Theory of Regulation." *Journal of Law and Economics* 19: 211–40.

Pertschuk, Michael. 1982. *Revolt against Regulation: The Rise and Pause of the Consumer Movement.* Berkeley: University of California Press.

Peterson, Ester. 1967. "Remarks of Ester Peterson." Consumer Federation of America, unprocessed, Consumer Movement Archives, Manhattan, KS.

Pew Charitable Trusts. 2012. "Payday Lending in America: Who Borrows, Where They Borrow, and Why." Retrieved from https://www.pewtrusts.org/~/media/legacy/uploadedfiles/pcs_assets/2012/pewpaydaylendingreportpdf.pdf.

Phillips, Kevin. 2002. *Wealth and Democracy: A Political History of the American Rich.* New York: Broadway Books.

Pierson, Paul. 1993. "When Effect Becomes Cause: Policy Feedback and Political Change." *World Politics* 45(04): 595–628.

Pierson, Paul. 2004. *Politics in Time: History, Institutions, and Social Analysis.* Princeton: Princeton University Press.

Polanyi, Karl. (1944) 2001. *The Great Transformation.* Boston: Beacon Press.

Potter, Rachel Augustine. 2019. *Bending the Rules: Procedural Politicking in the Bureaucracy.* Chicago: University of Chicago Press.

Prasad, Monica. 2012. *The Land of Too Much: American Abundance and the Paradox of Poverty.* Cambridge, MA: Harvard University Press

Puzzanghera, Jim. 2015. "Consumer Protection Bureau Cracks Down on Payday Lenders." *Los Angeles Times*, October 5.

Quinn, Sarah. 2019. *American Bonds: How Credit Markets Shaped a Nation.* Princeton: Princeton University Press.

Ramsay, Iain. 2007. "Comparative Consumer Bankruptcy." *University of Illinois Law Review*, 241.

Reese, Ellen, and Garnett Newcombe. 2003. "Income Rights, Mothers' Rights, or Workers' Rights? Collective Action Frames, Organizational Ideologies, and the American Welfare Rights Movement." *Social Problems* 50(2): 294–318.

Regulation E, 74 Fed. Reg. 59033, Nov. 17, 2009.

Riegle-Neal Interstate Banking and Branching Efficiency Act of 1994. P.L. 103–328, 108 Stat. 2338, enacted September 29, 1994.

Ripley, Randall B., and Grace A. Franklin. 1987. *Congress, the Bureaucracy, and Public Policy.* 4th ed. Homewood, IL: Dorsey Press.

Roosevelt, Franklin D. 1932. "Address at Oglethorpe University."

Roosevelt, Franklin D. May 14, 1934. "Message to Congress Recommending Legislation on Assistance for Home Repair and Construction."

Roosevelt, Franklin D. August 9, 1941. "Executive Order 8843 Directing the Federal Reserve Board to Curb Installment Purchasing."

Rose, Deondra. 2018. *Citizens by Degree: Higher Education Policy and the Changing Gender Dynamics of American Citizenship.* Oxford: Oxford University Press.

Rosenstone, Steven J., and John Mark Hansen. 1993. *Mobilization, Participation, and Democracy in America.* New York: Macmillan Publishing Company.

Sabatier, Paul. 1987. "Knowledge, Policy-Oriented Learning, and Policy Change: An Advocacy Coalition Framework." *Knowledge* 8(4): 649–692.

Sanders, M. Elizabeth. 1999. *Roots of Reform: Farmers, Workers, and the American State, 1877–1917*. Chicago: University of Chicago Press.

Schelkle, Waltraud. 2012. "In the Spotlight of Crisis: How Social Policies Create, Correct, and Compensate Financial Markets." *Politics and Society* 40(1): 3–8.

Schneider, Anne, and Helen Ingram. 1993. "Social Construction of Target Populations: Implications for Politics and Policy." *American Political Science Review* 87: 334–347.

Schooner, Heidi M. 2006. "Consuming Debt: Structuring the Federal Response to Abuses in Consumer Credit." *Loyola Consumer Law Review* 18: 43–83.

Schwartz, Herman M. 2009. *Subprime Nation: American Power, Global Capital, and the Housing Bubble*. Ithaca, NY: Cornell University Press.

S. 2755, January 7, 1960. 86 Congress, 2nd Session.

S. 5, January 11, 1967. 90th Congress, 1st Session.

Shelbourne, Mallory. 2017. "Durbin: Wall Street Hates Consumer Bureau like Devil Hates Holy Water." *The Hill*, November 26.

Skocpol, Theda. 1992. *Protecting Soldiers and Mothers: The Political Origins of Social Policy in the United States*. Cambridge, MA: Belknap Press of Harvard University Press.

Skocpol, Theda. 2003. *Diminished Democracy: From Membership to Management in American Civic Life*. Norman: University of Oklahoma Press.

Skowronek, Stephen. 1982. *Building a New American State: The Expansion of National Administrative Capacities, 1877–1920*. Cambridge: Cambridge University Press.

*Smiley v. Citibank*. 1996, 517 U.S. 735.

Sniderman, Paul M., and Sean M. Theriault. 2004. "The Structure of Political Argument and the Logic of Issue Framing." In *Studies in Public Opinion*, edited by Willem E. Saris and Paul M. Sniderman, 133–165. Princeton: Princeton University Press.

SoRelle, Mallory. 2018. "Will Republicans Be Able to Dismantle the Consumer Financial Protection Bureau?" Monkey Cage, *Washington Post*, February 13.

SoRelle, Mallory E., and Alexis N. Walker. 2016. "Partisan Preemption: The Strategic Use of Federal Preemption Legislation." *Publius: The Journal of Federalism* 46(4): 486–509.

Soss, Joe. 1999. "Lessons of Welfare: Policy Design, Political Learning, and Political Action." *American Political Science Review* 93(2): 363–380.

Soss, Joe, Richard Fording, and Sanford Schram. 2011. *Disciplining the Poor: Neoliberal Paternalism and the Persistent Power of Race*. Chicago: University of Chicago Press.

Staten, Michael, and Robert W. Johnson. 1995. "The Case for Deregulating Interest Rates on Consumer Credit." Monograph 31, Credit Research Center, Purdue University.

Stigler, George J. 1971. "The Theory of Economic Regulation." *Bell Journal of Economics and Management Science* 2: 3–21.

Stolle, Dietlind, Marc Hooghe, and Michele Micheletti. 2006. "Politics in the Supermarket: Political Consumerism as a Form of Political Participation." *Peace Research Abstracts Journal* 43(2).

Streeck, Wolfgang. 2011. "The Crises of Democratic Capitalism." *New Left Review* 71: 5–29.

Sullivan, Charlene, and Robert Johnson. 1980. "Value Pricing of Bank Card Services." Working Paper #34, Credit Research Center, Purdue University.

Sullivan, Leonor. 1967. "Remarks of Representative Leonor K. Sullivan," Consumer Federation of America, unprocessed, Consumer Movement Archives, Manhattan, KS.

Taibbi, Matt. 2012. "How Wall Street Killed Financial Reform." *Rolling Stone*, May 10.

Tarrow, Sidney G. 1998. *Power in Movement: Social Movements and Contentious Politics*. Cambridge: Cambridge University Press.

Teske, Paul. 1991. "Interests and Institutions in State Regulation." *American Journal of Political Science* 35(1): 139–154.

Teske, Paul. 2004. *Regulation in the States*. Washington, DC: Brookings Institution.

Thurston, Chloe. 2015. "Policy Feedback in the Public-Private Welfare State: Advocacy Groups and Access to Home Ownership Programs, 1934–1954." *Studies in American Political Development* 29(2): 250–267.

Thurston, Chloe. 2018. *At the Boundaries of Homeownership: Credit, Discrimination, and the American State*. Cambridge: Cambridge University Press.

Tocqueville, Alexis de, and Arthur Goldhammer. (1835) 2004. *Democracy in America*. New York: Library of America.

Traub, Amy, and Catherine Ruetschlin. 2012. "The Plastic Safety Net: Findings from the 2012 National Survey on Credit Card Debt of Low- and Middle-Income Households." *Demos*.

Trumbull, Gunnar. 2014. *Consumer Lending in France and America: Credit and Welfare*. New York: Cambridge.

Truth in Leasing Act of 1976, P.L. 94–240, 90 Stat. 257, enacted March 23, 1976.

Truth in Lending Simplification and Reform Act of 1980, P.L. 96–221, 94 Stat. 132, enacted March 31, 1980.

Truth in Savings Act of 1991, P.L. 102–242, 105 Stat. 2236, enacted December 19, 1991.

Tversky, Amos, and Daniel Kahneman. 1981. "The Framing of Decisions and the Psychology of Choice." *Science* 211(4481): 453–458.

U.S. House. Committee on Banking and Currency. 1934. *National Housing Act: Hearings before the Committee on Banking and Currency.* 73rd Congress, May 18–June 4 1934.

U.S. House. Committee on Banking and Currency. 1967. *Consumer Credit Protection Act: Report (to accompany H.R. 11601)*. 90th Congress. December 13, 1967. H. Rep. 90–1040.

U.S. House. Committee on Conference. 1968. *Consumer Credit Protection*

*Act: Conference Report (to accompany S. 5)*. 90th Congress. May 20th, 1968. H. Rep. 90–1397.

U.S. House. Committee on Financial Services. 2007. *Improving Federal Consumer Protection in Financial Services: Hearing before the Committee on Financial Services*. 110th Congress, June 13, 2007.

U.S. Senate. Committee on Banking and Currency. 1934. *National Housing Act: Hearings before the Committee on Banking and Currency*. 73rd Congress, May 16–24, 1934.

U.S. Senate. Committee on Banking and Currency. 1967. *Truth in Lending Act of 1967: Hearings before the Committee on Banking and Currency*. 90th Congress, April 13–May 10, 1967.

U.S. Senate. Subcommittee on Financial Institutions. 1968. *Financial Institutions and the Urban Crisis: Hearings before the Subcommittee on Financial Institutions*. 90th Congress, September 30–October 4, 1968.

U.S. Senate. Committee on Banking, Housing, and Urban Affairs. 2009. *Creating a Consumer Financial Protection Agency: Hearings before the Committee on Banking, Housing, and Urban Affairs*. 111th Congress, July 14, 2009.

Vogel, David. 2003. "The Hare and the Tortoise Revisited: The New Politics of Consumer and Environmental Regulation in Europe." *British Journal of Political Science* 33(4): 557–580.

Walker, Alexis N. 2014. "Labor's Enduring Divide: The Distinct Path of Public Sector Unions in the United States." *Studies in American Political Development* 28(2): 175–200.

Walker, Jack. 1983. "The Origins and Maintenance of Interest Groups in America." *American Political Science Review* 77(2): 390–406.

*Wall Street Journal*. 2007. "Politicians React: 'Not a Strong Advocate for Consumers.'" Real Time Economics, December 18.

Ware, Caroline. November 28, 1962. "Notes on Committee 6." Caroline Ware Papers Box 15, Folder "Economic Committee #6," Franklin Delano Roosevelt Presidential Archives, Hyde Park, NY.

Warren, Elizabeth. 2007. "Unsafe at Any Rate: Why We Need a Financial Product Safety Commission." *Democracy: A Journal of Ideas*, 5.

Warren, Elizabeth. 2008. "Product Safety Regulation as a Model for Financial Services Regulation." *Journal of Consumer Affairs* 42(3): 452–460.

Watzman, Nancy. 2012. "CFPB Launches Public Consumer Complaint Database." Sunlight Foundation, June 19.

Weaver, Vesla M., and Amy E. Lerman. 2010. "Political Consequences of the Carceral State." *American Political Science Review* 104(4): 817–833.

Weiner, Bernard. 2006. *Social Motivation, Justice, and the Moral Emotions: An Attributional Approach*. New York: Psychology Press.

Williams, Brett. 2004. *Debt for Sale: A Social History of the Credit Trap*. Philadelphia: University of Pennsylvania Press.

Williams, Raymond. 1999. "Consumer." In *Consumer Society in American History: A Reader*, edited by Lawrence B. Glickman, 17–18. Ithaca, NY: Cornell University Press.

Willier, William. 1969. "National Consumer Law Center Established at Boston College Law School." NCLC, Box 7, Folder 1, Consumer Movement Archives, Manhattan, KS.

Wilson, James Q. 1980. *The Politics of Regulation*. New York: Basic Books.

Wolfinger, Raymond E., and Steven J. Rosenstone. 1980. *Who Votes?* New Haven: Yale University Press.

Wu, Chi Chi, and Jean Ann Fox. 2006. "Pay Stub and Holiday RALs: Faster, Costlier, Riskier in the Race to the Bottom." National Consumer Law Center and Consumer Federation of America.

Yackee, Susan Webb. 2006. "Sweet-Talking the Fourth Branch: The Influence of Interest Group Comments on Federal Agency Rulemaking." *Journal of Public Administration Research and Theory* 16(1): 103–124.

Yackee, Susan Webb. 2014. "Participant Voice in the Bureaucratic Policymaking Process." *Journal of Public Administration Research and Theory* 25: 427–449.

Young, Nancy Beck. 2000. *Wright Patman: Populism, Liberalism, and the American Dream*. Dallas, TX: Southern Methodist University Press.

Zaller, John. 1992. *The Nature and Origins of Mass Opinion*. Cambridge: Cambridge University Press.

Zaller, John, and Stanley Feldman. 1992. "A Simple Theory of the Survey Response: Answering Questions versus Revealing Preferences." *American Journal of Political Science* 36(3): 579–616.

Zibel, Alan, and Annamaria Andriotis. 2015. "Lenders Step Up Financing to Subprime Borrowers." *Wall Street Journal*, February 18.

# Index

*The letter t following a page number denotes a table and the letter f denotes a figure.*